Praise for

PRODUCER

"Wendy Walker is a legend in the business and in PRODUCER, she gives not only a behind the scenes account of some of cable television's most memorable moments, but some of the hard-learned wisdom she has picked up over the years."
—Anderson Cooper, anchor, CNN

"What an amazing adventure! If you're a student interested in the world of news, a fan of Larry King or looking for a great [read] about a woman who has seen and done a lot, this is it! The life lessons at the end of each chapter are taped to my refrigerator!"
—Jeff Probst, executive producer/host, *Survivor*

"Wendy Walker reminds us all to look at life as an adventure. She says that around every corner something miraculous may happen, and she should know, she probably booked it."
—Lisa Gregorisch-Dempsey,
senior executive producer, *Extra*

"Every day for over three decades, Wendy Walker has held a clinic on how to produce the best television journalism. Now she reveals the insights she's gained so that every reader can have a stellar career as a professional and as a person. I learn from her every day, and you will, too."
—Jon Klein, president, CNN U.S.

"Wendy Walker has been one of the most influential people this world has known. From behind the scenes she has shaped the social culture of this world. In this book, not only does she share what she has learned with her many years of producing, but through her work she has helped to teach all of us to maybe be just a little bit more forgiving, understanding and compassionate of those who we share this planet with."

—James Van Praagh, spiritual medium,
author of *Talking to Heaven*

"If Stewie Griffin had read Wendy Walker's book, he would have taken over the world ages ago."

—Seth MacFarlane, creator of *Family Guy*,
American Dad, and *The Cleveland Show*

"Wendy has written a powerful book—one that I strongly recommend. Having worked with her for twenty years at CNN, I began reading this book thinking I probably wouldn't learn much—I was so wrong. I learned something on almost every page. She pours her heart out and offers lots of very useful advice. I have already started using some of that advice, and am grateful to her. In short, read this book and learn."

—Wolf Blitzer, CNN anchor of
The Situation Room

"Take simple, practical, yet profound advice, add fascinating stories of remarkable people, put in a pinch of humor, add a dash of moxie and you have Wendy Walker's recipe for a deeper, better, more harmonious life. PRODUCER is a terrific read that will help anyone achieve their personal goals."

—Mary T. Browne, author of *The Five Rules of Thought*

"Wendy was there for every big moment of the last thirty years. There are plenty of lessons for each of us from what she has seen and learned along the way. There's no better Producer than Wendy."

—Jeff Zucker, CEO, NBC Universal

"For decades, *Larry King Live* has been one of the best shows on cable television and Wendy Walker has been the secret of its success for the last sixteen years. In this highly entertaining book, Wendy takes you behind the scenes of the biggest stories and best interviews from her three decades in television— from the King of Pop to the President of the United States. This is one hell of a good story from one hell of an impressive woman."

—Haim Saban, chairman and CEO,
Saban Capital Group

"A highly optimistic, wildly entertaining, nakedly honest glimpse into the life of a great woman. Wendy's lessons will open your eyes, inspire you to reflect, and empower you to live your best life."

—Trish McEvoy, founder and makeup artist,
Trish McEvoy Beauty

"This is a terrific read! The behind the scenes stories by a major television veteran will hold you page by page. Enjoy!"

—Larry King

"I have known Wendy Walker for twenty-five years. She's one of the best television producers I've ever had the pleasure to be associated with."

—T. Boone Pickens, founder and chairman of
BP Capital Management

"In PRODUCER, Wendy Walker shares wonderful stories about extraordinary people, but her most amazing production has been her own incredible life and the lessons she's learned along the way. This is the most interesting and illuminating book I've ever read about how television news really works. She is a producer's producer. Highly recommended!"

—Dean Ornish, M.D., author of *The Spectrum,*
Clinical Professor of Medicine, University of California,
San Francisco

PRODUCER

*Lessons Shared from 30 Years
in Television*

WENDY WALKER

with

ANDREA CAGAN

with a Foreword by Larry King

CENTER
STREET

NEW YORK   BOSTON   NASHVILLE

Center Street
Hachette Book Group
237 Park Avenue
New York, NY 10017

www.centerstreet.com

Center Street is a division of Hachette Book Group, Inc.
The Center Street name and logo are trademarks of Hachette Book Group, Inc.

Printed in the United States of America

First Edition: November 2010
10 9 8 7 6 5 4 3 2

Library of Congress Cataloging-in-Publication Data

Walker, Wendy, 1953-
    Producer : lessons shared from 30 years in television / Wendy Walker with Andrea Cagan.
      p. cm.
    ISBN 978-1-59995-253-6
  1. Walker, Wendy.   2. Women television producers and directors—United States—Biography.   3. Television producers and directors—United States—Biography.
I. Cagan, Andrea.   II. Title.
    PN1992.4.W25A3 2010
    791.4502'32092—dc22
    [B]
                                                                    2010030833

To
my children,
Amaya and Walker,
who constantly teach me
new lessons about life and love

CONTENTS

FOREWORD

by Larry King

"Lessons" is a great word. Whenever I see it, I know that in the next few moments I'm going to learn something. And there is no better teacher than Wendy Walker, my senior executive producer for the past seventeen years. She really is the driving force behind *Larry King Live*. From early in the morning, throughout the day, and into the early evening, it's all on Wendy who stays on top of things by booking the show, making the calls, driving the crew, checking in with me, and putting out fires all along the way. Then when she's finished with her work, I get the last hour.

When I was ready to hire a new executive producer, the network narrowed it down to three possible choices. What a host looks for in a good executive producer is knowing she's right there, always at the helm, and always ready to stand up for me versus higher management. It's all about loyalty, an extraordinary trait which Wendy has demonstrated as long as we've worked together.

Before I met with Wendy, I favored a guy who worked on *Good Morning America* and was an avid sports fan, just like me. I liked him as a person and I liked the fact that he had no desire to leave his present job—unless he could work for me. I could imagine doing shows about sports each night since that was what I spent my days talking about. In fact, sports is my number one avocation. So much so, that if the *Washington Post* had a headline that read *Larry King's Secret Sex Life Revealed*, I'd turn to the sports page first.

But a meeting with Wendy changed my mind. At first it seemed impossible. Think about it. Jewish Sports Guy from Brooklyn meets WASP White House Producer from the Midwest. But I was amazed at her large array of letters of recommendation from past presidents, highly regarded newsmen, and other influential people. She had the contacts, that was for sure. Then it was the way she looked me in the eye and said, "I *really* want this job." I would learn about her loyalty later (that can only be proven with time), but I figured anyone who was that aggressive and offered me even more impressive recommendations if I wanted them fit the role of my executive producer. And we have worked together amazingly well ever since.

This doesn't mean we always agree. Quite the opposite. I often disagree with where Wendy wants to take the show, and we have some spirited discussions. But it wouldn't be healthy if we felt the same way about everything. As the host, I may want to talk about sports, but my executive producer is not a sports nut. She's thinking about the audience and what they want, something I never do because I don't have to.

This may seem strange, but I *never* go on the air thinking, "Will they like this or not like this? Are they enjoying this?" That would make me second-guess my questions. I see my job as being a conduit from the guests to the audience, asking the right questions, bringing out what the guests have to say and what they're thinking about. Then the audience makes up its own mind.

But the executive producer is *all* about the audience. While I prefer to talk about Manny Rodriguez, Wendy knows what will draw the highest ratings. This causes us to be at tangents. But the lesson you learn from Wendy is when to give and when not to. She knows when to win and when to lose, and she is impeccable in her loyalty at the same time.

When I heard that Wendy was writing a book, I immediately thought it was a great idea. I know she has something valuable to say, she has a great background, she's been through the ups and downs of the news business for the past thirty years, and she has watched television change right in front of her eyes. In fact, she has been and continues to be an integral part of that change. Nobody knows better than Wendy that there is no way to predict the news business, and no one can tell you what the media will look like in as little as five years from now.

In the end, it takes resilience and flexibility to be a great executive producer, traits of any good general and traits that I see in Wendy all the time. We are close friends, something that can work against us at times, because it feels like I'm at odds with a wife instead of a coworker. But really, I have never doubted my wisdom in hiring Wendy Walker as my executive producer, a woman whose loyalty and actions rise high above her job description.

So get ready to go back to school. It won't be as tough as it was when you were a kid, and you won't be graded. But you better listen well, 'cause you've got one hell of a teacher! And I love her with all my heart.

PRODUCER

INTRODUCTION

My name is Wendy Walker. Although you don't know me and probably don't recognize my name, you *will* recognize the events, tragedies, and celebrations in this book, since we all lived them. I am just one of the people doing my job behind the scenes and I'm a lot like you—except that I couldn't go to my college reunion because I had to produce the TV coverage for a US-Soviet summit. And I couldn't pick out the bridesmaids' dresses for my wedding because I was too busy covering the Bush-Clinton presidential campaign.

Throughout the years, I have had the privilege of working for Ethel Kennedy, ABC News, CNN, and Larry King. Beginning in 1983, I was CNN White House producer for a decade, and I have been senior executive producer of *Larry King Live* for the past seventeen years. As I have worked both in the White House and producing this amazing show for Larry King for such a long time, I have loved meeting world leaders, great authors, presidents and kings, extraordinarily influential people who have changed the course of the world as we know it. In fact, over the past thirty years, as I have told my stories, which constantly intrigued my listeners, many people have urged me to write a book. "Who else gets to meet these people?" they reminded me. "You have stories. You need to share them."

When I thought about it, I realized that as great as my stories are, I have something even more valuable to offer—the lessons I've learned, often the hard way, along the trajectory of my very challenging and active career. In an effort to share these priceless hard-earned life lessons, I decided to follow my friends' urgings. So I did it. Here I am, this is my book, and I have to say that I am way out of my comfort zone. But I'm doing it anyway.

I'm just not used to being in front of the camera or being the center of attention. I feel best in the background, behind the scenes, but with this book, that's changing. It has been a great learning experience for me, and reliving my lifelong adventures as an adult, rather than a kid, has been illuminating and a whole lot of fun.

In the pages of this book, you will find unique stories about lessons learned along the way, as I try to highlight the humor and some practical ways to lead a good, exciting, healthy life. There are stories involving many luminaries, such as Mikhail Gorbachev, Marlon Brando, and Yasser Arafat. Not to mention Larry King, an icon, one of the most famous and talented broadcast interviewers in the world.

When I began my work, I was a kid. Now I'm not a kid anymore, but with each day and each show I produce for Larry, I'm still learning a great deal about life and about myself. I feel excited about the years to come and about finding new ways to understand how connected we all are. In the end, I can see that the energy we give out in this life is exactly the energy we get back.

CHAPTER 1

Freaking Out Is Not an Option

My alarm clock woke me at 5:30 a.m., as usual. It was still dark outside as I reluctantly pulled back the covers, got up, and headed for the bathroom to wash my face and get ready for a new day. The digital readout on my clock told me it was Thursday, June 25, 2009, and I felt like I had a jump on the day.

The night before, when I went to bed, my staff and I had booked what I thought was a diverse and interesting *Larry King Live* show for tonight. I knew from experience over many years that if breaking news occurred anywhere in the world, we could and would shift our plans in an instant. That's always the case in the news business. But I was hoping for an easy day as I headed into my home office off my bedroom to check my e-mails. They were arriving fast and furious since it was a little after 8:30 a.m. on the East Coast. I scanned my incoming box quickly and checked last night's ratings.

I love living on the West Coast, and in the blush of a promising summer sunrise, I scanned the wires and various reports from my East Coast staff to confirm the morning headlines.

Then I went back to my e-mails. My production staff of forty across the country were streaming information to me from everywhere and would continue to do so—to the tune of at least two thousand e-mails daily. I know how impossible that sounds, but it's true. Imagine taking a half-hour walk or driving a kid to school in the early morning and having more than two hundred new e-mails waiting when you get back home. That's how it is with me, as I scan thousands of e-mails every day, eliminating what I don't need and making sure I respond to what is necessary and hopefully not deleting something important.

While I started answering the messages, my staff kicked in. They do myriad jobs that are all important; it's the old it takes a village concept. Since ten of the forty producers are bookers, when we decide in which direction the show will go that night they make the calls and do the intense work of booking the guests. When we were in the midst of reporting the deadly earthquake in Haiti in February 2010, for example, we had to decide who we wanted to interview concerning a massive world tragedy. Everybody got on board with ideas and suggestions, and we came up with names.

Among our staff, one producer is assigned strictly to knowing all the books that come out and which authors might be right for the current show. Two producers are in charge of the fifteen-minute water cooler stories, such as local tragedies that include people who are not normally in the news, which is how the Scott Peterson case began. Another producer handles celebrities and their agents and publicists. There are political bookers who work with Washington and the White House, and all of them have their A list: people we would have on at any time, such as Angelina Jolie and Brad Pitt or a sitting president.

In other words, we are always working simultaneously on whatever is going on today, the rest of the week, and way into the future. While we do this, one of the editorial producers does the research for the open of the show: Larry is extraordinarily well-versed since he watches news all day long, but he still needs specifics. So one producer writes the open, others produce the video components, and still others are in charge of the live show. That includes satellites, audio, graphics, phone calls, the rundown, content, remote locations, and breaking news during the show. There are publicists, cameramen, makeup artists; everyone is doing his or her individual job to create a live show.

And so each job is a piece of the whole, like a set of dominoes. It all has to fit together in harmony because if one domino goes down, so do all the rest. Everyone has to know what everyone else is doing, and we perform this intricate dance every day, all day long. If the show changes suddenly in the middle of the day, which happens very often, we start the process all over again, with less time and more scurrying around. But we always get the job done.

So far so good for this particular day. It seemed that *Larry King Live* would go forward as planned. On our roster, we had conservative Ann Coulter, Democratic strategist Donna Brazile, and Elizabeth Edwards, who was struggling with inoperable cancer and her ex-senator husband's stunning infidelity. I thought we might include some information on Governor Mark Sanford of South Carolina who was also embroiled in an extramarital scandal, so the show was off to a solid start.

I gave the go-ahead to check into the availability of Governor Sanford and a few others, but as executive producer I had to keep in mind that Barbara Walters was airing an ABC special about ailing actress Farrah Fawcett that night. In her advance publicity for the special, Barbara had suggested on *Good Morning America* that Farrah, who was struggling with the last stages of cancer, might not make it through the day. It sounded a little presumptuous on Barbara's part, but the actress had supposedly been at death's door for quite a while. If she died today, I would have to change the show. That was par for the course. I often changed the focus of a show when we were in the planning stages, since I had to respond to what was going on in the world at each moment. But I hoped I didn't have to.

I was in the middle of the morning booking call when, at 9:28 a.m., a flash showed up on my computer. Farrah had passed away. Barbara had been right and we had some adjusting to do.

Adjusting on a moment's notice is what this job has constantly demanded during the past seventeen years. Now we were facing the death of a beloved actress and we had to change the show. We did an about-face. There was no doubt that the show we originally planned was out. It was tough since we had to start from scratch again, but I didn't freak out. That would have taken up too much time and wasted too much valuable energy. We would replace show number one with show number two, which would be devoted to Farrah's death. We all got on the phone to reschedule our guests (we never cancel; we always reschedule) and round up the appropriate people for the tragic new show.

When a show suddenly turns on its head because something important supersedes our plans, each moment is crucial and we are filled with anxiety as we are required to book a whole new show in a very short period of time. It's not unusual for me to be ironing out the wrinkles of a show well into the late afternoon, which is edgy since we air at 6 p.m. on the West Coast. By the end of a day like the one I was presently facing, I have generally made hundreds of decisions, and the only way to do that is to remain calm. That would be the case today, I realized, reminding myself to breathe as we began drawing up lists of guests who knew Farrah, as well as checking their availability. Dreams of a simple day flew out the window as we began to prepare for show number two, but I had no idea how crazy the day would turn out.

Before I got back on the phone, I shot off an e-mail to my friend Lisa Ling, special correspondent for CNN, and *The Oprah Winfrey Show*. Her sister, Laura Ling, and a colleague, Euna Lee, had been detained in North Korea since March 17, 2009, for entering the country without a visa. They had been covering a controversial story on human trafficking, and on June 8 the women had been sentenced to twelve years of hard labor, having been found guilty of the "grave crime" of illegal entry into North Korea, even though they were told by their guide that it was safe to do so.

Lisa had been working day and night to try to bring her sister home, and we had booked her, her parents, and the husbands of the two detained journalists on the show to make a public appeal. I recall being very careful to accentuate Lisa's needs rather than making the show what *we* wanted it to be during that hour she talked with Larry. This was all about getting the women back, which overrode our desire for good ratings. All of Lisa's pleas and maneuverings needed to be handled with great delicacy because of how political and disturbing the situation was. I couldn't imagine how she was getting up in the mornings, so I e-mailed her daily, asking about her progress and if there was anything I could do. This morning, I wrote:

Hi. Have you heard anything more? How are you holding up?

Lisa wrote back:

Hey, Mama. [That's what she calls me.] I'm about to lose my mind.

This is so frustrating. I'll be ok, just venting about bureaucracy...

Back to Farrah. Time was flying by as we contacted various principals in her life and tried to book them. So far, we had gotten Dick and Pat Van Patten, Candy Spelling, Joan Dangerfield, and my dear friend Suzanne Somers. It was coming together, but I stopped for a moment when a provocative e-mail landed in my in-box. The popular TMZ Web site, a huge leader in entertainment news, had posted the following information:

1:44 p.m. We've just learned that Michael Jackson was taken by ambulance to a hospital in Los Angeles...we're told it was cardiac arrest and that paramedics administered CPR in the ambulance.

Oh, no. What was this? Please! I e-mailed the staff member who had sent it:

1:45 p.m. We might have to do something on this. Check it out please.

I got on a conference call with several of my producers while one of them phoned Jermaine Jackson, Michael's brother, to find out what he knew. She sent me this:

1:47 p.m. I'm on with Jermaine's wife right now. They had no idea.

I immediately e-mailed Lisa Gregorisch, my close friend and executive producer of *Extra*. She always got the celebrity breaking news fast and we often validated our information with each other.

1:48 p.m. I am sure you know this. An insider just told me that an ambulance just went into the compound of Michael Jackson's home. No details or for what reason or for whom. Minutes ago, the ambulance just left Michael's home with sirens sounding.

Lisa wrote back:

1:49 p.m. Yes, it could be cardiac arrest.

My staff continued booking the show about Farrah and I told them to keep Larry off all press calls, at home and on his cell phone. We had to find out the truth about Michael Jackson before he said a word to anyone. What if Larry answered his phone, was asked a question, and made a comment that was not true? When I was sure Larry would not answer any calls, I placed a call to criminal attorney Mark Geragos, a regular on our show and a former lawyer to Michael. "Mark," I said, "we're hearing that Michael Jackson might be very sick. Or dead."

Mark said he would check it out. Five minutes later he called me back. "I've been told he's dead," Mark said, "but they're not confirming it yet."

What should we do about the show? It was a tough call, but my gut told me this was more than a rumor, partly because I knew that Geragos had reliable sources inside the LAPD. It was after 2 p.m. when my staff and I started booking an alternative show, just in case the rumors were true, which was looking more and more likely. Show number three would feature the deaths of both Michael Jackson and Farrah Fawcett. It's hard to book a show when you don't know if someone is alive or dead. Imagine the sensitivity required in asking someone to come on the show "if and when" their loved one dies. Or if he has already died. And still, we had to do it.

My anxiety was at a high pitch when we had four hours left and we weren't even sure what we were going to do that night. I could lose my composure, which would waste precious time, or I could follow my gut, which told me that a tragedy of some sort was occurring around Michael Jackson. I had come to trust my intuition after so many years of depending upon it, and besides, I reminded myself, if it was a rumor, why would it still be circulating this many hours later? I felt the immensity of the situation. If Michael was really dead, similar to the deaths of Elvis and Marilyn, it would touch everyone on an international level. But we had to find out the truth quickly so we could put together the right show.

At 2:50 p.m., we got another e-mail from the TMZ Web site:

> We've just learned that Michael Jackson has died. He was 50. Michael suffered a cardiac arrest earlier this after-noon and paramedics were unable to revive him. We're told when paramedics arrived, Jackson had no pulse and they never got a pulse back.

Since it was TMZ, a celebrity and gossip entertainment site, it was still considered a rumor, but it was getting much too real to ignore. Should I continue to book guests for Farrah as well as Michael? There was no one to ask, so I made a quick decision. While the buzz about Michael's death continued to escalate, I sent out the following e-mail to my staff:

3:08 p.m., PST. Assuming the news is true, we will be going live at 9 and possibly at midnight. Concentrate on Michael Jackson...it is a bigger story because it is a shock. Do not book any more guests for Farrah unless they know Michael. It is about Michael.

Show number four was in the works, and the first order of business was to confirm that the rumors of Michael's death were true. Each of us made calls depending on whom we knew best. I called back Mark Geragos, who was getting the news from his sources. All of my producers and I were working in tandem with the network since they needed to get a production truck to the hospital and Jackson's home as we contacted every friend, colleague, and business associate of Michael's, putting out an APB on the guests we were trying to book at the last minute.

The hour was late and we were working on booking a long list of people when I pushed back from my desk, feeling light-headed. When was the last time I ate? I hadn't been this immersed in a story since Scott Peterson was convicted of killing his wife and his unborn child. I walked into the living room to find my daughter sitting on the couch, reading a magazine. Walker was on the floor beside her. "I'm pretty sure Michael Jackson is dead," I told them. "This is a moment you'll never forget."

I remembered exactly where I was when John Lennon, Marilyn Monroe, President Kennedy, and Princess Diana had died. I knew that if Michael really was gone, this was the same kind of monumental loss that would send the entire world into collective shock. But I had a show to book. I returned to my office and got back on the phone, so far removed from where I'd been when I woke up that morning, it was hard to believe it was the same day.

In the next half hour, the *Los Angeles Times* reported:

> Pop star Michael Jackson was pronounced dead by doctors this afternoon after arriving at the hospital in a deep coma, city and law enforcement sources told the *Times*.

It wasn't long after this bulletin that I was e-mailed a photograph of Michael's head, presumably dead. The photographer wanted money for it. He was wasting his time. Soon after, CNN made the announcement that Michael had died. Now it was official.

I dove headfirst into the business of finding out who knew Michael best and who we could get on the show in just a few hours. Show number four was in full production mode, and still, I had to do my regular job when a crisis arose about something else altogether. An executive producer wears a lot of hats, and it seemed that Billy Ray Cyrus had been on the show June 12 and had concerns about his segments. It was a rare occurrence when a guest was less than satisfied—I couldn't even remember the last time—so I wrote Billy Ray an e-mail to the effect that I was a little busy with the current breaking news but I wanted to apologize. I followed that with a short explanation of what had occurred and why. In essence, I took the blame, fell on my sword, and sent the e-mail.

It's a good idea to avoid blaming the other guy. If you made a mistake, just admit it. It might feel uncomfortable at the time, but owning your mistake will make you look a far sight better than coming up with a lame excuse that nobody believes anyway. For this very intense moment in time, it worked with Billy Ray. I got an e-mail straight back from him, saying he couldn't believe that on a day that two icons had died, I was still concerned about him. He thought that was amazing and he wrote, "We'll always have this moment of sharing the tragedy of the death of Michael Jackson. He was so important to me and I am so sorry."

I exhaled. Back to the work at hand. My staff had the tough and highly delicate job of letting the Farrah people know that we were preempting her for the death of a more famous and celebrated star than the woman they loved so well. Then an e-mail arrived from Lisa Ling. One would expect her to be completely wrapped up in advocating for her sister, but she was caring enough to have moved outside of her own tragedy and thought of me:

> I don't know if you know this, but Deepak was very close to Michael.

This was news to me. I shot out a thank-you e-mail to Lisa and got Deepak Chopra on the phone. I knew Deepak well, I respected him and his opinions, and he agreed to appear on the show the very next day. During that call, he stated to me in no uncertain terms, by the way, that he believed that drugs administered by licensed medical doctors had killed Michael. I scribbled down some of his comments as he told me that Michael had been taking a drug called Diprivan that was so powerful, it was only used in operating rooms. It created an effect that was about as close to dying as a person could get, and when someone was on the drug, they needed to be closely monitored in case they needed to be brought back from the throes of death. Deepak was furious at the doctors who he said he believed had administered such dangerous medications to Michael in his home without proper monitoring. He told me that Michael liked getting dangerously close to death and then brought back.

In a few minutes, Jonathan Klein, president of CNN, called me to confirm tonight's show and ask if we could run for a straight two hours with reruns at midnight and at 3 a.m. We agreed. This was a rare evening when I did not have dinner with my children. I stayed in my office and when Larry was ready to go on the air, we had booked enough star-studded guests, all stunned and upset by the death, to fill the show.

We started with Dr. Prediman K. Shah, Director of Cardiology at Cedars-Sinai Medical Center. Then we went on to singer-musicians Smokey Robinson, Céline Dion, Cher, Aaron Neville, Donna Summer, and J. C. Chasez. We had Tommy Mottola, former Sony music executive, Suzanne de Passe from Motown who had discovered the Jackson Five, and Shelly Berger, former manager of the Jackson Five. Larry also interviewed Kara Finnstrom, Ted Rowlands, and Richard Roth, all CNN correspondents, and Carlos Diaz, correspondent for *Extra*. Everyone had something to say.

We also had Thea Andrews from *Entertainment Tonight*.

KING: At the UCLA Medical Center, which is, by the way, a two-billion-dollar edifice, much of it named in honor of the late Ronald Reagan, Thea Andrews stands by. She's an *Entertainment Tonight* correspondent. Still crowds there?

ANDREWS: Many crowds, Larry. There are thousands of people here on all sides of the medical center. As you said, it's a huge facility. It takes up more than a whole city block. Getting here, trying to find your cameras was hard, because there are so many news people out here, thousands of crowds, helicopters buzzing overhead, and, of course, many supporters of Michael Jackson, many people devastated by this loss.

KING: What has the hospital said?

ANDREWS: The hospital has been mum. They haven't released a statement yet. What I can tell you is that *ET* has exclusively obtained the last photos of Michael Jackson, as he was being removed by paramedics from his home. As you heard earlier, it's very close to here, about six minutes away.

He was in full cardiac arrest. Paramedics attempted to revive him during transport here to the hospital, and they continued to attempt to revive him inside the emergency room. Obviously, they were not successful. But as you see the photo—I don't know if you have the photo up there, Larry. They're attempting to revive Michael. His eyes are closed.

KING: How did you get that photograph?

ANDREWS: I don't know, Larry. You'll have to ask my executive producer.

KING: That's a heck of a job of reporting. We'll be checking back with you.

Also that night, Larry interviewed Randy Jackson from *American Idol*, civil rights activist Jesse Jackson, and actor Corey Feldman. Two Jackson fans named Cheryl and Melvin came on the air, and musicians Sean "P. Diddy" Combs, Sheryl Crow, and Kenny Rogers called in. It was an impressive lineup as we checked in with people from all over the country and the world who were devastated and shocked by the sudden death of the self-declared King of Pop.

Cher called in and said, "You know, I was just sitting here listening to you talk. And I'm having a million different reactions.

Things that I didn't expect I would feel. When I think of him, I think of this young boy, that teenager that I first met. This adorable boy that I met who, you know, loved to look at my beaded socks. Yes, he was a great singer. You know, it's like God gives you certain gifts. And some people he gives different gifts, and some people he gives more gifts. And this child was just an extraordinary child, touched by this ability to have people feel him and feel people. And he just had that sense that you get, and you don't get it from a living person. You get it from someplace else. He had it."

Céline told Larry on the phone, "I am shocked like the rest of the world. It doesn't sink in right now. I'm overwhelmed by this tragedy. I have to say that Michael Jackson's been an idol for me all my life. I remember being in my house when I was very, very young and having his posters above my bed. He's been my idol all my life, I looked up to him, and my goal was to be maybe doing the same show business world as him."

And Liza Minnelli called in and said, "Oh, Larry, I couldn't believe it, honey. I got a call at two o'clock in the morning from a lawyer telling me that he's gone into cardiac arrest. They said he had been complaining of chest pains, you know? He changed show business. He hit with a force that was spectacular as he started to grow up. And then he grew and grew and grew. All the time. He grew all the time."

Talk about flying by the seat of our pants, we were actually booking guests while the show was on the air. Larry would say, "We just got this person on the phone," and he would launch into an interview with no preparation whatsoever. Michael's death finally felt real to me when I saw the live picture of the helicopter that was transporting his body to the morgue. And the news just kept on coming.

As the story unfolded, I noticed a rhythm that is often

present when we are dealing with breaking news. It actually takes on a whole different feel than a prepared show has when you know exactly what you are covering and with whom. With breaking news, you are constantly getting new information and an energy takes over as the story unfolds in a natural way. That was the case with the Michael Jackson story as we began to let the incoming news items guide us.

Somewhere in the midst of all of this, I went to tuck my kids into bed. Then it was back to my office, but now I was using my large office in another portion of the house that had been converted into a state-of-the-art newsroom with a dozen screens that allowed me to check breaking news on all the cable and broadcast networks, national and international. The news about Michael was spreading fast all over the world, and global reactions were pouring in about the shocking and untimely death of this musical icon.

By 2 a.m. it was all over—at least for the day. This was a story that would not end with a single day of coverage or even a week. I knew it would go on and on as accusations of drug overdoses and finger-pointing at so-called unscrupulous doctors began to dominate the conversations, along with relentless reports of Michael's bizarre and unhealthy lifestyle. And then there were rumors about Debbie Rowe, one of Michael's ex-wives, the mother of his two oldest children.

I dropped into bed exhausted and amazed that, once again, I had made it through a day that dealt me so many dips and turns I should have gotten seasick. After all, I had awakened with one show in mind and had booked three more before Larry went on the air. I'd answered thousands of e-mails, much more than my usual number, I had taken care of my kids, and we had all done our jobs. And the show had gone on.

The next night Deepak was among our guests. Here is a

segment of his interview, staggering in its directness and in Deepak's commitment to be the first person who dared to speak about this.

CHOPRA: In 1988, he [Michael] called me out of the blue and asked me to teach him meditation. I went to Neverland and we had a weekend together and became friends since that.

KING: What was he like?

CHOPRA: Magical. First time I met him, he was magic. He had a jukebox in his studio, with the traditional coins. So, we threw in a few coins and he said, choose the music. And I chose "Saturday Night Fever" and he started to dance...

KING: You complained, though, today about people around him. You've been very open and been critical of what?

CHOPRA: Well, in 2005, after the trial, Michael came and spent a week with me. And out of the blue he asked me for a prescription, knowing that I'm a doctor and I have a license, too. It was a prescription for a narcotic. I said, wait, why would you want a prescription for a narcotic? It suddenly dawned on me that he was getting a lot of prescriptions from a lot of people.

KING: Was he an addict?

CHOPRA: Yes, he was.

KING: Did people around him encourage that addiction?

CHOPRA: Yes, more so his doctors.

KING: Didn't he have migraine headaches, though? Wasn't he in a lot of pain?

CHOPRA: He was in pain. But there are many ways to manage pain. Even if you're on narcotics, there's a way to manage narcotics.

KING: Did he take a lot of pills and stuff?

CHOPRA: I know for a fact that he did. I saw bottles of OxyContin. I knew he was getting shots. I knew his doctors were enablers. What can I say? I confronted him many times with it. When I did, he would stop returning my calls until we changed the topic.

KING: Lisa Marie Presley, his ex-wife, writes on her MySpace blog that Michael once told her he was afraid he would end up like her father. Did he talk about that?

CHOPRA: He did...I'm discussing the problems in the medical profession which enables this kind of addiction. It's become a tradition in Hollywood.

KING: You're blaming the medical profession.

CHOPRA: Of course. There's a coterie of doctors right here in Hollywood that like to hang around celebrities. They perpetuate their habit. They make them drug addicts. We've got to really investigate this.

Decpak was the first to tell it like he believed it to be. When he went on the air and said what he did about the medical profession, people were enraged at him and they wanted to kill the messenger. But it came out later that Michael had had countless interventions that clearly did no good at all. And in the end, when Dr. Conrad Murray, Michael's primary doctor, was arrested for involuntary manslaughter, everyone had to admit that Deepak's suspicions may not have been unfounded.

Over the next few weeks, while we continued to cover this monumental death, it seemed as if a never-ending flurry of celebrities were dying. The list includes: David Carradine, Farrah Fawcett, Michael Jackson, Walter Cronkite, Ed McMahon, Robert Novak, Ted Kennedy, Dominick Dunne, DJ AM, and Patrick Swayze. We covered these deaths as best we could on *Larry King Live*, making sure we were honoring most of the people on this long list. In fact, the viewing audience tuned in to our show for that very reason. With so many deaths occurring and so much public grieving, they needed a place where they knew their favorite personalities would be given their due. That was how people looked at our show.

And yet, a piece appeared in *Vanity Fair* magazine, in September 2009, written by James Wolcott, criticizing Larry. In a snarky, critical tone, this writer called the show "the funeral parlor for the gods." He called Larry "America's chief mourner and grief counselor," and criticized him for "assuming the indispensable role of designated mourner to the stars, tollbooth collector at the last stop before the Hereafter, pallbearer beyond compare."

By the end, the author conceded that we needed Larry to help us get through these things. I suppose it was a back-handed compliment to have an entire article devoted to us in *Vanity Fair*, but the nature of the article was so negative, it implied we were doing it incorrectly. And then, this writer only referred to the deaths of Farrah, Michael, David Carradine, and Ed McMahon. What if he had waited until all ten celebrities were gone? What would he have said then? While we honored the rest of the people who had passed, should we have left out Teddy Kennedy? Or what about Walter Cronkite?

The truth is that millions of viewers have their eyes and ears trained on our show every single evening. When someone of importance in this country dies, the public assumes that Larry will have something to say about it. I take it as a compliment and a responsibility. These deaths were very important to the general public.

No matter what occurs and when, there is no crystal ball to tell us which direction we should take. There is no instruction book to turn to or anyone who has the answers. It's basically up to me and my staff, so we have to keep up with everything all the time to make the best decisions we can. We try not to second-guess ourselves. I go with my gut (it's usually all I have), I depend on my staff, and we book the best show we can produce. When it all looks impossible, I try to be the calm in the midst of the storm. Our reward is that each day, whether last night's show was great or mediocre, the palette is clean and we get to start all over again, a little wiser for what we learned yesterday. And a little bit more trusting of ourselves.

❖

FREAKING OUT IS NOT AN OPTION

When you have to make an important decision and there are a variety of ways to go, the only clear path is to channel your intuition. Check in with your gut. We all have that intuitive gift to some degree. My psychic friends assure me of this, and I know it's true. Some people just have it honed better than others.

So, when the stress-o-meter hits ten, remember that losing your cool is not going to help or change the situation. When things get confusing and you feel frazzled and upset, try taking a deep breath and calming yourself down. Do whatever it takes to accomplish this. You may need to leave the room, sit in a quiet place with no music where you can't be disturbed, and take a moment to go inside yourself. Then ask yourself, *What do I really want here? What feels right?*

When you lose your temper and freak out, that behavior negatively impacts others and can throw them off their game. Clearly, we all need to learn from our mistakes, and that includes reviewing the things that did not work, but it doesn't make sense to upset the apple cart when you're standing in the middle of it. You can't stop in the midst of a situation to figure out what happened in the past, because you have to be present and look forward. Once it's over, you can take the time to figure out what went wrong so it won't happen again. But screaming and freaking out will only take you further away from your goal of working things out. Losing it will intimidate people and push them away, which is counterproductive to what you are trying to achieve. The truth is that no one wants to work with a screamer, and that kind of negative energy never does any good for anyone.

When you take some time to get in touch with your feelings and you can hear yourself think, consider both the short-term and the long-term repercussions of any decision you might make. Ask yourself, What will this decision mean to me tomorrow, five days from now, five weeks from now, or five years from now? No matter the nature of the decision you need to make, go with your intuition. If it feels right, go with it. If it doesn't, walk away.

I once knew a woman who had five psychics at the ready whenever she needed advice. If the first one didn't tell her what she wanted to hear, she called the second one, and so on. At the end, she was still confused and she had no ability to make her own decisions.

Not that you should be isolated and never check with anyone else. Sometimes after you make a decision that feels right, you might want to clarify by checking with a smart friend who really knows you, understands your situation, and absolutely will tell you the truth. For the most part, however, when you go inside and trust yourself, you'll be amazed at how much easier decisions become. When you stay calm and take all the elements into consideration, a confusing situation will generally turn out a lot better than you might expect!

CHAPTER 2

Be Someone Others Want to Be Around

When I graduated from Hollins University in 1975, I didn't know what I wanted to do next, and neither did most of my friends. Back then, we really didn't plan our careers like college students do now. In fact, when I think back about my childhood, we didn't plan much. It was a sign of the times for girls to think more in terms of jobs than careers, and it all followed a somewhat logical plan, with marriage and children usually being the end goal.

But I was a little different. When I graduated from college, I wanted to leave home and work. My mom would have preferred for me to settle down in Jackson, Michigan, where she and Dad were living. But that didn't appeal to me. I had already lived in Paris and I wanted to move away and live on my own—despite a terrifying experience.

It was during my junior year when I joined a program called Hollins Abroad, an opportunity to spend a year in Paris and study art, which was my passion. I went to Paris with two friends, Torrey and Cynthia, and we all lived in the home of a lovely French family. I got pretty fluent in the language and I felt very grown-up, being on my own for the first time and traveling all around the city on the metro.

One afternoon, I was thrilled to meet Thomas, a cool American guy who suggested he and I meet at La Madeleine, a famous Roman Catholic church, to hear some music. I should have asked him to pick me up or meet me at my place so I wouldn't have to travel alone through the streets of Paris. Our dean at Hollins had warned us to be careful about being tricked and abducted, and he suggested we always travel with someone else.

Still, I threw caution to the wind. I hailed a cab by myself and got in. *"L'église Madeleine, s'il vous plaît,"* I said in French, feeling very cosmopolitan. As the cabdriver began to ask me questions in French, I felt proud of myself that I could answer him—until the nature of his questions began to concern me.

"What are you doing here in Paris?" he started quite innocently.

"I'm going to school," I answered him in French.

"Do you live in a dorm?" he asked. What business was that of his?

"No," I answered quickly. "I live with a family."

"Do they wait up for you?" he wanted to know.

Now I was beginning to feel anxious. "Yes," I said, "they wait up for me. Could you hurry, because my friend is waiting for me right now and he's probably getting worried and making some phone calls."

The cabdriver picked up speed as I had requested, but that only made me more anxious. Then, all of a sudden, he pulled over to the side of the road two blocks away from the church. I grabbed the door handle to jump out of the car but he turned, reached into the backseat, and placed his hand firmly over the lock. A small car pulled up behind us and stopped. A man jumped out of the car behind us and opened my door from the outside. He reached for me as if he were about to pull me out of the car when the driver stopped him. *"Ce n'est pas bon. On ne peux pas faire ça,"* he said. "This isn't good. We can't do this."

In an instant, the man who was trying to pull me toward him let go of me and slammed my car door shut. My driver took off, sped forward for two blocks, pulled up in front of the Madeleine, and I dashed out, slamming the cab door behind me. No one followed me as he sped away and I was breathless, standing in front of the church, scared to death. I had just come so close to being abducted I could hardly breathe, and I was grateful to be alive.

Despite my near abduction, I decided to leave the security of my family in Michigan and go to Washington DC, anyway, rent a cheap place with some friends, and find a job. I had lots of interests and I wanted to experience life and the workplace so I wouldn't end up being bored or boring. My father understood my desire to break away and he gave me the grand sum of forty dollars to get started on my new life. "Go to Washington," he told me. "If you don't find a job in two weeks, write yourself a check for a plane ticket and come back home."

When my five friends and I arrived in Washington, we found an inexpensive apartment to share in Georgetown, just outside of DC. That took care of my forty dollars, so I headed straight over to a popular clothing store called Brooks Brothers (it was very posh at the time) to apply for a job in sales. I needed some money coming in right away so I could eat. I wanted to continue at school to get my master's degree in art. But if I did, I would have to pay for it myself.

The job interview was my first real one, and I tried to present myself in a good light. I knew the position was competitive, so during my interview I made sure to be friendly, positive, and to look like I had something on the ball. After all, I had lived in Paris! I must have done okay because I was hired on the spot as a salesperson for Brooks Brothers. Although I knew this job would be temporary, at least I had a paycheck coming in. I had bigger goals than sales, but this was exactly what I needed to do right now.

I concentrated on being the best salesperson I could be. In the midseventies, there were very few women on the floor at a primarily men's store, not because men were considered better than women at sales. There was no way to know, because in the posh clothing stores back then, it was considered improper for a woman to ask a man, "What side do you dress on?" when he was buying pants that needed to be hemmed. I actually didn't know what that meant until a fellow salesperson told me. It seemed that any reference to a man's genitals was out of the question for a woman at the time, so we could not fit the men in suits.

Of course, that was where the money was. While a suit might cost a couple hundred dollars and in many cases, up from there, a shirt cost about $18.50. Ties, undershirts, and handkerchiefs were inexpensive and we worked on commission. I did the math and realized that I would need to sell a load of stuff to make any money at all, so that was exactly what I set out to do.

I served many a VIP during the time I worked at Brooks Brothers in Washington, including Ethel Kennedy, Nancy Kissinger, and Eunice Shriver. I always made sure I approached them with a good attitude. I was a popular saleswoman because of that, and I remember my very first customer, a distinguished man named Clark Clifford, former US Secretary of Defense. When I approached him on the floor to say, "Can I help you?" with a nice smile, it turned out that he wanted a large number of custom-made shirts with monograms. They were quite expensive, and my very first sale totaled a couple thousand dollars.

When a veteran salesman saw me serving ex-Secretary Clifford, he sized me up as a "just out of college chick," and he came over to rescue my sale that did not need rescuing. I *did* need him, however, to help me ring up the order since I was unfamiliar with the system as yet, but the commission was mine. Buoyed by making such a strong first sale, I continued my efforts and I swiftly became the highest earning salesperson on the staff, man or woman, without ever selling a suit.

One afternoon at about 4 p.m., after the manager of the store, Bob Mallon, had finished an afternoon cocktail, he called me to his office. "Okay, Wendy," he said, "how are you doing this? I want to know exactly what you're doing."

"Well," I said, "I walk up to a customer. I smile, and I say, 'If you need anything, I'll be right over there.' And I walk away."

"Why do you do that?" Bob wanted to know.

"I don't know about you," I said, "but I don't like to be bugged when I'm shopping at a store. I hate it when someone starts following me around. If I greet them with a smile and tell them where I'll be if they have any questions, they find me and ask. And they don't feel bugged or pressured."

"That can't be all," he said. "What else do you do?"

I thought for a moment. "Some of the sales staff don't go out of their way to make a sale for just a tie or a scarf that costs only about ten dollars. They prefer to talk with one another instead of waiting around. But in my mind, ten times ten equals a hundred dollars. I see each sale as important, and I make the customer's experience a good one. I don't care how many times I ring up a ten-dollar sale. I just know it adds up."

Excited, Bob went to a sales meeting in New York and told

his bosses about this interesting saleswoman who was making more than most of the men. I ended up working at Brooks Brothers for the next two years, earning annually about thirty-four thousand dollars in commissions, an unheard of amount at the time, especially for a woman who was not allowed to sell suits. I was thrilled, able to go out to dinner when I wanted, and I did my artwork, my first love, on the side. I had no idea how long it would be before I ever matched that salary again, and at the time, I took it in my stride. My dad, however, hoped I would stay on at Brooks Brothers for a good long time because he got tons of new shirts every month!

The trouble was that I got tired of being a sales clerk. True, I was earning a really good living and I was meeting interesting people. But there was only so far a salesperson could go. I wanted more. I wasn't sure what that looked like until one of my customers told me he wanted to open an art gallery. He and I had discussed art and he knew it was my first love. So he asked me if I was interested in leaving my present job to run the art gallery he was about to open. I did it. I left Brooks Brothers to manage a small new operation called the Huber Art Gallery for five thousand dollars a year, a fraction of the salary I'd been making. Looking back, it seems like an impulsive move and not the smartest thing to do, but I couldn't remain a sales clerk forever. I had started my master's degree work at George Washington University, but I stopped when I left Brooks Brothers. I just couldn't afford it anymore.

When I began working in the gallery, I did as much outreach as I could, but very few people wandered in. When they did, they usually walked back out pretty quickly since we really didn't have much interesting art to speak of. I spent most days alone, answering the few phone calls I received and keeping the place tidy, an easy job since we had so little foot traffic.

I was sweeping the floor one morning (again) for lack of anything else to do, when the telephone rang. I ran to answer it and I was caught off guard by the voice on the other end of the line.

"Is this Wendy?" asked a female voice.

"Yes, it is," I answered.

"This is Ethel Kennedy," she said.

I paused. There was simply no way Ethel Kennedy would be calling me. But I *had* served her at the store and we had carried on lively conversations. In fact, I was so stunned that at first I thought someone was playing a trick on me. Now, when I think back, I should have suspected it was Ethel herself, considering the way my life has played out. It seems like fate has had a way of placing me in circumstances that are unexpected and extremely foretelling.

Let me explain. It started when I was three months old and my family just happened to move into the same house in Chappaqua, New York, where the former president and Secretary of State Clinton live today. Then, about three years later, in 1956, we were living in Johnstown, Pennsylvania, when Richard Nixon was running for vice president for a second term.

He was on a whistle-stop tour when my mother took me to the station to watch his train come chugging in and slowly stop. There he was, standing at the back of the caboose, waving at people. It was chilly and I had on a pink flannel coat with a fur collar. Mom always dressed me impeccably in very short dresses and lovely coats. On this particularly cold day, however, I was wearing a pink number I called my "fat coat," because it was so thick and fluffy it made me look like a pink snowball.

Apparently, vice presidential candidate Richard Nixon noticed it, too. When the train pulled to a stop, he scanned the crowd for a moment and then swooped down, lifted me from my mother's arms, and held me up for a photo op. Mamie Eisenhower, the wife of the presidential candidate, was also on the train and she handed me a rose. Later, we dried it in an atlas where it remained for many years.

Of course, I don't remember the actual moment. I was only three. But what I *do* remember is seeing the newspaper the next day in Pennsylvania and there I was, in the arms of Richard Nixon in my fat coat. The man meant little to me at the time but I recall noticing that something could happen one day and end up in the newspaper the next. That was the first time I made that connection. Since his name was printed and mine wasn't, was that an omen that my life's work would be behind the scenes instead of in front of the camera?

Back at the gallery, Ethel spoke again. "Are you the Wendy who used to wait on me at Brooks Brothers?" she asked.

"Yes, that's me. I served you. How can I help you?" I asked politely, starting to believe that she really *was* Ethel Kennedy.

"How are you?" she asked.

"I'm fine," I answered. "How are you?"

"Great. Listen, I'm having a party tonight for Don Klosterman of the LA Rams. Would you like to come and be Joe's dinner partner?"

I inhaled sharply. The now late Don Klosterman (his name meant nothing to me at that moment) was a legend in the world of football, building winning teams in three different leagues throughout his career, I would learn later. Ethel Kennedy was asking me to be Joe's dinner partner, her handsome and savvy son with her late husband, Robert F. Kennedy.

"Can you come to dinner tonight at Hickory Hill?" she asked.

"Okay," I said haltingly.

The very name, Hickory Hill, carried with it a sense of

elegance and history. This colonial brick house in McLean, Virginia, built around 1815, was used as a temporary head- quarters by General George B. McClellan during the American Civil War. The home had originally been bought by Senator John F. Kennedy and his wife, Jacqueline, who sold it to Ethel and her husband, Bobby. Who didn't want to go to dinner at Hickory Hill?

"Where do you live?" Ethel asked.

I gave her my address in Georgetown.

"I'll have Caroline Croft pick you up and bring you to Hick- ory Hill."

I hung up the phone, wondering how on earth Ethel had found me. When the phone rang again (two calls made it a busy day at the gallery), it was my boss from Brooks Brothers. "Wendy, did Ethel Kennedy just call you?"

"Yes, she did."

"Good. She was looking for you and I gave her your num- ber. So what did she want?" he asked eagerly.

"She wants me to come over for dinner," I answered, hardly able to believe it myself.

I left work early and gathered my roommates together to tell them that I would be Joe Kennedy's dinner date that very night at Hickory Hill for a dinner given by Ethel Kennedy to honor Don Klosterman. I did the research to find out who Klosterman was but God only knew who else would be at the dinner and I had no money (thanks to my work at the gallery) and no decent clothes. When I put my head together with my roommates, Torrey and Cynthia, we decided that the nicest dress that any of us owned was rolled up in a ball on its way to the cleaners. I pulled the gray knit dress out of Torrey's car and I ran an iron over it. It was dowdy and conservative and it would have to do.

Then I called my mom. "Ethel Kennedy just asked me to go to Hickory Hill, that huge house in McLean, Virginia," I told her. "I'm supposed to be Joe Kennedy's dinner partner. She's sending a car for me."

"I don't want you getting into a car with a strange man," Mom said protectively. "You don't know those boys and I don't want you driving around with them."

"Mrs. Kennedy is sending a woman to pick me up," I assured her. "Her name is Caroline Croft."

That seemed to placate my mother. As I got ready for my big night, she told the rest of the family and one sister after another called me with advice.

"What are you going to wear?" said Peggy.

"How will you do your hair? You have to look really good," said Terry.

My third sister, Mary, being a little more scholarly than the rest of us, said, "Let me tell you about Joe Kennedy." She gave me a rundown, offering me all the information she had on this man, next to whom I would be sitting at dinner.

I was too nervous and excited to listen well. Why had Ethel Kennedy called *me*? When I finally stared into the mirror, with the addition of a string of very small pearls, a headband, and conservative heels, I looked like Alice in Wonderland as a matron: dumpy and all dressed up for a dinner party, looking the best I could considering what I had to work with.

I thought about the dinner ahead of me and how poorly prepared I felt. But I had earned this invitation and there was a reason. I had been funny and engaging when I met Ethel, serving her and making sure she had what she wanted. And she had considered me someone interesting enough to invite to dinner. Now, I was as ready as I would ever be when the lovely Caroline Croft arrived to pick me up in her long pastel silk shirt with flowing silk pants that looked somewhat like a caftan. I immediately decided she was the coolest person I had ever met. After all, she had worked for Senator Ted Kennedy for years. Now, she was executive director of the Robert F. Kennedy Foundation for which she coordinated fund-raisers. She actually managed to put me somewhat at ease, even though I knew I looked like a twenty-four-year-old dweeb. She was very kind to me and eventually, she ended up becoming a friend.

Of course I was in awe when we pulled up in front of Hickory Hill at dusk. I gazed at the sweeping grounds that I had seen only in photographs, swallowed hard, and entered through the front door to be greeted by Ethel Kennedy herself. After a moment of small talk, she introduced me to her son Joe, who was wearing a pair of nice dress pants and a blue jean shirt. He was close to my age and had a friendly face with a big Ken doll smile and a warm personality. He was a really nice guy and when he took a look at me, I could only imagine what he was thinking since I was clearly overdressed for the occasion as I stood there looking like a religious Barbie doll.

I wanted to retreat into a corner. I felt so out of place and awkward, but instead, I had a good time engaging with people in some great conversations. No sitting in the corner and just watching, I reminded myself. I needed to be interesting and interested. As a result, the evening was fun and I would discover later that this was just the kind of party that Ethel loved throwing. She was happiest when her house was filled with children, dogs, and appetizing smells from the kitchen. Wonderful historical paintings covered the walls in this beautiful colonial home, and Joe made lively dinner conversation and treated me with respect.

I scanned the dinner guests to see humorist and satirist Art Buchwald, Vernon Jordan, and Don Klosterman for whom the party was being thrown, and diverse Washington notables—a fun and rowdy group. I realized that Ethel had invited me because when we met she pegged me as an interesting person. Since she wanted some nice girls to attend her party that was overrun with men, she had called me, feeling that I would fit in. I was age-appropriate for Joe, but really, I was desperately out of my league with him and I knew it.

Toward the end of the evening, when people were starting to leave, I began to say my good-byes. I could hardy wait to get back home where my roommates were having a party to celebrate my dinner with the Kennedy clan. They were waiting for me to give them the scoop about the people who were there, the food, the decor, and of course, Joe. I politely thanked him for the evening and just as I was about to leave with Caroline, Joe said, "You don't really want to leave right now, do you?"

I was taken aback. Was he asking me to stay? Did he like me enough to want to spend more time with me?

"Why don't you stay for a while," he said, "and I'll take you home a little later?"

I considered my options. There was a group of people waiting for me back home, drinking beer and impatient to hear about my evening. I could play it safe and go home right then with very little to report about the night. Or I could stick around, have Joe Kennedy drive me home, and arrive with a terrific story.

I went for the story and I stayed for another hour while Joe walked me around the house and showed me the back rooms with photographs that were legendary. He was altogether charming, he was a perfect gentleman, and I was glad I had stayed behind. I soaked in all the historical references from my in-depth tour, but little did I know that in the not too distant future, I would be in Ethel's employ and Hickory Hill would be a place where I would report to work each day. But I get ahead of myself.

On that night, when the last people were leaving, Joe escorted me to a white convertible, opened my door for me, and went around the car to get into the driver's seat. "Oh, my gosh," he said, "I didn't realize I was so low on gas."

The sirens went off in my head. Oh, God, I thought, I'm in trouble now. Reminders of Paris flashed through my mind, but Joe managed to get me back to my little townhouse without getting stuck in the middle of the Georgetown Parkway. He parked in front of my house and when I reached over to hug him good-bye, the next thing I knew, he kissed me. I kissed him back. He was a great kisser, and we steamed up the car windows for a while. Suddenly, he said, "Don't you want to invite me in?"

I had never wanted anything more, but I couldn't invite Joe Kennedy up to my house where my friends were having a Wendy Went to the Kennedys' for Dinner party. It would look so lame. Instead, I kissed him one more time, thanked him, and reluctantly headed toward my apartment. When I turned to catch a glimpse of the back of his car disappearing down the street, I noticed something lying on the road. I walked back to find Joe's navy blazer that had fallen out of the car when I got out. I picked it up and thought, "This is a great souvenir of one of the most amazing nights of my life."

When I finally got inside, blazer in hand, my friends were all over me, wanting to know every little detail of what we ate, who was there, and how I liked Joe. I told them how the people looked, what they wore, what was served, and how queer my clothes were. When I finally got into bed, I looked at the navy blazer sitting on the chair beside my bed. I decided I would frame it with the caption, "I had one date with Joe Kennedy and all I got was this lousy blazer." Then I laughed myself to sleep.

Now I had a great albeit a bit embarrassing story to tell, but little did I know, it wasn't over. The night after the dinner party at Hickory Hill, I got back from the gallery and ate a light supper with my roommates. Three of us girls were hanging out in the living room and I had on a horrible flannel nightgown with lace around the neck, granny-style. We were enjoying a relaxing evening, knitting, crocheting, and gossiping about men. A total loser kind of night…

Suddenly, the doorbell rang. I jumped up and threw the door open to see Joe Kennedy standing there, smiling at me. "Hi," he said, "sorry to bother you, but did you find my blazer? I think it fell out of the car when I was dropping you off."

"Yeah," I said, returning his smile in spite of myself. "I found it in the street. Just wait a minute." I took off toward my bedroom, granny gown and all, got the blazer I was going to frame, and handed it to him.

"Thanks so much," he said, turned around, and he was gone.

I closed the door and headed back to the couch, picked up my knitting and thought, *First it was the Alice in Wonderland gray knit with the pearls, and now I'm in the mother of all granny nightgowns. Too bad Joe Kennedy will never know how way cool I really am.*

❖

BE SOMEONE OTHERS WANT TO BE AROUND

We're all attracted to people who are lively, stimulating, and fun to be with—the ones who see the glass half full. Don't you like being with someone who makes you laugh, treats others with kindness, and is funny and engaging? This kind of person is *doing* things in life as opposed to people who are not, and it doesn't take a rocket scientist to tell the difference.

Close your eyes right now, and think about two people you love to be around. Now think of two people you would *not* want to sit beside at a dinner party. We all know the type—they talk only about themselves, their energy is negative, and all they do is tell you about their problems. Do you want to be that kind of person, the one who gets your place card switched at a dinner party because no one wants to sit next to a complainer? Wouldn't you rather be the one whose place card gets switched because everyone wants you at their table?

When I was in the most painful part of my divorce, I spoke with Arianna Huffington, politico and founder of the Huffington Post. Having just survived a public divorce of her own, she told me, "People don't want to hear about my pain. So I don't talk about it."

I got the same lesson from Nancy Reagan when Larry and I had dinner with her one evening after her husband had passed away.

Larry asked her, "How are you doing?"

"I don't talk about it," she said.

"Why not?" Larry said.

"Because no one wants to hear about someone else's sorrow," she said.

So this was even true for Nancy Reagan who was talking about a president? Apparently so.

The key to being an interesting person is to stop complaining, step outside yourself, and be interested in others. Here are some basic rules that will work in your favor:

- When someone comes to your table, stand up and show your respect, whether they are older or younger.
- Remember what your mother taught you and listen well.
- Look people directly in the eye if you expect them to remember you.
- Shake someone's hand and let them know you're happy to see them.
- Smile.

My boyfriend, Randy, is a master at making people happy. He was trained to do this when he worked with the pharmaceutical company Eli Lilly, and it stuck. Today, he treats others with so much interest and kindness, no one ever wants him to leave, including me! The point is that when you make someone feel good about themselves, they will remember you and the fact that you have good energy. In a spiritual sense, that's what it's all about. Good energy attracts good energy. But you have to be real about it and not just pay other people lip service. Being available, interested, and interesting is a lifestyle, not a momentary action.

Do you know anyone in your life who says all the right stuff, who "acts" interested, maybe they remember your kid's name and they ask about you, but you know they really don't care? They're acting nice but the energy behind their actions doesn't lie. You can tell the difference when someone is truly engaged and when someone pretends to care, while in truth they're thinking only about themselves and what they can get from you.

I recently attended a seminar near San Diego at the Chopra Center for Wellbeing in Carlsbad, California. The seminar was entitled Sages and Scientists, and many scientists and philosophers spoke over the three days. There was a great deal of valuable information given out, but in my opinion the best advice of the weekend came from one scholar who got up toward the end and said very simply, "Be nice. You know, the Golden Rule!"

This does not exclude being strong, forceful, or creative. We can be nice, too, and that will make you feel better about yourself. If you run into a jerk in your life, you don't have to be one, too. Why drop to a level of negativity and rudeness that will hurt everyone involved, including you? As Sun-tzu says about the art of war, "Keep your friends close and your enemies closer." I would add, "And be nice to all of them."

CHAPTER 3

Details Matter: They Are Everything

I was still working at the art gallery when I got a call from a woman I didn't know named Suzy Wills. "Is this Wendy?" she asked in a fast-paced voice.

"Yes, it is," I said.

"I work for Ethel Kennedy," Suzy said, "and she was wondering if you were interested in becoming her private secretary. She needs someone to basically run her life. You know, make calls, set up meetings, help her with social events, carry out her correspondences, things like that."

Suzy went on to inform me that Ethel, a woman of about fifty, was extremely active and extraordinarily focused on details. I recalled her high energy level when I had waited on her at Brooks Brothers and at the dinner I had attended at her home. She got loads of phone calls every day, Suzy explained, and she was very busy with her huge family and running her charity—a humanitarian foundation dedicated to the memory of her late husband, Robert F. Kennedy, gunned down by an assassin's bullet on June 5, 1968. Ethel had been forty years old at the time. Now, in 1978, ten years later, was I interested in the position?

I didn't take long to answer. I was making so little money at the gallery, I could barely eat, and I was getting more bored every day. So I listened carefully when Suzy explained what the job would entail. "You'll be keeping track of what's going on at the house," she said. "Ethel needs all her calls, appointments, and phone numbers organized. There are a million details."

I smiled. I always had excelled in organizing. Maybe this would be a good job for me.

"For example," Suzy said, "Mrs. Kennedy needs help putting on a charity tennis tournament this summer where pros will play celebrities. It's a fund-raiser for her late husband's charity," Suzy continued. "It's happening in Forest Hills, New York, in August, and it'll be televised by ABC. Does that interest you?"

"Absolutely," I said.

"There's just one thing," Suzy added.

"What is it?" I asked, ready to hear the caveat that could burst the bubble of my sudden good fortune.

"You'll have to go to Hyannis and stay at the Kennedy compound for the summer," said Suzy. "Would that be a problem for you?"

I could hardly believe my ears. Staying at the Kennedy compound for the summer was no problem for me, I assured her.

She filled me in on some more details, like my salary, which would be $15,000 a year. Believe it or not, fifteen was a significant raise from the art gallery pay, and yet I saw the irony in the fact that when I was serving Ethel Kennedy as a customer at Brooks Brothers, I was making $34,000 a year. Now, as her private secretary, handling her personal affairs, my salary would be less than half that much. But compared to the gallery, this was a step up, both in salary and in excitement. I took the job, hung up the phone, and ran to my closet to evaluate my clothes. I had to make sure I had appropriate clothes to work as Ethel Kennedy's private secretary.

When I got into my light blue Chevy Chevette and drove up to Hickory Hill for my first day of work, I marveled at how much I hadn't noticed when I'd arrived at dusk for dinner just a few weeks earlier. I pulled into the parking area, got out of my car, and gazed admiringly at the beautiful white colonial home with soft blue shutters, glowing in the morning light. At least I was dressed more appropriately than the last time.

When I was shown inside my new workplace, the first thing I saw was Joe sitting all by himself in the dining room, having breakfast. We greeted each other and he said, "I hear you're going to work for my mom."

"Yeah, I am." I was relieved that my awful granny gown was not the last outfit he ever saw me wear.

Joe smiled, wished me good luck, and I was suddenly overwhelmed. Yesterday, I had worked at a mediocre art gallery that hardly saw a customer. Today, at age twenty-three, I was private secretary to Ethel Kennedy, whose name alone was completely daunting. But I had no time to wallow, thank goodness, as a house employee showed me the front room, my headquarters where I would be working for Ethel. I smiled at the decorations and fabrics in pastel peaches and pinks, colors for which my new boss and I clearly shared an affinity. I settled in for my first day and found that the work, although piled high, was pretty straightforward. And did Ethel ever need me!

I began by tackling her Rolodex that was utterly disorganized. I also helped with her concerns about the upkeep of her home. She liked that I was meticulously neat and artistic by nature, and I placed calls to her friends and to celebrities who were part of her latest charity event. How cool was it to get Chevy Chase on the phone and have him call me "dear." I was having so much fun organizing, and now, there was Chevy Chase. Wow! To me, comedians are more interesting than royalty.

When I had a break, I walked into the backyard to admire the towering old trees and the old Coca-Cola dispenser by the pool where you could get a frosty Coke. Strains of music from an old jukebox wafted across the property, Dolly Parton singing "Here You Come Again," and the Bee Gees' hit song "Stayin' Alive." There was also a Warhol photo screen print in the pool house of Jane Fonda, who would later marry Ted Turner. Who could predict that I would get to know her when I worked for CNN? It was another clue on the roadmap to my future.

I especially loved the drawing room where people gathered for events and entertainment. It seemed to have a life of its own. But I spent most of my time in the front room, on the phone, working for Ethel, a strong and demanding presence. She scrutinized everything I did to the tiniest detail, and the finished products of whatever she asked me to do were finely crafted and well thought out. She would accept nothing less, and this made a great impression on me.

When we left for Hyannis for the summer, I could only anticipate what was coming. In the largest of seven villages on Cape Cod, Massachusetts, the Kennedy name and Hyannisport had been synonymous starting in 1926, when patriarch Joseph P. Kennedy had first rented and then purchased a summer cottage there. Over the years, various family members such as President John F. Kennedy and his brothers Bobby and Ted also purchased properties, eventually creating the family compound that spread out over six acres of waterfront property.

The beauty of the setting was matched only by its historical significance. The JFK Hyannis Museum in the old town hall on Main Street featured the years that the president spent there. To this day, a waterfront memorial includes a fountain and a fieldstone monument with the presidential seal and the inspiring JFK inscription, "I believe it is important that this country sail and not sit still in the harbor."

Into the heart of the Kennedy legend I was headed, as my new friend and coworker, Suzy Wills, and I moved our things into the dorm that was located on the property (I had my own small room), between the residences of Ethel and Jackie Onassis. The bed linens in the rooms were hand-me-downs from various bedrooms past. They were feminine with flowers and scallops and they had been expensive. Now they were just a little bit worn. But so pretty. It was shabby chic style.

The homes within the compound were typical Cape Cod white frame clapboard, with well-tended lawns, sumptuous gardens, and a sweeping view of the ocean. I walked around the property, taking in the two circular driveways, flagpoles, a boathouse, and stretches of lawn where the family famously played touch football.

I remember early one afternoon, when I was in Ethel's kitchen, working on her mailing list. Just before his daily sail, Ted walked unannounced into the kitchen in baggy pants and a pair of old sneakers. He headed over to the stove and stirred a pot of clam chowder that was brewing. He took a taste and said, "Ethel, that's good chowder." Plain and simple. But it was one of those events in which my brain took a permanent picture of everything—the room, the chowder smell, and Teddy's voice. I was actually in Hyannisport in the kitchen with Ethel and Ted Kennedy talking about chowder! I just couldn't help marveling that this was the Kennedy family, and everything they did, including stirring the soup, seemed so exciting.

The preparations for the tournament were all-encompassing as I worked with Ray Benton, a sports attorney from Washington DC, who, incidentally, I already knew. It was another of those odd serendipitous occurrences, since I'd met him years before when I was growing up in Dubuque, Iowa. He happened to be the tennis pro at our local country club and I was his worst student. Really, I was horrible at tennis. In fact, I was bad at most sports except when it came to swimming and dancing. Those two things I could do, but just about any other sport, well, forget it. In school, I was the last to be picked as a member of any sports team for good reason. I was prissy and a lousy athlete.

I remembered Ray before his name carried much sway, trying to get through to me as the ball would come speeding at me and end up getting stuck in my curly hair. "Okay, Bird Legs," he used to call me for obvious reasons, "let's try it again." It was a humiliating period, since my boyfriend at the time, John Schrup, and some of my closest friends excelled at tennis. I was a dork, my forehand and backhand were equally ineffective, and Ray couldn't help but laugh at me. I decided to overlook it now as Ray and I joined forces to work on this RFK Pro-Celebrity Tennis Tournament.

"Oh, my gosh! Hey, Ray," I called to him. "It's me! Bird Legs!"

He broke out into a huge smile and I marveled that he hadn't changed a bit. He still remembered my nickname, but I must have looked completely different to him, since the last time he saw me, I was a kid. Now, with Ray coordinating the tennis talent, Suzy and I set up shop in a small garage on the compound that had been converted into an office. Suzy would go sailing with the Kennedys most days but I was usually too busy working, besides the fact that I wasn't invited. But when I think back, that was a blessing in disguise. The one time I was included in a sailing trip on the spur of the moment, I got so seasick, I couldn't speak. Worse than being seasick, which is hideously unpleasant, is trying to pretend you're not. I would have been mortified if they knew, especially Ted and Ethel, who were hard-core sailors. When we finally got back onto terra firma, I had done enough sailing for one summer.

I was generally holed up in the small garage all by myself to do the massive job of working on the tournament and type piles of personal letters for Ethel that never seemed to end. Admittedly, I was not the greatest typist in the world, and when I misspelled a word (there were no spell-check features on typewriters) and gave it to Ethel, it was right back on my desk. "I can't sign this," she'd say. "You misspelled a word."

I felt the sting of her judgment and I quickly made the correction, always eager to please. I felt a little better when I recalled a document framed on the wall back at Hickory Hill that had been written in President Kennedy's own hand. Jackie had scribbled on it, "Can you pick out the misspelled words?" Apparently, JFK had been dyslexic and when Ethel said, "Don't worry about it, Wendy. Jack couldn't spell, either," I felt redeemed by being compared to a president—especially that one!

As I was dyslexic, too, typing was my major challenge. I never formally studied typing, and it was a tedious affair since standard typewriters were not self-correcting and each mistake had to be whited out and typed over. Then I heard about a brand-new invention called the IBM Correcting Selectric typewriter. I had repetitive letters to send out and the idea of correcting each one separately sounded unbelievably work-intensive, especially since I was not a crack typist. I simply had to have one of those typewriters.

The part of me that would serve me as a future producer kicked in as I picked up the phone, called IBM, and said, "I'm calling for Ethel Kennedy. I hear you have a great typewriter with a memory."

"We do," they said proudly. "It's our Correcting Selectric version."

"How about donating one to the RFK Foundation for the summer?" I asked boldly. "We're putting together a celebrity charity tennis tournament."

The next thing I knew, the donated typewriter magically took its place in the garage right beside Ethel's newly organized Rolodex and the tennis tournament guest list.

And then there was Jackie. There are few times in this life I've been totally blown away about meeting someone. If I were the type to be regularly starstruck by celebrities or politicians, there is no way I could ever do the job I've done over the years, both as CNN White House producer and then producing *Larry King Live.* I was basically immune to celebrity worship and mostly I still am—with a few exceptions, mostly comedians.

The point is that each time I saw Jackie Onassis, the way she walked and dressed, I was instantly overwhelmed. There was simply no one like her, with her grace, her beauty, and her extraordinary and legendary fashion sense. She was a trend-setter from the moment we first found out about her, and I loved watching her leave her house and pass Ethel's house in her bathing suit, when she took her daily walk to the ocean. As hard as I was working on the upcoming tennis fund-raiser, I tried never to miss seeing Mrs. Onassis elegantly stride by Ethel's home to the beach. Always graceful, never in a hurry, she seemed to float from place to place and I never got tired of watching her. I know that many people share this feeling about her, because whenever I mention knowing the Kennedys, everyone wants to hear about Jackie.

One day when the electricity went out in Ethel's house, she said, "Wendy, go to Jackie's house and ask her if you can call the electric company."

Okay, I thought, *I'm on my way to Jackie's house.* I slowly walked over there in my pink flowered Lilly Pulitzer short shorts and knocked at her door. When she opened the door with a smile, I said, "Hello, Mrs. Onassis. May I use your phone? The electricity is off at Mrs. Kennedy's house and she'd like me to call the electric company."

Jackie could not have been more gracious as she invited me in and offered me a Coke. "Why don't you and Suzy work here today?" she offered in her inimitable voice as I stood in her kitchen, making a phone call. She was wearing a beautiful summery shift and she was barefoot and arranging flowers, a vision I will never forget. In fact, I will never forget a word she ever said to me or to anyone else.

I recall one evening in my room, in bed, when I caught the glow of Jackie's porch lights from outside my window. I sat up and watched through the window as she walked two guests out of her front door, lingering to say, "Good night, Maria. Arnold, I really enjoyed meeting you. Hope to see you again soon." It just seemed that whatever Jackie did or said, I found her alluring and as beautiful with no makeup as she was when she was done up for the public.

One day, when Ethel told me she was going to throw Jackie a party at the compound for her fiftieth birthday, I was thrilled. The rest of the world and I had watched this graceful woman as First Lady and as a grieving widow, veiled and walking in the funeral parade of her slain husband. I was ten years old when JFK was assassinated, and I wrote about it my diary:

Nov. 22, 1963

A very terrible thing happened, Kennedy is now dead. He was shot in the head and was dead at one o'clock. It's very hard to believe. It's so shocking. Each bullet was three inches. Now Vice President Johnson is President.

He was a wonderful man. I am so sorry he is dead and I'm sure everyone else is, too. I haven't written in my diary for 27 days. I thought this would be a good time to start. Even though I didn't want him for President, he was a very good President. I hate to think someone would do such a thing as to kill him.

Now it was Jackie's fiftieth birthday, and I would help to arrange the details for her party. The birthday guest list included Tom Brokaw and Walter Cronkite as well as many other luminaries in the news and political world. And all the Kennedys. It was a cloudy evening, there was a slight breeze, and drinks were served outdoors before dinner while the sun was setting. I remember watching some people doing the limbo on the lawn, and I was amazed when Walter Cronkite took a turn shimmying his body under the limbo rope! Then, when we were all gathered around the dining room table after the drinks and games, there I was, too, part of the celebrating committee, sitting at a side table with Suzy, eating and toasting Jacqueline Onassis. All I could do was ask myself what on earth I was doing there.

One afternoon before the tennis tournament, I was surprised

when Mrs. Onassis wandered over to the small makeshift garage office where I was sitting on the front stoop, going over some lists. She sat beside me and looked at the papers I was holding. She had on a navy top and a pair of white pants held together with a safety pin.

"Wendy," she slowly articulated, "what plane is John on for the tournament? Who's on the plane with him?" She looked directly into my eyes, something she always did when she spoke to anyone. After telling myself silently, *Mrs. Jackie Onassis is sitting on a step beside me*, I pulled it together and explained the flight manifest. I still recall her apparent discomfort as she wandered away looking less than satisfied. "I worry when he flies," she said over her shoulder. Her son was a teenager at the time and she seemed concerned. How could anyone have known the fate that was awaiting John Jr., as he and his wife and her sister would die in a plane crash many years later. It feels positively eerie today when I recall how nervous Jackie was that day.

To jump ahead, I was working for Larry in 1994 when I was at the Washington bureau and bumped into JFK Jr. There was a Democratic campaign office on the first floor of the building and John, now in his midtwenties, was leaving one afternoon as I was arriving with one of my staff producers. We greeted each other and he said, "Since CNN is in this building, do you think I could see the set? I always wanted to see those lights."

"Would you like to see them now?" I asked.

"Sure," he said.

I turned to the woman walking with me and said, "Please go to the set right now and make sure all the lights are turned on. We'll be right up."

She took off ahead of me while John and I waited for the

next elevator. By the time we got to the set, the lights were lit and I walked him around casually, as if I did this sort of thing every day. Like it was no big deal. The crew couldn't take their eyes off John as he viewed the set and said, "Funny, it looks so different on the air." When he went behind the desk and examined each colored light separately, I said, "I hope we get you to sit here sometime."

And so we did. Just as eerie and foreboding as Jackie's fear of her son flying was September 28, 1995, when Larry interviewed JFK Jr. on the launch of his political magazine, *George*.

KING: For the time being, do you want to stay with it [*George*]?

KENNEDY JR.: Well, I would hate to say that I am going to do anything until I am seventy. But I am going to be doing this for the foreseeable future.

KING: Do you ever fear for your own health?

KENNEDY JR.: Sure.

KING: There are nuts in this country. I mean, you Kennedys must think about it. How could they not think about it? Any Kennedy. In public life or not.

KENNEDY JR.: It's not something . . . like walking around wondering if you are going to be struck by lightning. It's . . . just not something that you really keep in the forefront of your mind.

KING: But it might affect decision making, like going into politics, mightn't it?

KENNEDY JR.: It might. But it doesn't.

KING: It seems not to for the five that are in it. But . . . if you went in, or thought about going in, the thought of being harmed by going in, would not enter into your thoughts?

KENNEDY JR.: That wouldn't be one of the considerations, no.

I was so impressed with JFK Jr. I thought he should have his own show on CNN so I arranged for him to meet with the late Ed Turner, a top CNN executive at the time. John strolled into the meeting holding a banana. He looked incredibly beautiful, but the powers that be passed on putting him on the air. Big mistake! He would have been a natural. In fact, if he were alive today, I'm sure he would have a popular political show on the air called *George,* after his magazine, which ceased publication about a year after his tragic death.

Back at the Kennedy compound in Hyannis, I recall a dinner one night when I met a White House producer for ABC news named Dorrance Smith. It was during the Carter administration and I was totally in awe of Dorrance's job. It was during a conversation with him when I thought, *This guy has a job that I'd like to have someday. I think I could do it.* For the time being, though, Ethel was keeping me very busy so how could I even imagine having a job like that? It was quite a coincidence that Dorrance was a producer for reporter Sam Donaldson, someone I would date in a few years. But during the time in Hyannisport, I had no idea who he was.

Toward the end of the summer of 1978, we were en route to Forest Hills, New York, on the various chartered planes for the August 26 tournament that would be broadcast on ABC. The turnout was fantastic and I was glad I had been a stickler for detail. Each little thing mattered when among the star-studded audience were crooner Andy Williams, Pulitzer Prize–winner Art Buchwald, actors Chevy Chase, Dustin Hoffman, and Lauren Bacall, and a load of Kennedys.

I ran into Jackie at the tournament, and this time, a compliment from her sent me over the moon. I had chosen to wear an extremely classic outfit that would still work today—a white silk shirt, khaki lightweight trousers, and a Gucci scarf wrapped around my waist as a belt. Apparently, the outfit pleased her as Mrs. Onassis said enthusiastically, "Oh, Wendy, I love your outfit."

"Thank you, Mrs. Onassis," I said, almost trembling with excitement. Knowing her fashion sense and her attention to beauty and detail, I was sure I would never get over it as I continued to scurry around, taking care of the logistics of this huge celebrity event that was being nationally televised. By the way, I never threw out that scarf!

This was the first time I saw a string of limos and tons of celebrities all gathered in one place. The air was electric as hundreds of observers kept arriving, and I was intoxicated by the energy of so many people coming together to raise money for Ethel's foundation. I was bit by the producing bug right then and there, as we all worked tirelessly to make the event a huge success. True, I was exhausted when it was over, and I had feared my lack of experience would get in the way of pulling this off. But pull it off we did. We had taken each thing as it came, made sure we had it all worked out to the smallest detail, and then moved on to the next.

When we headed back to Hyannis, exhausted and satisfied after a job well done, Ethel asked her inner circle of friends to write a critique of the tournament so she could make improvements for the next one. The only complaint she received was that there was no camera on Jackie—the one thing they thought she should correct the next time! That was a testament to our attention to detail, both large and small. Nothing had been overlooked.

My time with Ethel came to a close about a year after it began. I enjoyed working for Ethel and she asked me to stay on at Hickory Hill, but I ended up leaving because I had caught the producer bug and wanted to pursue it. I was sad when my time with the Kennedys came to an end, but I'm grateful for what I learned from being around one of the most famous American families, and to Suzy, who remains my close friend.

Among the many things I took away from this unique experience, and particularly from Ethel, is that details are everything. I learned to multitask and to write everything down—and I do mean *everything*. I took notes on each conversation I had so I wouldn't forget what I needed to do, and to this day, I don't understand people who don't keep lists and notes. If I had a hundred things to do for Ethel, and I finished ninety-nine of them, the detail I overlooked was inevitably the one thing that was most important to her. Keeping this in mind prepared me for the rest of my life as I left "all things Kennedy" with the tools to go into any situation and get the job done right.

❖

DETAILS MATTER: THEY ARE EVERYTHING

When you are creating something, anything, you want to leave a lasting impression. You want to present your idea and have somebody say, "Whoa. This is one great idea." So how do you stand out? It's all in the details.

Each time you have a presentation to do, think about the details that will make your work look better than the rest. You can hand in a generic computer printout of your presentation, or you can jazz it up with a special cover and attractive colors. People will see that you took the extra step and they will be impressed.

In order to be detail-oriented:

- Make sure you write down all the details that must be completed.
- Correct all spelling before you hand in anything.
- Take a second look at your work before you hand it in.
- Remember whom you are working for and what they want from you. And do it.
- Return all your phone calls.

If you can't manage this last one, there are several things you can do. Try picking up the phone and saying, "I'm on the other line but I saw your name come up on my caller ID. I can't talk now but I just wanted to check quickly in case you need something." That way, the other person understands that you can't talk now but you still made the effort to let them know.

If you have one, you can ask an assistant to let the person know that you are busy now but will call later. If you have no assistant, you can send an e-mail that lets the other person know you care but can't speak right now. Any of the above will keep you from being known as someone who doesn't return phone calls. Don't try lying and saying, "Oh, I just didn't get your message." With our current state-of-the-art technology, that one doesn't work.

Right now, we are trying to book a big star to do an interview on our show. But instead of just calling her assistant and asking for the interview, we're making a video in which Larry speaks to her personally, explaining why he thinks his show would be the best venue for her. In a similar fashion, we did videos for Jack Nicholson, Brad Pitt, Al Pacino, Bob Dylan, Eminem, Amy Winehouse, and John Edwards.

The point is that a job is never done until you've completed the last detail.

CHAPTER 4

Organize, Organize, and Then...
Organize Some More

I was at a dinner party recently at a friend's home. I knew some of the people there, others I had never met, and I took my place at the table with everyone else when dinner was ready. As we were all chatting, sipping wine, and enjoying some wonderful food, a woman sitting beside me, probably in her midforties, caught my eye and said, "What do you do?"

"I'm a producer," I answered.

A group of heads suddenly swerved in my direction. It seemed like everyone had gone silent, wide-eyed and expectant, waiting for me to tell my story. When I explained to my new acquaintance (and everyone else who was listening) that I had been the executive producer for *Larry King Live* for the past seventeen years, and CNN White House producer for ten years prior to that, so much attention got riveted on me, I might as well have said I just got back from walking on the moon!

I have discovered over the years that with the right kind of organization, a person can pull off just about anything, from a charity tennis tournament for the Robert F. Kennedy Foundation to a Soviet-US summit, to raising two active, demanding, and fabulous kids while producing one of the most watched television programs in the world on cable. Being extremely well-organized is a tried-and-true formula that I have counted on in just about every area of my life. In my opinion, it is the key to maintaining balance and success. Without organization, how could I be devoted to raising my children while producing a daily show that rarely goes as planned and often requires a total reboot with only a few hours to spare before showtime? Think Farrah Fawcett and Michael Jackson.

The *Larry King Live* show has gone through a number of cycles since its inception on June 1, 1985. You see, when Ted Turner first asked Larry to come on board with CNN and host the show, he took the offer reluctantly. After all, shooting a live show each night would mess with his baseball schedule. He would rather be at a game than anywhere else in the world. And I mean anywhere. He made the sacrifice, though, and his first interview was with then New York governor, Mario Cuomo. Larry wore no suspenders, he smoked cigarettes during the show, there were no colored lights behind him, and the production quality left a lot to be desired. CNN wasn't even seen in Washington since there were as yet no cable capabilities in the district. In fact, most people hardly knew what cable was.

When you fast forward to now, *Larry King Live* is an international show, presented in a highly produced, sophisticated format, with a famous colorful dotted backdrop and lots of video and fanfare. There is no smoking on the set, it takes a very talented staff to book and produce the show nightly, and this many years later, we have become a well-oiled machine with all of our moving parts communicating with all the others.

This takes an enormous amount of organizing since we have gone from a simple format in which we booked a guest and Larry talked with him or her one-on-one, to our current format in which we include e-mail questions, tweets, blogs, and podcasts, while Larry interviews from one person to a couple, from a small group to a large panel.

I always work with Larry to juggle his personal schedule with the requirements of the show. Someone may want him to give a speech or be in a movie, and I make time for him to do that while he still does the show every night. I also deal with the various network discussions on commercials, ethics, and legal issues that continuously arise. If guests are confused as to why we want them on, I am responsible for that explanation as well as explaining to more people than you could imagine why we are *not* asking them on the show.

To keep up with the zeitgeist, my staff reaches out to all avenues of communication to stay current with trends so we can book the show accordingly. The thing is, what worked ten years ago doesn't necessarily work today. And in five years from now (or even five days), something may come back and be in vogue again. I can't count the times when someone on my staff reminded me that I had said no to a particular topic last week, and now I was dedicating an hour-long show to that very topic. It's all about staying current with the changes, keeping our fingers on the pulse at all times, and making decisions according to what the public wants to see.

We all know that everything changes in this life, including the popularity of political issues and famous personalities. And no one person can keep up with all of it. I have to rely on my intuition, my staff, and my ability to organize. In the end, a successful show is the result of a dedicated group of people who are smart, flexible, and know what's going on in the world. I need them not only to find out what is happening out there and report back. I also need them to tell me when they disagree with decisions that I make. And I listen to them. In fact, I wonder what on earth I would do without them. But all that aside, being organized gives me the ability to focus creatively along with my staff so we can produce the best program possible. Without organization, great ideas would be lost.

A good example occurred in April 2002, when my staff suggested I book an eleven-year-old boy named Mattie Stepanek on the show. I didn't know much about him except that he had a rare inherited form of muscular dystrophy that was terminal (his older brother, Jamie, had already died from it) and Mattie was supposedly a poet. I didn't warm up to the idea at first, but when I saw how excited my staff was about him, I decided to take a second look. After all, I hired them because they were smart and if I didn't listen to them, that would be self-defeating. I heard their arguments and opinions and I decided to defer. On April 17, 2002, Mattie Stepanek appeared on our show, despite my initial reluctance.

STEPANEK: The doctors didn't think I would live one day, but I did. So they said, okay, he's not going to last six months. I did. Then they said, okay, we're drawing the line at two years old, three years, or he's going to die by then, and you might as well let him go now. And my mom said, no. I'm going to train this spirit. So I lived to be two, and they said, okay, five, five, five is it. Then I lived to be five, and then they said ten. And here I am, an eleven-year-old. So now they're saying teens or sometime as a young adult, but I plan to be 101. [When my sibling] died, I sort of didn't understand death. I wasn't expecting it. And I knew to say, my brother Jamie died. But I didn't know what it meant. And that's mainly how my poetry started.

KING: Yes, tell me about that.

STEPANEK: Well, I didn't even know it was poetry at first. I was just talking and playing. And 95, maybe even 99 percent of my early works were about Jamie's death. And then I learned it's poetry, my mom told me. And I asked her to write it down for me. And I said, wow, this is a way I can express my feelings, in a way that I can cope with this hard life and others can understand it.

KING: You never took writing lessons? So you are what might be called a natural poet?

STEPANEK: Yes…my poetry's about all kinds of different things. It began about Jamie and then it evolved into things like nature, friendships, challenges, hopes. And the big theme is peace. I talk about peace in many different ways so that everyone likes it, it appeals to all people and so that everyone understands it.

KING: What do you mean by *Heart Songs* [the title of his book of poems]?

STEPANEK: A heart song is your inner beauty. It's your inner message. It's what you feel you want to do. In my case, my heart song is to hear my heart song and help others to hear theirs as well. And teaching heart songs does not mean, this is my heart song, now it is yours. Everyone has a different heart song and the differences are what make them beautiful. And we are a mosaic of gifts. And we need to choose to put those pieces together, not spread them apart.

He recited an original poem called "Making Real Sense of the Senses":

Our eyes are for looking at things,
But they're also for crying when we are very happy or very
   sad.
Our ears are for listening, but so are our hearts.
Our noses are for smelling food, but also the wind and the
   grass,
And if we try very hard, butterflies.
Our hands are for feeling,
But also for hugging and touching so gently.
Our mouths and tongues for tasting, but also for saying
   words like
I love you and thank you God for all of these things.

I'm so glad I listened to my staff and changed my mind about booking Mattie. I really had no idea how profound and loving this eleven-year-old boy was, the effect he would have on everyone, including me, and how much the public would relate to him. In fact, this show that I very nearly passed on was nominated for an Emmy award.

Mattie and I attended the award show together in New York and we had a great time. He worked the room in his automated wheelchair, which I called his go-kart, and we held hands when they announced the winner. We didn't get the Emmy. My heart broke for him, but we both had a terrific night to remember. When Mattie died in 2004 at age thirteen, he left behind a legacy that we had featured on our show.

The point is, it takes a highly organized operation, including me and my staff, to pull off a different, information-filled show every day. The list of decisions I have to make daily would seriously surprise you, it is so demanding. And organizing is the only way to pull it off.

I even organize my purse by cleaning it out every single

day, which some of my friends find inconceivable and obsessive. How do I find the time to do it? they want to know. My friend Suzy admits that her form of organization is stacking her stuff into piles. She knows where everything is, but no one else does, and I told her I'd be afraid to look in her closet. You see, just like women think that dumping out my purse every night, throwing out what I don't need and refilling it with what I *do* need, is ridiculous, I find it inconceivable that any woman would *not* clean out her purse every day. How do you know what you have with you? I need different kinds of things with me on different days, depending on my schedule. I simply can't fathom arriving somewhere and not having what I need readily available. Of course, I leave out something now and then, but for the most part, my organization skills help me feel prepared for the inevitable and I get some peace and ease from that knowledge.

In 1993, for example, I got a page early one afternoon when a newly elected Bill Clinton was about to give one of his first televised presidential addresses to the nation. The networks take turns producing such an event. It so happened that CNN was pool (one network taking the responsibility for providing coverage for all the networks) for this national address, so I headed to the White House along with the CNN technical staff to prepare for the live presidential address.

I already knew how these things unfolded and what preparation was necessary, but the president's aides were still feeling their way around as best they could since everything was new to them. When President Clinton arrived in the Oval Office before his speech, flanked by Vice President Gore and his aide David Gergen, he was ready for us to put on his makeup. But there was no makeup artist. This administration did not know yet that for presidential addresses, the president's aides were responsible. When I broke the news that the networks hadn't provided a makeup artist, Dee Dee Myers, Clinton's press secretary, and I looked blankly at each other. Then I said, "Okay, Dee Dee, let's open our purses."

Since I had emptied out my purse the day before and refilled it that morning with what I needed today, I knew I had some foundation and a clean sponge with me. Dee Dee found some old tubes of makeup in the bottom of her purse, so I cut the sponge in half and she and I went to work. While I did my best to cover a presidential blemish on Clinton's nose, he seemed unconcerned that two nonmakeup artists were applying his makeup before he addressed the nation on television. And one of us was a press person to boot! When he finally went on the air, Dee Dee and I decided we had done a pretty good job. Of course, it helped that he wasn't so bad looking to start with!

It has always given me a sense of balance to keep my life in order, and that bleeds over into my work world. Without deep organization of all the moving parts of my life, I would never be able to pull it all off and maintain a sense of decorum. Or even get my job done, for that matter. In essence, my life is about making decisions, tons of them all day long, and the only way I keep track is by keeping everything in some kind of order.

Luckily, being organized has always come naturally to me. I was a self-motivated kid, and I loved keeping my room clean and organizing my drawers. When Katie Couric's husband, Jay, died of colon cancer, her closest friends rallied around her to do what we could. Besides being there emotionally for her, we also jumped in to help organize the funeral arrangements. As much as I had driven Katie crazy with what she called my "almost OCD" ways when we lived together (more on that later), she was relieved to delegate the details to me when it really mattered.

"Wendy was there for me emotionally," says Katie, "in terms of doing research to find some options when Jay was still here. Once he was gone, at the funeral, I have a vivid memory of Cardinal O'Connor entering the church in his full cardinal garb. And there was Wendy, standing in the church, organizing everything, one of the things she does best. I used to call that her neat freak behavior when we were roommates, but I was really glad to see her there when Jay died, taking care of things. She even managed to make me laugh."

When it comes to the show, organization is at the crux of it all. It starts with those thousands of e-mails each day. I answer some of them, I check my long and detailed lists, I make my calls, I check things off and make more lists, and I do my best not to second-guess myself. I keep in mind that, first and foremost, we are a business, we have to sell airtime to commercial sponsors, and we have to respond to demographics and households. As little as twenty years ago, there were very few available venues for someone who wanted to get a point across, making it relatively easy to book any guest we wanted. But now, with the explosion of electronic communication and the Internet's digital extensions, all that has changed and the competition has become fierce. We have to work much harder to get the people we want, because these days we are not the only ones vying for interviews. Hey, people don't even have to go on shows at all anymore if they don't want to. They can just tweet or blog.

Incidentally, for anyone who thinks the escalation of technology is not a good thing, let me remind you about the aftermath of the earthquake in Haiti in 2010. During the 9/11 tragedies in 2001, our advanced technology allowed us to see what was occurring in the moment. It allowed Ted Olson to speak to his wife before she died on the plane that crashed into the Pentagon, and it allowed us to keep track of reactions all over the world. But by 2010, when the earthquake devastated Haiti and killed so many people, technology was allowing us to save people as they tweeted or e-mailed their locations to rescue workers.

Today, with the benefits of the most advanced technology to date, we take pride in the span of the topics and people our show covers. While we might interview a movie star one night, we might book the Dalai Lama for the next night. I recall when Nelson Mandela was freed from the prison cell in which he had spent the last twenty-seven years, and we were told he was willing to do an interview for our show. Larry and I flew to New York together that very night on a red-eye so we would arrive in time for the interview. This was one of those moments when I realized how major an impact our show could make on the world. We do pop culture (societal trends) and water cooler (the current buzz at cocktail parties). And we also do Nelson Mandela and the Dalai Lama, people who transcend cultural limitations, race, or color.

As you can see, our palette is so diverse, I have to be ready for anything. Good thing I have some habits in place that help me out. But even with the best organization and readiness, things happen over which we have no control. Since Larry takes his interviewer role so seriously, one of my greatest challenges occurs when we've booked a guest who arrives late to the studio. There is no degree of preparedness or organization that can eliminate the angst when a guest is late.

In 2001, we had booked former Vice President Al Gore to appear for the whole hour. He was a hot ticket for the show, we were thrilled to have him, but it was 8:45, the show was set to begin at 9, and Gore and his wife were stuck in traffic. There was no way he could make our airtime, so I had to figure out how to fill in the first segment of the show while we waited. My alternative was to run a show on tape, which would be such a waste since the Gores were "almost" there.

What should we do in the meantime? My staff and I racked our brains for someone we could throw on in New York or Los Angeles to fill in the time while we waited, but we couldn't come up with anybody. There were no famous people in our various news bureaus and we had minutes to fix this problem. As luck would have it, though, it was Larry's birthday and his wife, Shawn, and their two kids, Chance and Cannon, three and a half and two and a half at the time, were at the studio. "Let's start with the kids," I said suddenly.

We carted the kids onto the set and when the show aired, Larry proudly introduced his boys and let them wish him happy birthday for the first segment.

KING: They're expected [the Gores]. They're on the way. But one of the problems in working live, and I love working live, is that sometimes traffic difficulties get in the way. And Al and Tipper Gore were in Los Angeles. Pretty humid in LA today. I don't know if that had anything to do with it. Temperature's in the mideighties. But the Gores have not yet arrived...So we decided to spend those three promised minutes with my two kids and my wife. Today is my sixty-ninth birthday, so on the left on your screen is Chance King. He is three and a half years old. In the middle is Shawn King. On the right is Cannon King. He's two and a half years old. And I thought maybe we could sing "Happy Birthday."

CHANCE: I want to do a Halloween song.

KING: Okay, a Halloween song. Which one?

CHANCE: And Halloween and Halloween and Halloween.

KING: Okay. And what do you want to sing, Cannon?

CANNON: A ghost.

They continued to talk for the next few minutes until we cut to commercial. The kids had been very cute and when Larry went back on the air, Al and Tipper Gore had arrived and were sitting opposite him. Whew!

KING: What happened? Where were you?

TIPPER GORE: Traffic in LA. Misjudged the time, perhaps. We came from the East Coast today. We wanted to give your kids a chance to have their network debut.

KING: In the old days, there would have been flashing lights... Do you miss the trappings? You would not have been late if you were vice president... or president... I mean, what's it like to come from the life of that to not having the life of that?

AL GORE: I've joked about it a lot, but the truth is... it's great to be out of the so-called bubble and to be able to go on your own. There are disadvantages like being late here. I'm sorry.

KING: Don't you miss the trappings?

TIPPER: No. No, not at all. It was a privilege when we had them and when Al was vice president. And it was great. But that's over with. We've moved on. And it's nice to have our freedom back and be able to, unfortunately, get lost or be in traffic.

Besides a guest being late for the show, I am very uncomfortable when Larry or the show itself becomes part of the story. I believe that our show is about presenting the facts in a neutral way, and then the audience can draw their own conclusions. Larry agrees. I always try to keep him out of the foreground, but there are times when it's unavoidable and it just doesn't work out that way, no matter how prepared I think I am.

It was November 1993, when I got a phone call from one of my bookers. He had been on the phone with Al Gore's people and it seemed that the vice president wanted to challenge financier Ross Perot to debate the NAFTA trade agreement on *Larry King Live*. Were we interested in hosting the debate?

This highly controversial trilateral agreement, a hotly debated topic, was on track to be signed by the United States, Canada, and Mexico, to supersede the existing Canada–United States Free Trade Agreement. Gore was for the legislation, Perot was against it, and they wanted the debate to occur on our show. How could I say no? Gore was a sitting vice president, and these two men were extraordinarily powerful and influential.

Aware of the opportunity as well as the obstacles, I contacted Ross Perot to see if he was interested. He was game, and we figured it would be a great night of television, an unprecedented experience for us. But when we made the announcement that we would host this debate, it exploded into an international news story. Larry and I both ended up on the covers of a load of global newspapers and we were part of the story, exactly what I had hoped to avoid. Speculation was rampant as to who would win and how we would know who won. Now that we were part of the story, how would we end up convincing everyone that we were nonpartisan? I quickly realized that the scrutiny of our show was about to escalate intensely. In order for that to work in our favor, I needed to do absolutely everything right. I had to fall back on my organizational skills as I started making lists and springing into action.

First, I got permission from Tom Johnson, CNN president at the time, to extend our usual sixty minutes to ninety minutes.

Check.

Next, I called a meeting with the White House and with Ross Perot's people.

Check.

We were all on the same page, so to speak, and on November 11, 1993, Gore and Perot arrived at the studio about a half hour before the show.

Check.

I assigned a different person to take care of each man and make them both comfortable in private rooms that were the exact same size and filled with the same number of sandwiches, drinks, and other snacks. They did a coin toss for the privilege of choosing the seat closer to or farther away from Larry. Al Gore won and chose the seat closer to Larry. But once they were ready to go into the studio, I was up against another obstacle. It seemed that while Ross Perot had arrived at the studio on his own, Al Gore had Bob Squier with him, a personal friend and political adviser, but I couldn't allow him on the set.

I recall some years back when I got onto the Reagan press plane in Santa Barbara in tears. I had been dating a notorious womanizer named Carter Eskew who had been Bob Squier's business partner at the time. Carter had unceremoniously dumped me by cell phone just before the plane took off and I was devastated. One of our flight attendants, M.A., a friend of mine by then, whisked me into the lavatory on the plane to wash my face and help me stop crying. M.A. was so helpful, she actually pulled me down on her lap on top of the toilet seat cover to keep me safe during takeoff.

The point here is that right before the NAFTA debate, Carter

Eskew, in his inimitable fashion, left his partner, Bob Squier, just as unceremoniously as he had left me, going off on his own. Now, Al Gore knew that Bob and I had an inside secret— we had both been dumped by Carter Eskew. When I went in to greet the Gores and Bob, Al said to us, "Now you two really have something in common." Bob laughed so hard.

Ross Perot took his seat on the set with Larry when there were only about five minutes left until showtime. Where was Al? It seemed he had made a quick pit stop and Bob stood outside the men's room, waiting for him.

"Bob," I said, "you have to get him out here right now." I was looking at my watch and getting nervous.

The bathroom door opened and out came Al Gore looking extremely anxious. He seemed to be on edge about this debate and I hated to make him even more nervous by asking him to go out there alone. But I had to stop Bob from walking onto the set. "You can't go into the studio with him," I told Bob.

Bob looked at me and realized I wasn't kidding. He glanced over at Ross Perot, then he looked at Al, and I saw a smile break out on Bob's face. He leaned in and whispered in Al's ear, loud enough for me to hear, "Just remember one thing, Al," he said. "Everything on your body is bigger than his."

Al broke into a huge belly laugh and walked onto the set, looking completely confident. Who expected such a thing would end Al's anxiety? That day, I learned a good lesson from Bob Squier:

If you can't say something nice, say something funny!

The poignancy of this comment was well demonstrated seven years later, when Bob passed away from colon cancer on January 24, 2000. Before he died, I recall how pissed off he was that a thing like cancer was getting in the way of his great passion—running a winning campaign for presidential hopeful Al Gore.

The cancer got him in the end and I was honored to be asked to speak at his funeral at the National Cathedral in Washington. It was a well-attended funeral, with speakers like President Clinton, and then there was me, Wendy Walker, once again feeling way out of my league. I recall shyly walking in the procession and taking my seat just behind the president and the vice president. As I prepared to get up and take the podium, I looked down at the lovely black suit I had bought for the occasion, only to notice that my fly was open, the zipper was all the way down, and peeking out were my pink underpants. I turned the color of my underwear as I attempted to pull the zipper up. As I pulled myself back together, one zipper tooth at a time, the sound resounded throughout the silent cathedral. I was embarrassed but I couldn't help but smile. Bob would have really appreciated this bit of humor, I realized, which made it all the more sad that he was gone.

Back to the debate. We timed every comment with a stopwatch to make sure no one got more time than his opponent. We even took callers on the show and made sure their questions were equally distributed as well. When it was over, I was confident no one could complain that Larry had favored either candidate, although public opinion leaned in the direction that Al Gore had won. I was satisfied that we had pulled it off, it had been a success, and we had accomplished our goal of no favoritism. I owed it all to organization, for which there is no substitute.

I got home that night, exhausted but happy that we had worked so hard and had done such a good job of being fair. I was elated when I found out we had received the highest ratings for a cable show ever, and I fell asleep feeling contented. I expected to sleep in late that morning, but I was awakened around midnight by a call from a *Washington Post* reporter. I reached for the phone a little bleary-eyed and said, "Yes?"

"We have it from the highest sources," he told me, "that you rigged all the calls during the debate."

"What are you talking about?" I asked him. I sat up.

"We got this from a very reliable source," he went on.

"You know I would never do that," I told him. "You know our policies for the show. Where did you hear this?"

"We listened to a recording," he pressed on.

He was referring to a comment that the radio shock jock Howard Stern had blurted out earlier that morning on his undisciplined show. I got up and had the tape sent to me. When I listened, it was nothing more than the indomitable Stern prodding his listeners with criticisms and rumors, accusing us of political manipulation. Still, during that whole day, when I should have been able to revel in our success, I had to deflect call after call from reporters who were trying to depict us as cheaters. As hard as I had worked to keep everything fair and equal, nothing ended up looking equal until the Stern group finally admitted they had made the whole thing up.

For obvious reasons, I'm much happier when we book a standard show, which may be one person, or may include a panel of five. What interviewer besides Larry do you know who can talk with as many as five people at the same time and give them all equal time?

The additional logistics required when Larry interviews a group rather than an individual are considerable. But it is in our favor that Larry has such an innate relationship with time that we call him Mr. Clockhead. While the rest of us have to set clocks, Larry always knows in his head exactly how much time he has given to each person, and he does his best to keep it fair and square. It really bothers him when he inadvertently gives more time to one person than to another, so he makes sure that doesn't happen.

In the end, there is no randomness as to what topic or person I finally choose for the show. All decisions are based upon strategic calculations among Larry, my staff, and me. Most evenings, before I go to bed, I know some of what will be on the show tomorrow, which may have nothing to do with what we aired tonight. Or it may. I might wake up tomorrow, study my notes and lists, and scrap all my previous ideas for the show. Or I might go forward with a theme, like when we covered the trials of OJ Simpson and Scott Peterson, or the mysterious death of Michael Jackson. In cases like these, the same topic might go on for days, weeks, or in a rare case like the OJ trial, months.

Besides that kind of ongoing event, the uncertainty is considerable each day. There are countless stories and guests who never make it on the air because someone more important trumped them, no matter how much time we may have spent planning. But at least I don't have to suddenly get on a plane for Geneva, Moscow, or Reykjavik like I did when I was White House producer. Back then, I had to schedule time to go to the bathroom, which requires a whole different set of organizational skills.

❖

ORGANIZE, ORGANIZE, AND THEN... ORGANIZE SOME MORE

The most successful people I know are usually the most organized. Case in point, Ross Perot happens to be one of the most organized men I ever met. In my world, any success I can claim in this life is the result of meticulous organization. I really would not be able to manage my life without it, and I was lucky because it came naturally to me. I can only assume that when "they" were giving out the O gene, as in Organization, I was at the head of the line.

But don't despair because organization can be learned. Start very simply with the following:

- Make lists of tasks in a notebook and check each one off when it's completed. You get a nice sense of accomplishment when an item gets taken off the list.
- Copy the list at the end of the day and add what was not accomplished to tomorrow's list.
- Keep pens and paper all over your house, beside each telephone or computer.
- Keep a pad and pen by your bedside all the time, especially at night. If it's late and you think you're going to remember something in the morning, believe me, you won't. Take the effort to write it down and it won't be lost the next day.
- Update your schedule and color code it on your computer. For example, things to do with your kids can be red. Work appointments can be blue. Personal things can be green, and so on. If you don't keep your schedule clear, you can easily end up double booking yourself, which is embarrassing for you and rude to the other person.
- Take extensive notes—it's hard to trust yourself in a meeting if you don't take notes. How will you remember the details that will make all the difference later?

Being organized will help you emotionally, as you feel more confident and in control of your schedule and your life. I have come up with a great way to organize clutter in my home. This might work for you at home or in your workplace. So let me share it with you.

My kitchen drawers are always organized, and I have no junk drawers in my house. But I do have four junk boxes, three in the pantry (one for each kid and me) and one in my closet, where I store things that are temporarily out of place. That means I don't necessarily feel like filing them right then or putting them away. Maybe it's a letter, a report card, a child's toy, a CD without a jacket, or an article of clothing, a receipt, or a photo. Into the box it goes until, once a week, I go through it all, put everything in its place, and then I start all over again. Things are rarely lost in my house. They are usually in one of the boxes instead.

My kids and I have a story that pretty much sums up the value I pace on organization and my obsession with it. We once received a phone call in the middle of the night that we were being evacuated from our home due to fires that were raging close by, in the San Diego area. As we rushed out of bed and grabbed the things we most treasured, Amaya and Walker stared at me wide-eyed as I quickly made the beds, rinsed off the dishes, and put them in the dishwasher. Then I grabbed the kids, the animals, a handful of photos, and we all took off. They love to tell that story because it says it all.

CHAPTER 5

You Are Paid to Do a Job, So Do It

For a White House producer, organizing the coverage of a summit is a massive undertaking that is both political and historical. The amount of effort required to pull one off is almost impossible to fathom. Imagine hundreds of people gathering in a foreign country, often with questionable communication technology, and working under severe conditions for weeks on end, on an average of three hours of sleep a night. Bumps in the road are more like boulders and there is never a guarantee of success.

When a summit was over, everyone involved would drag themselves to the press plane and collapse from exhaustion. It could be called a thankless job if you happened to be looking for comfort, praise, or recognition. I wasn't. I kept my eye on the larger picture and I did my job, regardless of what it entailed. There were no assurances of anything and we were always alert for sudden catastrophes, which cropped up all the time and had to be unraveled tactfully and swiftly. We did the best preparations we knew how, but in the end, all we could count on was losing sleep, having major communication crises, and flying by the seat of our pants.

We appreciated having time to plan these highly demanding undertakings, but we didn't always get it. I recall a summit in Helsinki, Finland, starting on September 9, 1990, for which we were given five days to prepare, start to finish. John Towriss, CNN special events producer, a good friend of mine since we did so much traveling and producing together, was with me in Helsinki for this summit. He recalls, "The local Helsinki newspaper did a story on CNN, the crazy American network that was trying to set up in less than a week," he says. "We were in the midst of the Gulf War, and I'd been in Saudi Arabia where the average daily temperature was 155 degrees, when I was asked to fly to Helsinki, Finland, for this summit.

"In order to get to Helsinki from Saudi Arabia, I had a stopover in Frankfurt, Germany. I had all the wrong clothes after being in the heat of the desert. It was so cold in Frankfurt, I bought a sweater at the airport, which turned out to be the only cold-weather clothing I had the entire time I was in Finland. The local newspaper there took pictures of Wendy and me in our CNN jackets," he reminisces, "and when I look back today, we looked like a couple of college kids in our varsity jackets, shivering from the cold. But we were carrying a lot more responsibility than a college kid does. We were doing our part in setting up coverage of a summit that could literally change the world."

Among numerous summit challenges we faced was the fact that each of the four networks vied for the prime anchor locations. There were huge differences in the relevance of the locations, and the costs varied according to which sites offered the best view of the main event. Of course, each network wanted the advantage, which meant acquiring and paying for the prime positions for their reporters. But there really was no way to make these important allotments in a fair way so we used a draw.

We would put numbers in a hat from 1 to 4, and someone from each network would pull one out. Whoever got number 1 had the right to choose the best location, and it went backward from there. I always considered Towriss to be lucky since he had drawn much better numbers than I had over the years, so he was the one who inevitably drew the straw for CNN. And he often pulled the best numbers. He had pulled a prime location for this Helsinki summit and I was relieved because it promised to be monumental.

The thing is, while all the networks were like family and we smiled and supported one another overtly, we also were trying to outmaneuver and outfox one another all the time. In fact, we watched each other and our own backs like hawks, which added to the ongoing stress and battles against time we all waged. That's known as good old American competition, which is pretty foreign in a communist country. I remember being in Moscow when we needed setups for the four networks. The Russians had a controlled press corps and it was difficult for them to grasp the concept of a free press. Why did we need setups for four cameras instead of one? Couldn't we all share? We had to educate them about how we did things in America, and they had to educate us about what they could provide and what they couldn't.

But the considerable discomfort, confusion, and pressure of these events on so many levels was always offset by the fact that those of us who were there saw history being made right in front our eyes. What an opportunity for a group of youngsters (only someone young could keep up with such insane scheduling and loss of sleep!) who knew we were changing the way the world communicated.

So much of producing summit coverage, wherever they were, was getting accustomed to the local timing and logistics. For example, at a 1988 summit in Moscow, I met with the CNN Moscow bureau chief as soon as we arrived there. It was early in the morning, I was ready to hit the ground running, when he said, "First things first. We need to make reservations for lunch. When would you like to eat?"

Exasperated, I said, "There's so much to do, I really don't care about lunch right now. Don't bother with reservations. When we get hungry, we can go pick something up."

"You don't get it, Wendy," he said. "You're in Moscow. Food runs out here. We have to make reservations so you and your people have something to eat. Unless you want to work on empty stomachs all day."

I was shocked but I acquiesced. We made it to our lunch reservation and I have to say that the food was horrible, fatty brown meat and wilted lettuce, but at least we got to eat.

I recall being in Beijing, China, when one of my close friends and colleagues, CNN reporter Charles Bierbauer, and I butted heads. I had the occasional disagreement with my colleagues because we worked too closely under strained circumstances for us to always see eye to eye. The flare-ups were petty and they amounted to nothing in the end, but I have to say, this disagreement with Charles taught me a good lesson.

We were walking down the street in Beijing, short on sleep, when we got into a heated (and ridiculous) argument about who needed to be more focused, a reporter or a producer, a topic that would be compelling only when you're exhausted, running on empty, and you need to do something to let off steam.

Charles was busy telling me that his job was to observe, ask, synthesize, and then give his report. He described my job as "simple logistics," which angered me.

"Well, whatever you call it," I argued, "you owe me a lot. I do all this work on the setup and production so you'll look good."

"No, you don't," he replied. "You do your work because it's your job. We both do this because it's our job. I don't do it for you and you don't do it for me. Nobody gets any personal praise or recognition. I just happen to be in front of the camera and you're behind it. If I fail or stumble or if you do, that affects us both. We owe everything to our jobs and the people who pay us. Beyond that, we don't owe each other anything."

He was right, I knew that, but I was too annoyed to admit it right then. I rolled my eyes, a habit I had that drove him crazy. He wagged his finger at me (a habit *he* had that drove *me* crazy), and he said, "Don't you dare roll your eyes at me."

"Don't you wag your finger at me, then," I responded curtly.

And so I rolled, he wagged, and eventually we got to our location and stopped arguing. I guess we were so attuned to each other, we were like an old married couple. We knew each other well enough to have a good fight, but when the chips were down, we were there for each other 100 percent, and we never decided who owed what to whom.

Charles was also with me in 1992, when we landed in Tokyo where President George H. W. Bush was scheduled to attend a state dinner for 135 diplomats. Right after we landed in Japan, a reporter from each network was given a short interview, a five-minute sit-down, with the president, and when it was Charles's turn, he informally asked the president how he was doing.

"It was a long trip," Bush said. "I feel a little tired and achy, to tell you the truth."

"We're all worn out," Charles told him reassuringly.

About two hours later, President and Barbara Bush arrived at the home of Prime Minister Kiichi Miyazawa where they were greeted warmly. The dinner was covered by a pool camera, and CNN was pool that night so I had to monitor the dinner. As the president and the prime minister sat down to eat, the producers and reporters sat in our work space where we could see the action inside the banquet room on a monitor from that one small camera feed. We all relaxed a little bit as we chatted, had a bite to eat, and got ready to shut down for the night.

Not so fast! I was chatting with Charles about something insignificant, thinking about going to bed soon, when someone said, "Hey, did you see that? Where's the president?"

We all stared at the monitor. There was the table, there were the prime minister and his guests, but the president was nowhere to be seen. It seemed that he had vomited on the prime minister and then fainted, slumping to the floor beneath the table. Barbara, his wife, had rushed over and gotten on the floor beside him, trying to revive him. We had no idea what had just happened and we all picked up our phones to find out. That was when a call came in from Atlanta. One of the network's health correspondents said, "We just heard that the president died. And that they're flying his body back home. Is it true?"

"No. I don't think so," I said. "I haven't heard anything. But I'll find out." I called around to anyone who might have the information. If it was a rumor, we needed to nip it in the bud before it got reported. If it was true—well, I didn't even want to think about that.

I got in touch with a reporter standing outside the prime minister's home. "What's going on?" I asked. "Is the motorcade moving?"

"Yes. But we're not sure where they're going or who's in the car."

As we continued to make calls and tried to verify what was happening, we all received a computer file saying, READ ME! I froze for a second. This was our message alert system, letting us all know that there was an important message that we needed to read right away. When we opened it, it said something to the effect that although we had no confirmation as yet, there were rumors circulating that the president had died.

At CNN Atlanta, anchor Don Miller, who has since passed away, had been on the air. The network was on a commercial break when he got the READ ME! message. Looking troubled, he asked his producer, "Are you sure you want me to report this?"

"Yes," his producer said. "But we don't have much information. Can you ad-lib the story when we're back on the air?"

While this was going on, I called Dorrance Smith. Remember him? I had met him at Ethel's and wanted to *be* him? Well, now I had his job and he worked for the White House as part of President Bush's team and was with us in Japan. "Dorrance," I said, "we're getting reports in Atlanta that the president is dead."

"He isn't," Dorrance said with assurance. He had just seen the president. "He's alive and he has a nasty flu."

Don Miller was getting ready to report the unwelcome and disturbing piece of news as he somberly looked at the camera and said, "This tragic news just in from Tokyo."

But I had gotten a call through in time. At that point, his producer interrupted him and literally shouted into his earpiece, "No. Stop. Don't read it."

Thank God Don knew how to think on his feet. He managed to stop himself in midsentence and say, "Well, we'll get back to that story." And he went on to something else. We all exhaled. If that report had gone on the air, it would have been catastrophic. So, in effect, we nearly killed off the president that night, but we rescued him and ourselves in the nick of time. Good going, Don!

Perhaps this false rumor had spread like wildfire because it came on the heels of President Bush's diagnoses of atrial fibrillation and Graves' disease during the preceding twelve months. But this was typical of how the news worked. I can't tell you how many times something like a simple dinner with little to no import in the larger scheme of things suddenly became an international story. And we had managed to avoid spreading rumors and causing America and the rest of the world to panic. Who took the credit for that? None of us and all of us.

In 1989, I produced coverage for a US-Soviet summit in Malta, an archipelago in the middle of the Mediterranean Sea. Summits were always an exercise in controlled chaos and this one was no exception as we quickly realized the limitations of Malta's technology. We were all pushed to our limits, it was freezing cold outside, and John Towriss and I were in the work space well past midnight, arranging everything for the talks that would begin at 6 a.m. the next morning. "Wendy," John said, looking at me through bloodshot eyes, "I'm going up to my room and try to knock out a few hours of sleep."

Anxious to grab whatever sleep was possible, I went to my room, too. But sleep didn't last very long for me or for John.

"I lay down on the bed in my clothes," says John, "and I dropped off immediately without even turning off the lights, only to hear the phone ringing. It seemed like I just fell asleep five minutes before when I reached out to grab the telephone. I sat up with a start and said, 'What's going on?'"

CNN anchor, Bernard Shaw was calling John. A quick glance at the clock confirmed to John that it was not his imagination. He truly had just lain down.

"I tried to wake myself up fully," says John, "while Bernie droned in a slow, narrative kind of reporter-speak, 'Hi, John. This is Bernie.'"

"What's up?" John asked him, still groggy.

Bernie went on, "Well...I'm looking outside the window."

It couldn't have sounded more bizarre as Bernie continued speaking, using his words slowly and clearly, as if he were doing an on-the-air report. "A storm of terrific ferocity is blowing here. Our satellite dish is moving. Yes, now it's flipped over. It's broken. The satellite dish is broken. And our set seems to be taking a lot of water. Yes, water is now washing over our set."

While Bernie was talking, John ran over to the window and looked out. A monsoon of massive proportions was crashing down from the heavens, and he gazed with horror at our beautiful set on a ledge out over the water as the downpour lashed up over the TV cameras.

I got the same call from Bernie, maybe in not such a formal manner. I dragged myself out of bed, threw on some clothes, and ran down to see what was going on. As soon as I saw the problems, I quickly called various crew members and woke them up. "Get down here right away. We have to get all the lights down and the cameras need to come inside."

We all got pelted by the storm while a crew member climbed a ladder. With three guys holding the ladder against the wind, this agile man meticulously detached the lights and pulled them down. He made it back down the ladder and we all stared with horror at the mess in front of us. We were in a storm to end all storms, we were physically wiped out and drenched and so were our cameras, and the gales had flipped over our satellite dish that now lay on the ground, smashed to pieces. And we were scheduled to be on the air in five hours.

We called Atlanta to report our problem and find out what help they could give us. They called all around Malta, waking everyone up, to see if anyone had any spare satellite dishes. No one did. Then we began to call our colleagues at the other networks to see if they had unused time on their satellites. We wanted to know if we could connect to theirs until we found a way to broadcast. We came up blank again. Everyone was using every minute of available time they had.

Finally, John called the owner of our hotel. A lovely and cooperative man, he offered to call his brother who was a local sheet metal worker. When this angel in rain gear arrived in the middle of the night with advanced electronic knowledge and some used parts, he began picking up pieces of our broken satellite dish. He took the struts, banged them against soggy trees to straighten them out, and used a rivet gun to cobble together a makeshift dish with pieces of sheet metal he brought with him. He formed them into the rough shape of a satellite dish, our technicians connected the electronics, and amazingly, the thing worked! John and I were a little worse for the wear, but we got the job done. In fact, we always did, by hook or by crook, as they say. And we did it because that was the job we had been hired to do.

In line with what Charles Bierbauer had articulated to me in Beijing, getting this job done took every one of us putting our heads together and making it work. No one owed anyone a thing except for our shared obligation to CNN, which had hired us and paid our salaries. We did our jobs, and with the help of a few angels along the way, we were up and running when the time came.

Along with John and Charles, I have to add Gary Foster, head of the White House press corps, and CNN reporter Frank Sesno, to my list of colleagues whom I think of as brothers.

When we landed in Geneva for the very first Soviet-US summit in 1985, possibly the end of the Cold War, Gary stood at the bottom of the stairway, sending each of the network crews and producers to various camera setups that had been prearranged. As I recall, the energy in the air was palpable since no one knew what was about to happen and most everyone had their doubts and confusions.

The truth was that in the early years of Ronald Reagan's presidency, his opponents saw him as a cowboy, an anti-Soviet crusader who was dangerous, ill informed, and just might precipitously start a war. A large part of his platform throughout his presidency was his stance that America was seen as weak among other international powers. A great many Americans were fearful that this "cowboy" leader might decide to build and employ new generations of nuclear weapons.

This was a logical conclusion since during his first term, President Reagan, "Mr. Tough Guy," never met with a Soviet leader. Instead, he sent George H. W. Bush, his vice president, in his place. When he was taken to task for this, he famously said, "They keep dying on me." That was true. A number of Soviet leaders died in office, and Reagan was criticized for not attending the funerals and not making an effort to meet the successors.

Judging from his rhetoric, his attitudes, and his desire to build a nuclear shield in Europe, a pet project he called Star Wars, it appeared that there was no way this president would ever talk to the Soviets, much less try to negotiate a peace agreement. But the president's rigid stance eased when he had a talk with his close friend and ally British Prime Minister Margaret Thatcher. Thatcher and Reagan, both hard-core conservatives, had been close before Reagan came to power. Some even went so far as to call them soul mates. Now that the prime minister had declared that Gorbachev, the new Soviet leader, was not "doddering," like others may have been, but rather someone the West could do business with, Reagan was ready to meet with him. A new era was dawning, and a summit was planned in Geneva that would see these Cold War foes searching for a way to communicate.

There were worries about how well Ronald Reagan had been briefed for this all-important summit. Frank Sesno, our anchor that day, recalls the summit in Geneva vividly. "I was standing in clear view of the meeting place from my stakeout position," he says. "The building was a mission called Martha's Château. Gorbachev had already arrived, he was inside, and there was Ronald Reagan, walking deliberately into the mission, followed by his military aide who carried the nuclear codes in a briefcase, which we referred to as the 'football.' How incredibly dramatic to see the president who had labeled the Soviet Union an 'evil empire' walking into the lion's den with the nuclear codes in tow that could launch missiles capable of destroying the planet."

Each leader had his own agenda, but the story reported that day was a simple and life-changing one. It was about establishing whether these two previous enemies could see their way clear to working with each other. They seemed to be making progress as they left the château and took their famous hour-long "walk in the woods" through the Geneva heartland behind the US Embassy. That was followed by a bilateral talk in front of a roaring fireplace. We all could see that these men had established a rapport.

When they finally showed up for a joint business conference on a huge stage with flags from both countries raised overhead, they met in the middle and shook hands to thundering applause. Suddenly, they were on a first-name basis,

Ronald and Mikhail, and the sound of clicking camera shutters was deafening.

"As the leaders signed documents together," Frank Sesno says, "I realized that we were coming out of a deep freeze, into a warming trend, with a good chance of clearing."

On January 1, 1990, many years later, President Reagan came on *Larry King Live* and spoke about his legendary relationship with Soviet President Gorbachev:

KING: The liking of Gorbachev. Was that a real sense of affection? Did you, like, like him?

REAGAN: Yes. As you know...he was the fourth. There were three leaders before him, of the Soviet Union, and I didn't have much to do with them. They kept dying on me, but he was totally different than any Russian leader that I had met before, and I think that there was a kind of a chemistry there that set up. Now, on the other hand, I knew too much about communism to believe in words. I said that I would make my decision as to whether we were getting along on the basis of deeds. Every meeting that we ever had, I presented him with a handwritten—my handwriting—list of people that had been brought to my attention who wanted to emigrate and for [other] reasons to get out, and I would give it to him, and...

KING: He came through?

REAGAN: Yes...He is a likable person. You find yourself liking him. But again, knowing the difference between our two systems...I'm not a linguist, but I learned one little Russian phrase and I used it so often that he used to clap his hands over his ears, and that was *doveryai, no proveryai*, which means "trust, but verify."

We all were well aware of how fond Reagan was of saying, *"Doveryai, no proveryai."*

To which Gorbachev would say, *"Vi vceda eto gavorite."* "You always say that."

Then Reagan would come back with, "Well...I like the sound of it."

This kind of bantering among world leaders indicated a comfort level between them that would support continuing negotiations. The Cold War thaw officially had begun. Now, with each summit, there was progress being made between the two superpowers that previously had been enemies.

When I look back, I know that each leader involved had his personal agenda and each tried to do what he considered good for his country. There were no instant gains expected, they did not do it for each other, and no acknowledgment or personal praise was ever offered to anyone in particular who helped bring about this summit and make it a success. We were all just doing our jobs, and that is exactly the way it should be.

❖

YOU ARE PAID TO DO A JOB, SO DO IT

It really is that simple. Do you find yourself mulling the following questions?

- Do they like me?
- Do they like what I did?
- Did they say I was good?

If you waste time and energy worrying if someone likes what you did, if they're going to fire you, or if you're going to get a raise, you're on the wrong track. My advice is to not think about those things at all. Just do your job the best way you can.

I can't tell you how many times someone has said to me, "I thought I did a great job but I didn't hear a word about it."

The truth is that you didn't hear from anyone because you shouldn't hear from anyone. You were hired in the first place because they expected you to do, not just an adequate job, but a great job. And that doesn't come with praise or recognition. Just do what you were hired to do, and if you don't, believe me, you *will* hear about it. If you get an attaboy once in a while, that's a nice compliment. I try to give attaboys whenever I can, because generally when you hear from your boss, you did something he or she would like you never to repeat. If you do get called out, remember the value of constructive criticism. When it really is constructive and comes from someone smart and experienced, it's a priceless gift. How else can you keep on improving?

We all have insecurities that we have carried through our lives, but you can learn to put them on the back burner and just do your work. If you have a gift, concentrate on it instead of whether or not someone likes you. The more you get distracted with waiting for compliments, the more you get hung up on it, and you only get more insecure. It's a vicious cycle and getting out of it is a relief.

When someone complains that no one picked up a phone to tell them how great they did, I say it's time to grow up. Welcome to the real world where your boss is sure to call you out for a mistake, but when you perform well, no news is good news.

CHAPTER 6

Work Harder Than Anyone Else

By 1978, I was set on becoming a television producer, inspired by having helped organize the RFK Pro-Celebrity Tennis Tournament. At the time, there were three major networks: ABC, CBS, NBC. I decided to take my chances at ABC, not a choice that resulted from doing research and comparing my options. Rather, I chose ABC because the only producer I knew had worked there. But I never asked for his help. One day I just walked in cold and said to the ABC receptionist, "Hi, my name is Wendy Walker and I'd like to apply for a job."

"What would you like to do?" asked the receptionist.

"I'd like to be a producer," I said.

"Do you have any experience?" he asked.

"Yes. Well, no, not exactly." I explained the charity tennis tournament I had helped to arrange.

"You're going to need a lot more experience than that," he said. "But if you'd like to apply for an entry level position, you can do that and work your way up. Would you consider becoming a secretary?"

"I guess so," I said as he handed me a load of paperwork to fill out. At twenty-five, I was applying to become an entry level secretary at ABC, with no clout at all. But I was trying to keep my eye on the big picture, even though I didn't know exactly what the big picture was. I just knew that I was willing to do what it took to find out.

I took the typing test, I passed it (thank you, IBM Correcting Selectric typewriters), and I applied for a couple of ABC secretarial jobs. I got one! That was when I met a pretty, young, dark-haired woman and we introduced ourselves. Her name was Katie Couric, she told me, she was twenty years old, five years my junior, just out of college, and she was starting with ABC on the same exact day that I was.

"We were like two lost souls looking for a normal person to talk to," Katie explains. "It was her first day and my first day and we just sort of clicked immediately. I remember it was really fun to meet somebody who was completely on the same page as I was professionally, in terms of just starting out in television."

But while I sat at my desk as assistant to Kevin Delaney, deputy bureau chief, helping people sort out where they belonged, Katie, a desk assistant, was rushing all over the newsroom. She once told Larry during an interview, "Basically, when I started, I got Frank Reynolds his ham sandwiches and Xeroxed and answered telephones and made coffee and gave newspapers to the correspondents."

I made a little more money than Katie did (the only time that has been true throughout our careers), but her job was more fun than mine since she was in motion most of the time. When I look at Katie today, she looks pretty much the same as she did in that newsroom, and we still share a similar sense of humor and a drive to do the best we can at all times. We've both always had that drive and I only wish we had known back then that we really *could* do whatever we wanted to do. No one ever said to Katie, "If you want to be the first female network news anchor, you can do it."

Rather, people went out of their way to discourage her. Katie says, "When I started, the notion that I would have the job that I have today was laughable. I've always tried to enjoy and appreciate whatever job I'm in. While I had definite career goals, I wanted to be a network correspondent by the time I was thirty. I never imagined I would ever be an anchor. I just wasn't anchor material."

That was what they told her. So Katie and I simply followed our designated career paths, never realizing how far we could and would go. We kept at it, we worked as hard as we could, and we encouraged each other to take chances. We were both competitive by nature, we always acted like professionals, and we fell back on our humor to get us through the tough periods, sometimes acting silly together when we were sure no one else could see us. We needed to be taken seriously and we did what was asked of us, like making sure Frank Reynolds's cigarette was out when his show started.

After a month or two, Katie moved in with me. She had been living with her parents since she was out of college, and I was renting a town house in Georgetown. Now, as roommates, workmates, and friends, we egged each other on.

"We became even closer," says Katie, "because we were living in the same house and working at the same place. We could have gotten on each other's nerves but we didn't. Or maybe I got on *her* nerves. I'm very messy and Wendy is so organized, I think she might be slightly OCD."

The truth was that my room was in the basement of our Georgetown town house, so in order to make it cozy and feel

like a nest, I put sheets all over the walls and bought an inexpensive navy-and-white duvet cover from Bloomingdale's.
Once, I got home from CNN late at night to find Katie balancing an overly full cup of black coffee on my new duvet cover
while she was trying on my clothes and systematically tossing
them on the floor. A scene from *The Cat in the Hat* by Dr. Seuss
comes to mind whenever I think of that night. One look at her
room, strewn from bed to floor with random articles of clothing, explained why she was in mine. There was no place she
could sit in her own room. And she made sure to throw all of
my stuff around, too. It was so bad and comical, I once found
chicken bones in the pocket of a jacket she was lending me.
Our Felix and Oscar relationship was in full swing.

"We really were the odd couple," says Katie. "Wendy had
her sweaters organized by stripes and colors. Then I would
come into her room and throw a striped shirt in the solid pile
on her shelf. God forbid! Wendy called me Pigpen, not because
I was dirty, but was I ever messy! I'm better these days," she
adds, "but I still throw things around a little bit. And Wendy
still organizes my bathroom when she comes to visit, because
she says it looks like a drugstore."

Katie and I had bought identical gray Honda Accords and
mine was clean and tidy at all times. I never left a coffee cup
or a piece of paper in my car, while Katie's had half-full cups
in all the holders, and articles of clothing were strewn across
the backseat so you couldn't get in. Even her glove box was
so full, she couldn't close it, so it just hung open, offering easy
access to the pile of junk she had stuffed inside it.

It was so bad that at one point, Katie's mom came over to
have a talk with me. Katie was only twenty, she explained,
and this was the first time she was living away from home. She
asked me to please not throw Katie out because she was so

messy. I told her I had no intention of throwing Katie out, but when I tried to help her, she wasn't interested.

Mostly, though, we had a great time as roommates. "I would wake Wendy up to borrow a skirt," recalls Katie, "and she would wake me up to French braid her hair. When she had to tell off a boyfriend, I would create a script with her so she could call him up and know exactly what to say."

When Katie moved out into her own place, I came over to help her organize it, but it was futile. From the boxes all over the place to the impossible tangle of her gold necklaces in her jewelry box, it was a lost cause. The main area where Katie and I connected was in our work ethic. Although we had fun together, we were all work and very little play since we were both so focused on our careers. In fact, on Sundays, instead of hanging around our apartment or meeting friends for brunch, we went into ABC to volunteer our time. There, we wrote copy, logged tapes, went out with camera crews to various locations, and basically, we learned every phase of the business. All for no pay. We called it Sunday School, and we spent as much time as possible learning the news business and increasing our "skill sets," a term no one used back then. Whatever you called it, my motivation was clear. I wanted to learn everything I could as quickly as possible in order to figure out what I was really good at. If I had to work harder than anyone else, that was fine with me, because I knew that the harder I worked, the better chance I had of getting promoted.

Even as a secretary, I loved the feeling of being in the newsroom, the dimmed lights, the conversational buzz, and the constant clicking sound of the ticker tape. Everybody was puffing away on cigarettes (the room was always filled with layers of smoke), we communicated on big old telephones that were hooked into the wall with thick, coiled black wires, and I had a dinosaur of an electric typewriter on my desk, which was located at the very back of the newsroom at the Washington News Bureau.

Nevertheless, there I was, in Frank Reynolds's newsroom, where live TV news broadcasts were aired every night. Little did I know that one day I would be the White House producer for his son, Dean Reynolds, or that Dean and I would date for a few years. At the time, it was all new to me and truly alive with lights, the teleprompter, and massive motion and activity. I would watch various people scrambling around to get those pieces out as the news broke. Producers were editing at the last minute, suddenly changing something, and then literally racing down hallways, yelling, "We've got it, we're coming." And into the tape deck the video would slide, just in the nick of time. Just like a movie, but this was real.

My desk sat at the end of a long hallway just outside bureau chief George Watson's office. Once a show was ready to air, if you had enough clout, you were invited into the bureau chief's office to watch the show from there. I was not in a high-enough position back then to be invited into George's inner sanctum, but I watched with envy as other people ran in and out of there, wondering what eventual piece of this pie might be mine.

In the meantime, I worked nonstop on scheduling for the various production assistants, directors, and assistant directors who all needed to be at work at different designated times. I became the go-to girl to find out what time each individual person needed to show up, so I met and talked with everyone every day, since they all had to check in with me. ABC was airing news shows constantly, including a Sunday public affairs show called *Issues and Answers* which eventually turned into the much fancier show: *This Week with David Brinkley*.

One Sunday, George came in to ABC to finish up some work. Since my desk was located directly next to his assistant's empty desk, he noticed me right away and said, "Wendy, what are you doing here on a weekend?"

"I always come in on weekends," I told him. "So does Katie. We call it Sunday School."

When it came out of my mouth, I thought it sounded lame. But George was impressed while I continued to soak in information and revel in the bustle of the newsroom. Getting promoted was always on my mind, so after several months, I applied to be the booker for *Good Morning America* (GMA). Susan Mercandetti, the GMA booker and a dear friend, was being promoted and I had my eye on her job. I had never booked a show, but it didn't seem beyond me. The truth was, it was a lot different back then, since there were so many fewer venues for guests and so many people were eager to get on the air. Susan was the best booker in the business.

I would be remiss here, by the way, to omit the fact that Susan Mercandetti gave new meaning to the term "Rolodex." People had real ones back then, not virtual Rolodexes on the Internet, and Susan lugged her huge one around with her wherever she went. I remember being with her at Martha's Vineyard when she pulled out that crazy Rolodex. It really was the real thing! I didn't end up getting her job, which mortified me at the time, but when I look back, I see that I didn't deserve it. I needed some more experience.

The next job I didn't get but I think I actually *did* deserve was replacing one of our PR staffers, Jan Smith. Since she wanted to be a reporter, she was leaving her post as ABC public relations assistant to go to Kansas City, to "work on her reel." When someone wanted to become a reporter, it was common practice to go to a smaller market to get experience and create a reel of film. Then you would come back to the big city and land a job in the larger market, using your reel as an audition tape. I was eager to make the jump to PR assistant, but I didn't get that job, either.

Then one afternoon, my boss, Kevin Delaney, walked over to my desk and said almost apologetically, "Wendy, I need you to take a cab to Capitol Hill right now. Our correspondents Charlie Gibson and Ted Koppel are there, the phones are ringing off the hook, and they can't get any work done. They want somebody to come and answer phones. Would you mind doing that?"

Quite the opposite. It sounded great to me, and I jumped into a cab and headed for Capitol Hill to answer phones and do whatever else anybody needed. I only did this once but I loved being where the action was, it was the coolest thing ever, and I wanted to do more of it. The only hard part was jumping in the cab since, after my Paris incident, I am incredibly frightened of them to this day. But that was how much I wanted it!

It was 1979, during the Iranian hostage crisis, when Roone Arledge, the head of ABC news at the time, created a show called *America Held Hostage*. Roone had made a commitment to do a special every night that the hostages were in captivity. The show was expected to last for a couple of weeks, but the crisis went on for a tragically long period of time, 444 days, and so did the reporting. In the beginning, several different anchors were used, but ultimately, Ted Koppel, who anchored the show more than anyone else, became the permanent host and the show was eventually renamed *Nightline*.

When *World News Tonight* had finished airing in the evening, I would pick up my massive typewriter and carry it down to the editing booths to help with whatever else anyone needed. My job description at the time did not include editing, but I

went to the edit floor every night anyway, partly to learn editing and partly to enjoy the catered dinner that was served at
night, which encouraged everyone to keep working.

At that point in time, Katie and I were so broke, we shopped
at Loehmann's discount store and shared our outfits, wearing a
different scarf and hoping no one would notice. At the end of a
long day of work, our dinners were generally chicken pot pies
or spaghetti because that was all we could afford. We were so
poor, we would go to a restaurant in Georgetown, get a table,
order coffee, and ask cute guys sitting near us if we could
have a bite of whatever they ordered. Seriously! I have a hard
time believing it, but we really did that because we were broke
When we stayed late at ABC to help, however, they brought in
roast beef, mashed potatoes, fresh veggies, and pies. Getting
a free dinner back then was a big deal, and I made sure to
take advantage of it while I also learned the art of producing
a story on tape. Like a scene out of a movie, I would stuff my
pockets with rolls and chicken to take home and put in our
refrigerator.

Eight months after I began working at ABC, when I was just
getting the hang of things, George Watson called me into his
office and shut the door. "No one knows this yet," he said quietly, "but I'm about to leave ABC as bureau chief."

I was stunned. He was the last person I had thought would
ever leave, but when he explained further, I was intrigued.
"I'm taking a new job," he said. "I'll be helping Ted Turner start
the Washington bureau for his new venture called Cable News
Network. He wants to launch the first network that airs only
the news for twenty-four hours a day, seven days a week on
cable. And I'd like you to come with me."

This offer, which would eventually change my life for the
better in countless ways, was a complete surprise. At first, I

wondered, why me? Why didn't George choose someone with more clout? I was a neophyte, a mere assistant to the deputy bureau chief. I was not someone with prime contacts back then, and I did not have an influential voice in the news business. But I always worked harder than anyone else, and I had proven that to George. Today, when I review the amount of sweat, hard work, and moving mountains it took to do this impossible thing with Ted Turner, I probably would have hired me, too, considering the fact that I worked harder than anyone else.

❖

WORK HARDER THAN ANYONE ELSE

If your company is doing layoffs like so many are, they are going to lay off the people who don't work hard and have bad attitudes. The people who work the hardest and don't complain make their bosses' lives easier, so they get to keep their jobs. Which one are you?

This really is a no-brainer. The harder you work and the better your attitude, the more people will notice you and the more indispensable you will become. It's all about your work ethic.

Do you find ways to go above and beyond what is required of you, even if it takes a little longer?

Or are you tapping your foot, willing the hands of the clock to move faster so you can go home the instant your eight hours are officially up?

Here are some tips that will serve you well:

- Get in to the office earlier than your boss and stay after he or she leaves. I believe that when

my boss, George Watson, saw that I was coming
in to the office on Sundays, he felt secure that
he could depend on me to do a job with more
responsibility.

- Don't complain. Complaining is contagious and
  it brings everyone down, including you. No one
  wants to work with a complainer, no matter how
  talented you are. When a complainer leaves my
  staff, I am relieved. Of course, you may need to
  vent about certain things, so call a friend and tell
  him or her how you feel. Then it's back to work
  with a good attitude. It's so much easier to get a
  job done if you are someone other people can
  get along with. When a better position becomes
  available, you will be passed over if you have the
  reputation of being difficult.

- Don't drop the ball: Be a team player. If you are
  on a staff, every job will have some kind of over-
  lap with the next job. You have to get along with
  other staff members and keep the ball rolling. If
  you are someone who does his or her part and
  you are working with someone who drops the
  ball, instead of complaining and blaming, pick
  it up. People will notice. Don't waste your time
  being pissed off about the people who aren't
  working as hard, just because you're one of the
  people who does work hard.

- Offer your boss good suggestions without being
  asked. Be part of the solution. I expect my staff
  to present me with original ideas. I want people
  who are going to challenge me and be chal-
  lenged. It's a strong person who can say to their

boss, "I heard what you suggested and I don't think that's the way to go. I would do this."

If you have an idea about how to save money or improve on a product, speak up. It's all in the attitude. I would avoid complaints and irritation such as, "This is all wrong. We need to make it right." Nobody wants to listen to an employee who is irritable and grumpy. Instead, how about saying, "I'm curious. Wouldn't it work better if we did it this way?" This is being part of the solution.

And then, after you have spoken your mind, it's a strong person who can let it go if their boss does not agree, because he or she has the final word. Whether the boss followed your suggestion or not, you will be remembered as a creative thinker. Then, when that promotion comes up, who do you think will get it? Someone who did very little to speak of, or you, who came up with some revolutionary ideas? I think you know the answer.

Bosses feel a level of comfort when they have people on their staff on whom they know they can rely. These are the people who will get ahead because they work harder than anyone else, and they will get the job done right and on time. If you do these things, if your work ethic is beyond reproach, people will know. Believe me, one way or another, they always know.

CHAPTER 7

Mentor Yourself

When I first began my White House producing job for CNN in 1983, we had two desks in the White House basement press room, one for correspondent Dean Reynolds and the other for reporter Jim Miklaszewski (we called him Mik). I had no desk so I stood between them most of the time, happy just to be there. But I kept urging my bosses to ask the White House to assign us a glass booth with sliding doors and a small office inside, like the other networks. Maybe I would even have my own chair. The three large networks each had a booth and we needed one, too, but where would we put it?

I went on a search and discovered a small area in the basement of the press room. A kind of "crazy old lady" radio reporter was using that space to hoard old newspapers and magazines. I asked for the space and when the White House granted us permission to put our booth there, this woman was incredibly pissed off. She got so incensed, I had to take matters into my own hands and move her magazines and papers for her. It was the only way I could get it done.

And so, over Christmas that year, I spent most of my time overseeing the construction of our much-desired booth. When I look back, I wonder what in the hell I was thinking, spending my Christmas vacation at work in the basement of the White House. But back then, work was everything, and it was all trial and error since I had no one to show me what to do.

I would arrive at the White House in the morning about 7:30 or 8. I made coffee and got organized, made calls, checked the president's schedule for the day, and then I'd go to the morning briefing with my tape recorder. If there was a major news story, I'd type up my notes and fax them to CNN on our clunky fax machine.

The other producers at ABC, CBS, and NBC had one evening news spot to do while Mik, Dean, and I had to find live shots to feed the news beast all day long. That's why we needed to have a full-time producer stationed at the White House. I was like a short-order cook for CNN, leaving other people free to make calls and do the rest of their work.

I spent the entire day at the White House, acting as liaison between the administration and CNN. After the morning briefing, if the president was going somewhere, I might go, too. Then someone else from CNN would take my place at my desk. But I always stayed in contact with the main news desk. If the president was going out at night, we did what we called a "death watch," making sure someone always represented CNN in case something happened, such as the Reagan assassination attempt. We refused to be left high and dry any longer, so someone always stayed on "death watch" until the president was back home again. It usually ended up being me because nobody else was willing to stand on a street corner, waiting. For me, it was all about learning as I went along.

In fact, I had only been there a few months when I found

myself in a very embarrassing position. I was crossing the White House lawn on my way to the press room when I noticed a large crowd hovering around someone so small, you couldn't see who it was. When crews and reporters surround someone who is newsworthy and shoot out random questions, we call it a gangbang for lack of a better term. And this was just that—a gangbang on the front lawn of the White House. My first one.

Toting my huge walkie-talkie, too large to fit into a pocket or even an oversize purse, I made my way through the group of burly cameramen to see Mother Teresa, three inches shy of five feet tall, in her blue-striped head covering, discussing the meeting she'd just had with President Reagan. I marveled at how such a tiny woman could make such a huge impact on the world, as she clutched a handful of prayer cards.

Each time she spoke to someone, she handed him or her a white-and-blue card, colors that matched her clothing, with a painting of Jesus on the front. Anyone who received a prayer card took it and said, "Thank you, Mother Teresa," in reverent tones. When I got in close enough, she handed me a card, too, which I framed later as an offering from a living saint.

Card in hand and breathless, I stepped away from the circle and got on my walkie-talkie with a guy named Vito at the CNN assignment desk. "Vito," I gasped much too loudly, barely able to contain my excitement, "there's a gangbang with Mother Teresa on the front lawn."

I cringed when I heard my own words resound. It was pretty obvious that when it came to Mother Teresa, "gangbang" was not the right thing to say. I still had a lot to learn. But how would I learn it when there was no one around to mentor me?

Although there was a lack of an official mentor in my life, there were some great characters in the newsroom who had been around the block, and I learned what I could from them.

I think most everyone would agree that no one was more interesting, knowledgeable, and eccentric than Susan Zirinsky, who
is currently executive producer of *48 Hours* on CBS. She had
such a powerful reputation and was such a colorful character, the blockbuster movie *Broadcast News* starring Holly Hunter,
William Hurt, and Albert Brooks was based on this woman
whom we all called Z. I learned a great deal from her, like
making sure my reporters had three newspapers waiting for
them in the mornings and getting the typed-up notes to them
that explained where we were going that day and the various
phone numbers they would need.

I learned it all from Z, and she and I were quite competitive,
mainly because we were cut from the same cloth. That meant
that above all else, we both wanted to get "the story." She was
already a big deal when I arrived at the White House, and I
looked to her experience and her willingness to help, despite
her edge of competitiveness. She had one up on me because
when I was growing up, I had never engaged in sports in order
to learn the art of healthy competition.

Z once said to me, "Wendy, if you want longevity in this
business, you have to learn to cry." That comment sparked a
famous scene in *Broadcast News* where Holly Hunter's character
came in early to take a few minutes to sob loudly at her desk
before the business of the day took over. I appreciated Z's sen-
timent, but I already knew how to cry. I just had to make sure
I did it at the right time and in the right place so I didn't look
like a wimp.

The thing is, we all have our own styles and Z's style was
exciting and explosive, perfect fodder for a Hollywood movie.
When they were doing research for the film, costar and writer
Albert Brooks asked me if he could come to a presidential
event. He showed up in Santa Barbara to hear the president

speak and the director of the film, James L. Brooks, asked me if he could come to my Washington apartment to see how a producer lived. I invited him to see my Georgetown apartment, which was in a mansion that was now divided into four separate homes. Mine included the front door, half of a living room, and a tiny bedroom. He walked around, asked me a ton of questions, and took notes, and I have to say, I loved the movie. I was honored that the director even wanted to see my apartment. And it was great to see a movie based on Z.

I still had so much more to learn when bureau chief George Watson called me into his office in 1980 to tell me he was leaving ABC to be bureau chief at Cable News Network, Ted Turner's baby, and he wanted me to come with him. "Picking Bernie Shaw as the main anchor is easy," he said, "but I don't know the secretaries or the assistants here. I'd like you to be my assistant, and I need you to tell me whom we should hire from ABC. By the way, I know you want to be a producer, and at Cable News Network you can learn that by being hands-on, as opposed to staying here at ABC and watching everybody else do it. You'd eventually become a producer here at ABC, but it would take a lot longer."

I was a little taken aback since I had no idea what this new position would require. Did I have the experience and wisdom to help George make the right choices? I didn't know, but George's argument was convincing enough for me to seriously consider the offer. I checked with several of my coworkers at ABC who all encouraged me to go for it. I turned to my friend, reporter and anchor Sam Donaldson, to get his opinion because George had approached him to come over to Ted's new network. He declined the offer, which made sense, since ABC was treating him much too well for him to leave and join an upstart fledgling network. Still, Sam assured me that the door would remain open for me at ABC and I could come back after I'd gotten some producing experience.

After serious consideration, I went back to George and told him I was on board. "My roommate, Katie Couric," I said, "wants to be a writer. I think she'll come over with us. And I like Scott Willis, a really talented producer. He's a director at ABC and I think he'd be a great guy for us." I still recall my reluctance to leave ABC at that time, which was even tougher when I learned that Carl Bernstein, a reporter in his thirties, was taking over for George Watson as bureau chief.

The names Woodward and Bernstein were huge at the time (they still are), ever since the Watergate break-in and the revelation of the surreptitious whistle-blower whom these two reporters called Deep Throat. Little did I know at the time that more than twenty-five years later, I would be in charge of the very show that would get the only interview with the real Deep Throat, a man named Mark Felt.

Here is an excerpt from that rare interview that happened shortly before he died, on April 26, 2009:

KING: Were you surprised that it was a secret for so long?

FELT: Yes, I guess I was.

KING: Did you like being called Deep Throat?

FELT: Well, yes. In some ways, I do. I'm proud of everything Deep Throat did. Yes, I like being related to him.

KING: So you have no questions of yourself as to why you did it?

FELT: No. No.

KING: Because there were some who said that you were kind of like a traitor to the cause. There were a few—certainly on the Republican right side, who complained that you were turning the tide on your boss.

FELT: That sounds like the Republican approach.

KING: Why did you do it?

FELT: I don't remember doing that. I mean, I tried to go along with whatever I thought was correct and 100 percent accurate, but if that happened to bring somebody in on the side, that was just the effects of the facts.

KING: Why did you decide to help Woodward? Why did you decide to do what you did?

FELT: Because he was doing a good job.

KING: No other reason?

FELT: No other reasons.

KING: Did you always trust Bob Woodward?

FELT: Pretty much so, yes. Pretty much.

KING: You never feared that he would reveal your name at a time that might have been...

FELT: I didn't have that fear, no.

KING: Why did you come out?

FELT: Well, because with politics moving the way they did, I had no choice, really, but to come out and put everything on the line, both plus and minus on the line.

KING: Do you think you upset Mr. Woodward?

FELT: Well, maybe a little. A little, but I think he understood. When it was all laid out on the table in front of him, he understood.

KING: Because he always said, you know, they'd never reveal it until Deep Throat passed away. And obviously, you didn't pass away.

FELT: No. I hope I haven't.

As part of that interview, Larry spoke with both Bob Woodward and Carl Bernstein:

BERNSTEIN: I certainly salute him [Mark Felt]…I think that he did a great thing under difficult circumstances and I wish at a time of another aberrant presidency we had more people with his values, as he expressed them during Watergate, today.

WOODWARD: There are a lot of people in the FBI who were critical of Mark Felt, and I think I'd just like to take a moment and talk to them because I've heard from a number of them. Go to the seat that Mark Felt had at the moment of Watergate. Hoover just died. Nixon was putting tremendous political pressure on the bureau. There was evidence of concealment and cover-up and criminality, all of the tentacles of Watergate.

Felt saw those, the attorney general, former attorney general, the White House counsel, as we now know the president himself, all the key people in the White House, quite frankly, were involved in a criminal conspiracy. What do you do? Do you sit there on your ass and do nothing? A lot of people would say, well, yes, those are the rules. Well, sometimes you have to break the rules and this is somebody who was willing to step over the line and I think, given his training and position in the bureau and being there so many years, probably one of the hardest things a human being ever did, but he did it.

Everybody wanted to be in close proximity to these legends who were famous for keeping a secret while they broke open the Watergate scandal. But when Carl Bernstein also encouraged me to go to Ted Turner and said I could come back when I wanted to, the debate was over. Still, it was a very sad day when I walked out of ABC carrying my little brown box filled with the things from my desk, climbed into my Chevy Chevette, and drove away.

I knew very little about Ted Turner, the person, although he had definitely made his mark in business. A highly competitive and controversial figure, Ted was a unique entrepreneur who helped change the way the world interacts with the media, particularly the news. Both hated and loved for his flamboyant style, Ted (notorious for, among other things, marrying actress Jane Fonda, which ended in a high profile divorce) was a Southern businessman with a penchant for taking risks that helped him establish a corporate empire with holdings in every area of the entertainment industry.

An accomplished sailor, Ted took part in sailing competitions from the time he was eleven years old at the Savannah Yacht Club in Georgia. He so excelled in this field, he competed in the Olympic trials in 1964 and successfully defended the America's Cup for the United States as skipper of the yacht *Courageous*. In the 1979 Fastnet race, in a deadly storm that killed several participants, he skippered his craft *Tenacious* to victory.

Sailing, however, was not the only arena in which Ted Turner competed and won. In 1970, he purchased an Atlanta UHF television station which, along with CNN, became the Turner Broadcasting System (WTBS). No one knows what he foresaw when he dreamed up Cable News Network and started implementing it. But he must have had an inkling of its extraordinary potential for success, or why else would he have risked so much time and so much of his own money?

It was an uphill battle to get the network launched and make it relevant. Today, however, CNN has revolutionized the news media, arguably making its name in January 28, 1986, when we were the only network to have live coverage of the launch of the space shuttle *Challenger*, which exploded just seventy-three seconds after liftoff. Seven astronauts, including schoolteacher Christa McAuliffe, were killed in the disaster and CNN became a household word. Since I had interviewed Christa McAuliffe on the White House lawn when she visited President Reagan, I felt the loss personally as well as collectively.

President Reagan consoled the nation from the Oval Office with heartrending words written by his speechwriter Peggy Noonan, who borrowed an image from John Gillespie Magee's poem "High Flight" to describe the disaster: "We will never forget them [the crew], nor the last time we saw them this morning, as they prepared for their journey and waved good-bye, and *slipped the surly bonds of earth, to touch the face of God.*"

Some years later, CNN's coverage of the Persian Gulf War in 1991 clinched our standing as the essential news network. Today, everyone knows about CNN, both in and out of the United States. Our kids have grown up with it, and like computers and cell phones, they can't imagine life without twenty-four-hour news channels, whether or not they watch them. Before we were known worldwide, however, all we could do was scurry around to find employees for this revolutionary undertaking. Katie joined us as an assignment editor and Bernie Shaw, a highly respected reporter who was in Iraq during the hostage crisis, came on board as anchor.

March 11, 1980, was my first day with Cable News Network, which was about three months before its launch. Without a clear job description and no one to tell me what to do, I bought myself a Rolodex and began to gather names and numbers. I really didn't know how to begin, and there was no one to ask. So my first order of business, I decided, was to cold-call the Washington agencies and various news organizations, telling them that Cable News Network existed and we were entitled to receive their press releases. I also contacted Capitol Hill and the National Art Gallery, asking them to send us their press releases, too, like they would any other news organization. No matter that we were being ridiculed and called the McNetwork and a lot of other names such as Chicken Noodle News.

Our first Washington newsroom was on Wisconsin Avenue in Georgetown, and our employees had all come from some kind of news experience. Local news people and veterans from ABC arrived at Cable News Network with their unique set of skills and did whatever they could. In the meantime, a ton of résumés were pouring in along with audition tapes from reporters. I viewed them all and used my gut to make decisions. I often found myself in the position of having to trust my intuition since I had no solid idea of what I should do and no one who came before me to show me the ropes. I simply had to mentor myself, so that was exactly what I did.

I thought about what ABC used to do as I gathered some good people together for George, and he generally listened to me as to whom we should hire, like a young man named Sandy Kenyon, who eventually became Bernie Shaw's producer. There was a fair amount of naïveté at the time among our fledgling staff as we grabbed local news anchors who were big deals and various other reporters from here or there. We simply had to move forward as if our network was a done deal, but it was mostly trial and error. We ended up with some really inefficient people, some really good people, some terrible reporters who didn't belong on the air, and some solid ones who were sophisticated and deserved to be on the air. I chalked it all up to growing pains, and we tried to stay positive as we raced against the clock to launch Ted Turner's dream. Now it had become our dream, too.

When the furniture arrived to fit out our brand-new newsroom, we laughed at the grungy spotted chairs and old desks that Ted had sent us from one of his offices in Atlanta. The sofa for the bureau chief's office had such horrible stains on the cushions, we really didn't want to imagine where they came from. No one could ever have predicted the high-tech, wealthy, global communications center that we would become one day. For now, we were happy to have torn, stained chairs and broken-down desks so we could sit and work in between scrambling around. We had three months to prepare for the first day of twenty-four-hour news and we worked our butts off, but we were pathetically underequipped. I remember bringing in Ajax and old rags, trying to get spots off the old metal desks before our staff saw them.

We had inadequate answering machines back then, there was no call-waiting, and we had one big old fax machine that was such a dinosaur, we could barely lift it. Was it ever an old clunker! You'd put a piece of paper in the paper feed, push a button, and a lever would start making a *cha-chonging* noise. It took about a minute and a half to send a simple fax, groaning and chugging all the while, on paper that curled up at the edges, and it took about the same amount of time and noise to receive one. But at least we had our very own fax machine.

In fact, that was about all we had because with next to no money, we needed to justify every little purchase we made. We were computerized, attached to a system, but we couldn't take a computer on the road or to any of our homes. There were no portable computers back then, and there were no hard drives, so you could save a few things along the way but there was no storage for data. You may be thinking, *But Ted Turner was loaded. Why did you have to scrimp and save every penny? Was he cheap?*

No, he wasn't. Just keep in mind that starting a news network is a huge undertaking. In fact, it's astronomical, since it has to include various newsrooms throughout the nation and Europe. To create CNN, Ted had to upgrade his original newsroom in Atlanta, create another in New York, one in London, one in Los Angeles, and of course, a bureau in Washington. Ted was funding this venture personally, and as we put together the Washington bureau, he was the only one who was certain it would work. Everyone chuckled under their breaths that this was a shot in the dark, that it would never work, so why was Ted bothering?

He clearly didn't care or pay any attention to the naysayers. A revolutionary thinker and inventor, he just kept moving forward, building up the center in Atlanta and setting up all the others. Ted once said to me with a big smile and a long drawl, "There are going to be a lot of ladies working here because I can pay them less." As chauvinistic as that sounds, it was true. Women earned less than men, and hiring them could and did help him save money. But with so many women on staff, his suggestion that we needed to use less toilet paper was laughable. A group of women skimping on toilet paper? I don't think so.

In the spirit of saving every penny when we first began, along with directives to skimp on toilet paper, we were not allowed to buy Styrofoam or paper cups. How would we drink coffee, the mainstay for weary reporters and workers who often missed sleep when the news cycle got heavy? I had received a gift of six cups for my college graduation so I brought them in to the bureau.

As we labored to create this revolutionary concept, I met Ted Turner for the first time with George in a restaurant that was part of the Hilton, which would eventually come to be known as the Hinckley Hilton because of the assassination attempt. At first, I judged this forty-three-year-old man. Ted was handsome, sure, but he was old. Actually, at twenty-six, I thought I was old, too. Ted had a deep drawl when he spoke, and even though I had lived in Virginia when I attended Hollins University and had heard plenty of Southern accents, Ted's drawl was so thick, it was almost cartoonish. One of the first things I heard him say was, "Remember, George, I want a lot of happy news on this network. Happy news. We're always faced with a lot of sad news, so I want just as much happy news."

I was a little put off by that, but of course, I kept my mouth shut. Whenever I saw Ted, it was a big deal since he came around so seldom, and we were all on our best behavior. Even my friend Gail Evans, a former White House Civil Rights unit staffer who had assisted the special counsel to the president, said that when she first met Ted, she was filled with angst. Ted appeared on Larry's show on May 14, 1991, and spoke about the beginnings of CNN.

KING: Let's go back to the origins of this network...The concept of CNN—how did that begin?

TURNER: I was in the radio business before I got in television, and even though we only had small-market radio stations and none of them were big enough to support all-news operations, I was aware that there were formats in the major cities like New York that had all-news radio stations, and they worked. It just made sense to me that on cable, which was going to have lots of channels, that an all-news channel would be a benefit both to the cable systems and to the viewers.

KING: When people laughed at it, which they did when it started—did that bother you? That other networks said it wouldn't last and—

TURNER: ...you've got to remember, other networks were hoping it wouldn't last...if it did work it was going to lead to the death knell of their news dominance that they'd had up until that time.

KING: Did anything turn the tide at CNN? One event or series—

TURNER: Not that I can think of. It was a good concept, it worked from the beginning, and it's just gotten stronger as time went by and people learned about it and then learned how to use it.

KING: Well, I'm interested in what moguls think because you're on a different plane than the rest of us.

TURNER: Well, I don't consider myself a mogul. And one thing I don't do is give advice publicly over the air to my competitors.

KING: All right, tell me what's coming as you envision it—2000, what can we see at home? What is it going to be like?

TURNER: Well, right now, when you really think about it, a lot of cable systems have forty, fifty, or more channels and the video stores have unlimited viewing options there. We already have a bewildering array of choices in television, but I'm told now that technologically they are increasing the number of channels that they can get onto cable in fiber optics and that the number of channels may double or triple by the year 2000.

KING: So we'll have a hundred and one choices?

TURNER: Sounds like it.

KING: So do you envision this as a less profitable business, or a more profitable business?

TURNER: Well, I think that the very smart will figure out a way to profit and prosper, but it's going to be tough for a lot of people.

Ted was a man of the future, and he made an impression on everyone, not necessarily a good or bad one. He was just

Ted, a largely invisible figure with clout and power reminiscent of Charlie on *Charlie's Angels* who was known for remaining invisible while he ran things. In a similar way, Ted hovered in the background, he wanted it that way, and when he hired a president for the network, Reese Schonfeld, he told him, "Hey, Reese, I'm giving this to you. I'm not into micromanaging. Just do it your way." I was lucky that Reese, the first president of Cable News Network, and I got along.

When Sunday, June 1, 1980, came around and it was time to go on the air, it felt like we were cranking up a three-ring circus. We were poorly coordinated (how could it have been otherwise?) and we were hideously unsophisticated. But it was official. We were going on the air.

At 5 p.m. EST, Cable News Network was launched with no mentors in sight. First on the air was an introduction by Ted Turner saying, "We won't be signing off until the world ends. We'll be on, and we will cover the end of the world, live, and that will be our last event...and when the end of the world comes, we'll play 'Nearer, My God, to Thee' before we sign off."

At the time, Jimmy Carter was in the White House and the United States was reeling from a protracted hostage drama in Iran. That was covered in our first newscast, anchored by husband and wife team David Walker and Lois Hart. *Money-line*, a financial show that survived in its original format for over twenty years, premiered in 1980. Over time, the show moved more toward general news along with economic and political commentary, and it was renamed *Lou Dobbs Moneyline* and later *Lou Dobbs Tonight*. This program remained on the air until the end of 2009, when Lou Dobbs did his last show for CNN. *Evans and Novak*, a weekly Saturday interview program, was also created in 1980, hosted by conservative syndicated columnists Rowland Evans and Robert Novak of the *Chicago Sun-Times*. And still, we were the laughingstock of the news world.

I was surprised when I found out that my friend Gail Evans, who lived in Atlanta and was tapped by Ted as an editorial assistant, was having a very different experience than I was. It seemed that the Atlanta news bureau was getting as much encouragement as we were being ridiculed. In the Atlanta headquarters of Turner Broadcasting, Cable News Network was located in the basement. Originally a Jewish tennis and swim club, Ted had converted it to offices. He installed satellite dishes adjacent to the old swimming pool, and Gail's office used to be a locker room, believe it or not. The Georgians, particularly those living in Atlanta, knew all about Ted and they were excited about his latest idea. In fact, they expected it to work, which was a shot in the arm to the people there who were putting it together.

In Washington, however, a city that was jaded and competitive as hell, we had to fight the odds every single day. We were ridiculed regularly and maybe the strangest part of all was that, as yet, Cable News Network was not being televised in Washington, even though we were broadcasting from there.

The 1980 Republican National Convention, like all conventions, separated the relevant from the irrelevant news agencies, and our brand-new network was struggling against the tide of the cooler and well-established agencies. George Watson, Bernie Shaw, and I were sitting in our makeshift anchor booth in Detroit, feeling inadequate and staring with envy at ABC, CBS, and NBC in their large, well-equipped booths, the reporters wearing their bush jackets (all the rage at the time) with stopwatches around their necks. And there we were, in our pathetic excuse for a booth as we scurried out on the floor, scouting and begging for interviews. Bernie Shaw's producer, Sandy Kenyon, and I would ask different people, "Can you come be interviewed on Cable News Network? Please?" And then we had to explain what it was.

We had to escort each delegate to our modest booth that was poorly soundproofed. I wistfully looked at the lavish set-ups of food at the other network booths and then back to us, where we had a pathetic cheese platter with cheese cubes so old, they had turned shiny. I got so hungry after a long day and evening, I remember picking up a cheese cube and tossing it in my mouth. Then, when I absentmindedly brushed my hand against Bernie Shaw's leg, it left a greasy mark on his pants. I looked at him, he looked at me, and we both started laughing out loud. Bernie was the highest person on the totem pole of CNN and I was the lowest. Imagine how he felt, having left ABC with a huge soundproof booth and catering that would make your mouth water, to join CNN that could boast only greasy cheese cubes. Thank God we both had a sense of humor, because we could have been working at that big ABC booth but we had chosen to be where we were.

In June 1982, a political debate show on late night television, *Crossfire*, was launched on CNN, hosted by liberal Tom Braden and conservative Pat Buchanan. These two men had debated on a daily radio show since 1978 and they were so popular, the show was elevated to prime time. When Pat Buchanan left in 1985 to become communications director for the Reagan White House, conservative columnist Robert Novak took his place. He was already the host of a talk show on our network as well as a regular contributor on *The McLaughlin Group*.

Today, our network has thirty-six bureaus (ten domestic, twenty-six international), more than nine hundred affiliated local stations, and several regional and foreign-language networks around the world. But from July 14 to July 17, 1980, when we attended the thirty-second Republican National Convention at the Joe Louis Arena in Detroit, Michigan, we were beginners in a field of die-hard veterans. Former California governor Ronald Reagan was being nominated for president, with former Texan congressman and CIA director George H. W. Bush as his vice president, running on the slogan "Make America Great Again."

When I look at the historical origins of CNN, I realize that if I had waited around for someone to show me what to do, I would still be waiting. I never studied political science or communications in college. I just used the old trial and error method as did my colleagues, and we got back what we put out. March 2010 marked my thirtieth year at CNN, and I can say without reservation that just about everything that has occurred in my adult life has had something to do with CNN.

❖

MENTOR YOURSELF

We are each blessed individually in this life. Some of us are lucky in love, others have great mothers, still others have terrific kids, and then there are the people who are graced with mentors. The rest of us have to mentor ourselves.

Anyone who has a real live mentor is truly fortunate, but that is not the tipping point of whether or not we can become successful. I managed to build a wonderful life and a rewarding career and I never had a mentor. I just wasn't that lucky and you may not be, either. But there is no cause for alarm. If you are not fortunate enough to have met up with a live mentor, you can relax because they are everywhere.

You have only to go on the Internet to find information on any topic you can dream about: how to lose weight; how to dress on a budget; how to stop your kids from throwing tantrums; how to have great sex; how to get your PhD at home. You name it; someone is offering it to you. If you have favorite geniuses like Warren Buffett or Bill Gates, read up on them. Pick up a copy of *Fortune* and find out who the most powerful people in the world are. How did they get there? What are their hobbies and who are their friends? That is one publication I would turn to if I were trying to mentor myself these days.

If you love to write and have a favorite author, take a leap of faith. Look him up on the Internet and send him an e-mail. For all you know, you may end up meeting this person. But if you do nothing, you will be eliminating possible opportunities. The point here is that the Internet, magazines, and instructive television programs are all over the place and they are filled with mentors. Have you checked out the Horatio Alger Awards? The Horatio Alger Association rewards successful people who started with nothing and are focused on giving something back—like actor James Earl Jones who started his life as a stutterer. One man I read about in *Fortune* was raised in an orphanage, got his first pair of pants when he was fourteen, and today is the CEO of a major corporation.

There are no more excuses about why you can't learn to do anything you choose. Pick up some biographies and see the obstacles that successful people have managed to overcome with their own wit and work ethic. Just be observant and watch for what works and what doesn't. I have read extensively about one of our Founding Fathers, Thomas Jefferson, who is a great role model for me. The point is that living or dead, the world is full of mentors and their teachings, so we all have access to whatever we are interested in. Take advantage!

And always thank anyone along the way who helped you become who you are today. Never forget these people. This is very important. It says a lot about who you are.

CHAPTER 8

Think Bigger Than Big

What I love most about Ted Turner is his penchant for thinking bigger than big, and fighting for what he wants. No one could talk him out of creating CNN, and he ignored naysayers, taunters, and anyone who tried to talk good sense into him. He had a huge vision and he followed it. I didn't know Ted when I first began working at ABC in 1979, but in a very short time, he would be a major influence in my career as someone who thought so far outside the box, we lost sight of the box.

When I first got my job at ABC, I reveled in the bustle of the newsroom. There was constant activity, the space was filled with smoke, and the ticker tape was clicking constantly. The personalities were larger than life and I remember feeling a virtual energy explosion when I met reporter Sam Donaldson for the first time. He burst into the newsroom on my first day, jumped on top of my desk in a navy blazer and a red tie, and shouted, "Where are my nuts? My pistachio nuts. I've misplaced them." He pulled a package of pistachio nuts out of his pocket, but I had a pretty good idea where the other set was when I looked upward to see his long, skinny legs straddling either side of my typewriter!

Born in Texas, Sam had grown up in a small farming community in New Mexico. As ABC chief White House news correspondent for the previous twelve years, Sam was in his heyday and he loved making a ruckus and getting a lot of attention. He would growl loudly when he entered the newsroom, and he was a biter. I'm speaking literally as he liked to teasingly bite people to get their attention. That would never be allowed these days; he would have been a human resources nightmare as someone would have slapped him with a harassment lawsuit. Back then, though, people put up with it. And while some of the staff were annoyed by his aggressive behavior, I have to admit that I was mesmerized by him, his energy, and his unconventional looks.

Sam was a thin man, all legs, with a Mr. Spock kind of face with heavy dark eyebrows that made his expression always seem intense. He would arrive at my desk and say much too loudly, "What's going on?" When he did, you better know what was going on, because he really intimidated everyone. Actually, he was an odd combination of class clown and a determined, highly knowledgeable, and powerful reporter who had his finger on the pulse of whatever or whoever was making news at the time. Sam endlessly teased me throughout my life, and he likes to tell people, "Her relationship with Ethel Kennedy and their work together ended as friends. I don't think Wendy stole any silverware or anything like that."

Thanks, Sam, for your vote of confidence.

In an effort to stay current, Sam constantly pissed off his producers by waiting for the last minute to make changes in his evening stories. It was common practice to see someone running through the newsroom, holding that precious tape that was late, all because of Sam. He was always in a hurry, running into the Washington bureau at Connecticut and L Street to set up his next piece and then rushing back to the White House lawn to do a stand-up. The looks on the faces of Sam's staff were classic while he was cavorting back and forth, never quite sure that he would make it.

I had a crush on Sam for quite a while, and we dated on and off. I was smitten back when I started as White House producer for CNN, but Sam and I had separated by then and I was none too happy about it. I made a decision to immerse myself in work and forget about him.

On my first day in my new White House job, NBC reporter Lesley Stahl came running downstairs. "Ladies," she said, "Please come over here." We all gathered around and she proceeded to let us know that she was giving Sam a luncheon to celebrate his upcoming marriage. Then she addressed me and said in a nice enough way, "You just started here, Wendy, so you don't really know Sam. You don't have to come. I'm just inviting the people here who have worked with him and who really know him."

Little did she know how well I *knew* him before I ever joined CNN. While the other women went to lunch to celebrate Sam's upcoming nuptials, I buried myself in my relentless work. But I bumped into him constantly, as fate would have it, since we worked in the same place. And we were eventually able to forge a friendship that continues to this day. And he has been married ever since then to his lovely wife, Jan, to whom he is incredibly devoted.

Cut to March 30, 1981, before I worked at the White House, the morning when President Reagan and three other people in his entourage were shot. Sam told me he had been a little grumpy that morning since he had to show up early at the Hilton Hotel in Washington to cover a speech by Reagan. To make matters worse, Frank Reynolds of ABC had called Sam, also at ABC, and said, "This really is a nothing speech Reagan is giving. He's just talking to the building trade union. Send your number two guy and let's have lunch."

Sam was tempted but he decided he better be there. ABC counted on him to do stand-ups wherever the president went, so despite his reluctance, Sam went off to the hotel to do his job. A consummate professional, he always showed up, even if he was grumbling about it. Meanwhile, I was at home in Georgetown having a day off.

But just as I began to settle in, I discovered that the electricity in my apartment was out. I walked across the street to a phone booth at the fire station to call the power company when I noticed a number of firemen standing around, staring at a TV monitor, with long looks on their faces. There was a familiar face on the screen, with his head tipped downward like he was dead. There had been an attempt to assassinate the president and apparently Jim Brady, his press secretary, had gotten caught in the crossfire. I had met Jim one week earlier at a Georgetown party that he was hosting and I'd found him to be pleasant and vivacious. Was that really the same man whose head was drooping after being seriously wounded during an assassination attempt on the president?

My electrical problem got relegated to the bottom of my priority list as I drove straight to CNN to find everyone in a panic. The events had unfolded like this:

Reagan had been in office for sixty-nine days when he spoke at the Washington Hilton. Ironically, his topic that day concerned government's role in protecting society. It was 2:25 p.m., the talk was over, and he stood at the side entrance of the hotel at T Street NW, ready to get into his limo, when six shots rang out.

The first bullet hit White House press secretary Jim Brady in the head. The second one hit DC police officer Thomas Delahanty in the back. The third bullet overshot the president and hit the window of a building across the street, while the fourth hit Secret Service agent Timothy McCarthy in the abdomen. The fifth hit the bulletproof glass on the open side door of the limousine. Finally, the sixth bullet ricocheted off the side of the limousine and hit the president in his left armpit, grazing a rib and lodging in his lung, stopping about an inch from his heart.

Sam was there when it happened. He'd told his cameraman to stay behind for some cutaway shots while Sam stood by the door, waiting for the president to exit. When the shooting occurred, since the ABC news bureau was only five blocks from the Hilton, Sam gave the first report among the big three networks:

Here at the Washington Hilton, shots rang out as President Reagan was leaving the hotel and about to enter his limousine. At least one person was hit and fell to the sidewalk with blood coming from his body. It was not the president. I don't know whether the president was hit. I do not believe he was. His car left rapidly under police escort. The shots were fired by someone in the crowd of people watching the president depart. Five or six shots rang out. It sounded like a pistol shot. At least one person has been hit and fell to the sidewalk. I do not believe the president was hit, but I'm not certain. His car drove off rapidly.

No one knew for sure that Reagan had been hit in the armpit, not even the president himself, until he was taken to George Washington University Hospital. Almost as quickly as he was spirited away, the police nabbed the shooter, John Hinckley, Jr., placing him in custody and confiscating his Röhm RG-14 .22 caliber blue steel revolver. We would soon find out that his motivation was to get the attention of young actress Jodie Foster. It had nothing to do with the president at all, which would explain why Hinckley asked his arresting officers whether that night's scheduled Academy Awards ceremony would be postponed due to the shooting. He was a stalker of the worst kind.

In the early days of Cable News Network we didn't have enough people to assign a reporter to be with the president every day in case something happened. No one could predict what would occur on any given day, but since we had missed taping this sudden and astronomical event, how would we get hold of the coverage so we could contribute something? Unsure what to do, I thought about what ABC would have done.

Today there are endless places to obtain information on a story like this. Back then, however, since there were only three networks, I got three TV sets and set them up side by side. Then I sat there, watching each set on a different network, and writing down what the other networks were reporting. I gave my notes to Scott Willis, executive producer and a colleague of mine back at ABC. Bernard Shaw, another ABC veteran, was in the anchor chair.

Here is Shaw's original Cable News Network report on the shooting:

Wielding a .22 caliber "Saturday-night special," John Warnock Hinckley shoots President Reagan in the chest outside the Washington Hilton Hotel. The twenty-five-year-old drifter with a history of psychological problems also shoots the president's press secretary, James Brady, in the incident. The president is rushed to George Washington University

Hospital and quickly recovers, although the gunman's bullet inflicts severe damage on Brady.

I spent the next several days and nights in the newsroom, watching the other networks and preparing our coverage. The actual assassination attempt had been captured on video by ABC, while our CNN camera crew had been broadcasting Reagan's speech live moments earlier. Since we had only one crew, they were still inside the hotel so we missed taping the shooting. We were still so underequipped, we needed help, but we sure weren't about to get any from the other networks.

The three major networks had what they called a pool: a small group of reporters, a still photographer, a network correspondent, and a small crew. The pool was arranged by the White House to shoot cutaways close to the president and to ride in the motorcade. There is no way the entire press corps could do all of that, so one network would shoot the events of the day and share it with the other two. That meant that every three days, one of the networks shot tape. All of the big three could use the pool tape, but no one outside of the three networks was given access. That was a problem for us, because Cable News Network was still on the outside.

We were all working overtime to cover this huge story, so I hadn't seen Sam for a couple of days when I met him at a restaurant near the hospital where President Reagan was recovering. I joined him for lunch and Sam said smugly, "So, Wendells (a nickname he gave me), how's it going over at Cable News Network? What are you guys doing over there? Here we have the biggest story in the whole world and you don't even have tape of the assassination attempt."

"Oh, yes, we do," I said, ready to meet his attitude with my own.

"No, you don't. You don't have access to the tape," he said adamantly.

"I just told you we do have access," I repeated.

"What do you mean?" he exploded in a booming voice. He was enraged as he said, "That was pool tape. Pool tape is only shared with the three networks. You know that, Wendy. We pool our resources together and that tape belongs to us."

I nodded my head calmly, uncomfortable at his outburst. And yet, it felt satisfying to say, "Well, we got it."

Sam would not let it go. He made a huge fuss, calling us every name under the sun. "This is the lowest thing I've ever seen in the history of the news business," he said. "How can CNN survive and hold its head up when it has shamed itself beyond recognition?"

True, Sam had a penchant for drama, but maybe he felt ownership rights since he had been the first person to report the shooting. He continued to question me, saying, "Now wait just a minute here. I want to know right now how you got that tape, because you shouldn't have it."

"The pool gave it to us," I said.

"No, that didn't happen," he said. "Nobody in the pool would ever give it to you."

He continued to glare at me as I asked our waiter to bring a phone to the table so I could call Scott Willis at my network. "Scott," I said, "I'm here with Sam and he wants to know how we got the pool tape."

Willis said something about the tape being given to us. When I repeated it to Sam, he stood up, outraged. "That did not happen," he repeated.

"Hey," I said, "I'm not sure how we got the tape, but Sam, you're going to get me fired if you keep going on like this."

"It isn't your fault, Wendy, but you should never have had

access to that tape. It's a White House tape" (meaning that only he and the other two networks had the right to use it). In the next moment Sam got up and left the restaurant abruptly, taking gigantic strides out the door and heading straight over to the ABC bureau in Washington. He got on the phone to ABC in New York and demanded to speak to Roone Arledge, then chairman.

"Roone," Sam said, "you might want to find out whose tape CNN used during the shooting coverage."

Roone sent a telegram to Ted Turner, asking him if he had used the White House pool tape. But if he thought he might be successful in intimidating Ted Turner, he was dead wrong. The response was typical Ted Turner as he wrote back, "Hell, yeah, we used that tape. In fact, we're suing the White House right now to be part of the pool. We asked and you said no, but we have every right to the tape and to be part of the pool."

We rolled that infamous tape in Atlanta and used it over and over again. I am proud to say that as much as Sam was fuming, I was one of the people in a small group who prompted Ted Turner to sue the White House for CNN to become bona fide members of the White House press corps and, therefore, a member of the pool. We won the suit, much to the despair of the other networks. Ted had proven that he was not going away, so they might as well make room for us. From the day we won the lawsuit and joined the pool, our access and ability to report the news in a timely fashion escalated, thanks to Ted who knew what he was about and was not afraid to claim his place.

Now there would be four networks instead of three in the pool, and the rotation would give each network access every fourth day instead of every third. No wonder Sam and the others were upset. They didn't need any more competition, but we were here to stay.

It took the president thirteen days in the hospital to recover from the lung puncture as his medical team administered intravenous fluids, oxygen, tetanus toxoid, and chest tubes.

He later described that night on our show on January 10, 1991:

REAGAN: I didn't know I was shot. I heard a noise when we came out of the hotel and headed for the limousine, and I heard some noise, and I thought it was firecrackers. And the next thing I knew, one of the Secret Service agents behind me just seized me here by the waist and plunged me headfirst into the limo.

I landed on the seat, and the seat divider was down, and then he dived in on top of me, which is part of their procedure to make sure that I'm covered. As it turned out later, the shot that got me careened off the side of the limousine and hit me while I was diving into the car. And it hit me back here, under the arm, and then hit a rib, and that's what caused extreme pain, and then it tumbled and turned—instead of edgewise, it went tumbling down to within an inch of my heart.

But when I got in the car, I hadn't felt anything. He landed on top of me, and then the pain, which now I know came from the bullet hitting that rib, that terrific pain, and I said: "Jerry, get off, I think you have broken a rib of mine." And he got off very quickly. And just then, I coughed. And I had a handful of bright, red, frothy blood. So I said: "Evidently, the broken rib has pierced the lung." He simply turned and said, "George Washington Hospital," and we were on our way.

When First Lady Nancy Reagan arrived in the emergency room after being informed that her husband had been shot, Reagan famously remarked to her, "Honey, I forgot to duck." He borrowed that line from boxer Jack Dempsey, who said that to his wife when his opponent Gene Tunney knocked him out.

Jim Brady lived but was not as lucky as Reagan since he was permanently disabled. Hinckley was found "not guilty by reason of insanity" and lives in a psychiatric facility, St. Elizabeths, to this day, while they are allowing him extended visits with his mother.

As for Sam, he wrote a book some years later, in 1987, called *Hold On, Mr. President*, and I was surprised to see that he was still angry about the pool tape. The following is an excerpt:

> I got to the Hilton in time to hear Reagan's speech. We had two camera crews there, one set up on a tripod to photograph the President head-on, a second to roam through the ballroom getting reaction shots to use in editing the report. The second cameraman was Hank Brown, his partner carrying the videotape machine, Harry Weldon. I told Brown that when Reagan finished, I wanted him to stay on until the President left the room. I told him I would go upstairs and save a spot for him on the rope line outside to get Reagan's departure from the hotel. "Get up there as fast as you can," I said, "but I want the pictures of the President leaving the room, and if you don't make it outside in time, I'll work around that." Brown got outside and into place on the rope line about thirty seconds before Reagan appeared.
>
> I have often thought what might have happened to my career if he hadn't made it. Later, when the furious postmortems would have been conducted as to why ABC News had none of its own pictures of the assassination attempt, Brown would have to say it was because I had told him to linger downstairs. Of course, Cable News Network had none of its own pictures that day (it hadn't scheduled a camera crew

outside), but it didn't stop CNN; it just "lifted" ours off the air and used them as its own. No one at ABC knew it until a week later when a CNN producer friend of mine, Wendy Walker, told me how nice she thought it was for ABC to give permission for them to use our tape. Permission, hell. Walker wasn't aware of it but it was pure theft.

Like it or not, we had become a permanent member of the pool and our status was rising steadily. All thanks to Ted, who thought bigger than anyone else dared.

❖

THINK BIGGER THAN BIG

When I come up with an idea and I need courage and inspiration, I think of Ted Turner as the archetype for thinking big. Imagine the mind of someone who makes a determination that what the world needs most is a network that will provide the news twenty-four hours a day, seven days a week. Ted thought so big, so outside the box, that today, none of us could begin to imagine a world without being able to turn on the news at any time of night or day. And he didn't care what anyone else thought. In fact, Ted was ridiculed, marginalized, and made fun of constantly while he allowed his mind to create a network so large and all-encompassing, it would become a household word.

This kind of man doesn't care what anybody else thinks and is guided by his ability to think bigger than anyone else. And so, it made perfect sense that once Ted had created his idea of CNN and actually implemented it, he was fully prepared to sue the White House to be allowed in as part of the pool. While everyone was ridiculing him, he was busy creating a massive empire, based solely on what he had envisioned, which existed nowhere else in the world.

Did you know that one of our most common household items, the Post-it, was invented twice? The first man who thought of it, Spencer Silver, felt it was not useful because it didn't have enough glue, and he let it go. Then, some years later, a forward-thinking man named Art Fry found a way to utilize Silver's invention to locate certain passages in his church hymnal. In the end, these two mad scientists got together and became wealthy for creating something no one else believed in.

There are people all throughout history who took risks and thought bigger than big.

- Think about Ronald Reagan, an actor who became president.
- Computer genius and billionaire Bill Gates said, "The value of having everybody get the complete picture and trusting each person with it far outweighs the risk involved."
- President Barack Obama said, "It's only when you hitch your wagon to something larger than yourself that you will realize your true potential. And if we're willing to share the risks and the rewards this new century offers, it will be a victory for each of you, and for every American."
- Author T. S. Eliot said, "Only those who will risk going too far can possibly find out how far one can go."

The late Bob Novak circa very early 80s having bad makeup put on by my intern. We could not afford makeup artists so we trained interns! *Courtesy: Elissa Blake Free*

Party to open the second Washington DC News Bureau on Massachusetts Avenue. Funny picture because Larry and I did not know each other. He was with his guest Geraldo and I was with the White House correspondent, Charles Bierbauer. *Courtesy: CNN*

The reason I am a producer! This is July 4, 1983, where I was reporting live on Wayne Newton singing on the mall. Nice shoes! *Personal photo*

The late John Holliman and I looking at the plans for the very first Washington DC Bureau. This was of course before the network was on the air! We were sitting on furniture that was sent from Ted Turner's various offices! *Personal photo*

I am delivering a letter from White House cameraman Reggie Selma's many admirers somewhere in the United States on a presidential trip via the Pan American Press Charter. Some girl was looking for him and all she found was me! *Personal photo*

On the podium at the Dukakis Democratic Convention. I am a bit top-heavy with that old headset! *Personal photo*

Interviewing President Reagan during his radio address in Santa Barbara. I was so green that didn't even know I was supposed to be nervous! *Courtesy: Reagan Presidential Library*

This is one of my favorite pictures! Mrs. Reagan is holding a photograph of me all dressed up in my pink suit with President Reagan and my baby. And fast forward to my baby Amaya, now a young girl, in the same pink suit meeting Mrs. Reagan! I sent this to my sales person at Chanel to show off three Chanel suits. *Courtesy: CNN*

Vice President Nixon held me in 1956 when he was running for a second term on a whistle stop tour in Johnstown, Pennsylvania. I thought the coat made me look fat. It starts young! Even at three! *Personal photo*

Ethel Kennedy with Senator Ted is escorting then President Carter's daughter Amy around Hickory Hill for her charity pet show. My claim to fame is as her assistant, I made Ethel's T-shirt! *Personal photo*

My only state dinner invitation and I was actually sitting at President Bush's table! I thought they had me mixed up with one of his relatives since my name is Walker. I kept thinking someone was going to move me to another table. But they didn't! *Courtesy: Bush Presidential Library*

Producing an Oval Office live televised address to the nation. *Courtesy: Bush Presidential Library*

Dee Dee Myers and I putting makeup on the President minutes before an address to the nation. I love Mack McLarty's face...so worried about a producer applying presidential coverup! *Courtesy: Clinton Presidential Library*

This is me outside my home in Chappaqua, New York, which just happens to be the Clinton's home now! What are the odds? *Personal photo*

This was moments before the famed NAFTA debate, having a laugh with our mutual friend, the late Bob Squier. I really miss him. He was the one who taught me, "If you can't say something nice about someone, say something funny." Great advice! *Courtesy: CNN*

First Lady Hillary Clinton in my Washington DC office admiring a wall of guests that have appeared on *Larry King Live*. Everyone always loves looking at the pictures! *Courtesy: CNN*

My daughter and crew after President Bush's interview at the Beverly Wilshire in Los Angeles. The beautiful woman on my right is Shawn, Larry's wife. Amaya loved skipping school for this! *Courtesy: CNN*

Meeting President Obama at the White House before his interview with Larry. *Courtesy: CNN*

One of my favorite pictures in the world, Marlon Brando kissing me like he kissed Larry! I will never forget that moment! *Courtesy: CNN*

My first big get for Larry as his executive producer, landing an interview with Yasser Arafat thanks to my great friends, Sabih and Hani Masri. *Courtesy: CNN*

It was a thrill meeting the Dalai Lama. What else can I say? *Courtesy: CNN*

We flew all night to interview Nelson Mandela in New York. It was a chance of a lifetime to meet him. *Courtesy: CNN*

This was when my staff surprised me with an interview with Jim Carrey. The way to my heart is truly through comedians! *Courtesy: CNN*

My all-time favorite guest was President Gorbachev, because of the history we had that he never knew! *Courtesy: CNN*

Oprah told me she liked my outfit! I was in heaven. It doesn't get better than having the two greats together on the set. *Courtesy: CNN*

Paul, Ringo, and Yoko getting together to talk about Cirque du Soleil's production; *The Beatles, Love. Courtesy: CNN*

Preparing for the live Beatles show with Larry's staff in Las Vegas. *Courtesy: CNN*

Larry and our friends raised ten million dollars doing a telethon for Haiti. The Larry King staff put their hearts and souls into this event and it paid off. *Courtesy: CNN*

We did a great show with the cast and creative crew of *Avatar,* showing our viewers exactly how they did it! *Courtesy: CNN*

My son skipped school for this one, to meet his hero James Cam-
eron! *Courtesy: CNN*

It took us sixteen years to land an interview with Mick Jagger. This
was at the Carlyle Hotel in New York. Sometimes even after doing
this job forever, you meet someone that you have grown up with
and you think...*wow...I'm talking to Mick Jagger.* This was one of
those moments. Larry loved this interview. *Courtesy: CNN*

A nice moment in Larry's office on his seventieth birthday. I love the guy.
Courtesy: CNN

This was a publicity photo of us, one of my favorites. I got to wear suspenders!
Courtesy: CNN

Larry and his beautiful wife Shawn on the set. I love this picture of them.
Courtesy: CNN

Red carpet at the White House Correspondent's Dinner in Washington DC, with our guests, cartoon genius Seth MacFarlane and *Survivor* host, Jeff Probst. *Courtesy: Photo by Linda Davidson/The* Washington Post *via Getty Images*

My parents, Russell and Miriam Walker on their honeymoon. They look like a Hollywood couple. *Personal photo*

Sam Donaldson and I in Santa Barbara. What I would give for those legs back! I mean, mine! *Personal Photo*

Katie and I in New York. *Personal photo*

My fiftieth birthday party, surprised by Paul. I can never lie about my age since my birthday became my fifteen minutes of fame! *Courtesy: Kandice Brown*

My children, Amaya and Walker, the absolute joys of my life. *Courtesy: Boyd Harris*

Two of my favorite guys... Larry and my son, Walker. *Courtesy: Michael Spengler*

June 30, 2010, right after he got off the air and told the world that he was hanging up his nightly suspenders. A very emotional day for all of us. *Courtesy: CNN*

CHAPTER 9

Should You Really Care Who Gets the Credit?

When it came to pulling off TV coverage of summits that involved hundreds of crew, producers, and reporters, no one person could ever take credit for anything that happened. It was a group effort with so many twists, and so many fires that needed be put out, that it took all of us to untangle the confusions and extinguish the proverbial flames. And when a summit was over, I couldn't believe we had gotten through it!

At the 1987 NATO summit in Berlin with the Soviets, for example, I recall the anticipation of waiting for Reagan's speech at the Berlin Wall. CNN White House correspondent Charles Bierbauer was in a prime stand-up position on June 12, where he could see everything as it occurred. Charles, incidentally, was a perfect choice because he had lived in Germany for five years, working for CNN. An avid student of the Cold War, he was on the platform in front of the Berlin Wall as the anticipation for Reagan's speech escalated.

Frank Sesno, also a CNN White House correspondent, was doing the pool and he and I were in the makeshift control room. We had gotten an advance copy of Reagan's speech and there was a line that made all of us cringe. "I don't know about him asking Gorbachev to tear down the Berlin Wall," Frank said. "It's so in your face that it could be interpreted as a cynical cheap shot. I don't know how people are going to take this."

We weren't the only ones who felt that way. We didn't know at the time that Reagan had just finished a raging debate with the State Department and his aides who also advised him to take out the provocative line. In fact, they came as close to insisting as they could manage, but Reagan would not budge.

That turned out to be a golden decision on his part since his appeal to the Soviet leader, "Mr. Gorbachev, tear down this wall," would eventually become the definitive signature line of his eight-year presidency. A signature line stays with a president for better or worse, and some other presidents have not been so lucky. Think about George H. W. Bush, whose signature line was, "Read my lips. No new taxes." Or Bill Clinton, whose unfortunate signature line was, "I did not have sex with that woman."

We sat there in the control room on the fourth floor of a building that overlooked the Brandenburg Gate. It was really creepy to peer over the wall from where we sat and gaze down at what looked like a prison camp. During the pre-advance trip, Gary Foster, head of Reagan's press advance office, and I had been standing at the gate, discussing the staging for the talk to come, when I realized that Reagan would not be facing the wall. That meant his back would face East Berlin. Amid his Secret Service detail who were milling around and working out security arrangements, I said a little too loudly to Gary, "Aren't they afraid he could get shot from East Berlin?"

Gary literally put his hand over my mouth. He was mortified that someone from security would make us leave.

Now, with his back to the gate, President Reagan delivered his highly dramatic appeal:

We welcome change and openness; for we believe that free-dom and security go together, that the advance of human liberty can only strengthen the cause of world peace. There is one sign the Soviets can make that would be unmistakable, that would advance dramatically the cause of freedom and peace. General Secretary Gorbachev, if you seek peace, if you seek prosperity for the Soviet Union and Eastern Europe, if you seek liberalization, come here to this gate. Mr. Gorbachev, open this gate. *Mr. Gorbachev, tear down this wall!*

"I looked at the sound man who was standing next to me," says Charles Bierbauer, "as we were hearing these words come out of the president's mouth. 'Nice rhetoric,' I said with sar-casm, 'but that's never going to happen.'"

Charles saw the rhetoric as a substitute for reality, the very thing that had torn apart the German nation. After all, he had lived there for years and in his opinion, "It felt like Reagan's plea to the Soviet leader was more like Kennedy saying, *'Ich bin ein Berliner.'* That was rhetoric, too, and the irony was that Ken-nedy didn't speak it correctly. The word 'Berliner' was also the name of a dessert. When Kennedy left in the 'ein,' that made the actual translation something you would say in Germany when you ordered a jelly donut."

Later in his speech, President Reagan said:

As I looked out a moment ago from the Reichstag, that embodiment of German unity, I noticed words crudely spray-painted upon the wall, perhaps by a young Berliner,

"This wall will fall. Beliefs become reality." Yes, across Europe, this wall will fall. For it cannot withstand faith; it cannot withstand truth. The wall cannot withstand freedom.

He also called an end to the arms race, which was met with polite applause. In fact, there was no wild reaction one way or the other until three years later, in September 1990, when former President Reagan returned to Berlin where he personally took a few symbolic hammer swings at a remnant of the wall.

I happened to be in Malta at the time, doing a pre-advance for an upcoming summit and I wanted to see this historic moment for myself. After all, I had been there when he gave the speech three years prior. I remember running around Malta, a somewhat isolated island, searching for a way to watch CNN. I finally found one hotel with communications that were advanced enough to pick up our network. As I watched the Berlin Wall fall, I remembered an inspiring motto that sat on President Reagan's desk in the Oval Office of the White House:

THERE IS NO LIMIT TO WHAT A MAN CAN DO
OR WHERE HE CAN GO
IF HE DOESN'T MIND WHO GETS THE CREDIT.

When I first saw it, I copied it down on a piece of paper that sat on *my* desk for a long time. It was also on my close friend Ali's desk. Today, they sell this adage on plaques at the Reagan Library, and as tough as it is, I do my best to live up to it every single day.

The lesson here is that the tearing down of the wall will always be seen as a defining moment in Cold War history. For me, watching Reagan beseech Gorbachev to end the boundaries between East and West Berlin was a moment I will never forget. But to this day, there is disagreement over how much influence, if any, Reagan's bold speech actually had. No one can say for sure who deserves the credit, but most people are relieved that the wall is down, whoever caused it to happen.

As a producer, I am like a ghost person who stands in the background. All my decisions are made strategically for the good of the network and the current situation. In the end, no one can take credit for anything because it takes a large group of people, including mostly unsung heroes, to create a summit and to pull it off. Since I am not in a position where people credit me for whatever success we are having, I have learned not to measure my self-esteem by somebody noticing my work. As a producer, that isn't going to happen. It's an old story: When you make a mistake, you get called onto the mat and everyone tells you about it. At CNN, we try to remember to credit the people who deserve it, but sometimes we get so caught up in what we're doing, we forget. That doesn't mean that people are not appreciated, though. When times are chaotic and you do something wrong, you'll be called out. But when you do something right and you hear nothing from anyone, that just might be the highest compliment of all.

A great irony is that after all the years I produced TV coverage for summits between the Soviet Union and the United States, I had never met or even seen Mikhail Gorbachev in person. I was always in the control room when he was onstage, and by the time it was over, he was gone. This was true in Malta, Geneva, and Reykjavik, as well as our other venues, because as much as I wanted to meet the Soviet president and shake his hand, I was too busy doing my job.

It is doubly ironic, then, that I finally met Mikhail Gorbachev years after I left my job as White House producer. Skip forward to when I was working with Larry. I thought that Mikhail Gorbachev would be our dream guest, so I sent him a book about Russian and American art. The card said, "I covered all of your summits and now, I'm producing *Larry King Live*."

Maybe he got it and maybe he didn't. But we eventually landed an interview with him on our show when he wrote a book he wanted to promote. I suggested to Larry that we take him to dinner before the show to break the ice. We agreed to meet at a restaurant called Duke Zeibert's, a DC political hangout on Connecticut Avenue, and I was in awe as I stood at the escalator, waiting for Mikhail Gorbachev to arrive. When I spotted his balding head and the telltale scar on his forehead at the bottom of the escalator, I was stunned at my good fortune.

He and his interpreter began to ride up, and when they arrived at the top of the escalator, I put out my hand. "How do you do, Mr. Gorbachev?" I said. "My name is Wendy Walker and I produced eleven US-Soviet summits for CNN from 1983 to 1993. And this is the first time I'm meeting you in person."

His eyes got wider and his smile became warmer. He looked like he felt that, just maybe, he was in good hands as I escorted him to the table where Larry was already seated. As we ordered and engaged in some conversation, I couldn't help but marvel at the way things had worked out. During a decade of summits, I had been all over the world with the Soviet president, in Geneva, Malta, Helsinki, Berlin, Reykjavik, and Moscow, and many more places. Now, after leaving the White House job and signing on with Larry King, here I was, meeting and having dinner with Mikhail Gorbachev for the very first time.

When anyone asks me to name the biggest guest we ever had on the *Larry King Live* show, I always answer, "Mikhail

Gorbachev." It meant so much to me personally because his appearance on our show represented so much history and so much effort to get to that moment.

On a CNN live special at the funeral site of President Reagan, in June 2004, Larry hosted a final farewell to President Reagan. Former president Mikhail Gorbachev spoke with Larry, through a translator, about his former friend and opponent:

GORBACHEV: I've been thinking again about many things that happened in the past. It was the will of destiny that at the most difficult time that the world was going through, when it seemed that only a miracle could stop the process of confrontation and of tension, we were able together to stop it, and this was done, thanks to the fact that the US leadership, particularly the president of the United States, President Reagan, and the Soviet leadership understood where the world was moving and how far the arms race had gone.

I remembered, when I was there, the history between us. It is really unique. It all began when, after the first meeting in Geneva, we even exchanged some bitter remarks. But in Geneva, two days were enough for us to begin to understand each other, and we adopted a statement saying that nuclear war cannot be won and must never be fought. It was a difficult dialogue. I do not want to be simplistic... But then trust emerged and it became easier to solve problems. And he turned out to be the person [with] whom we were able to get along and then to become friends.

He was a person who had a big heart, a person who had his values, and a person for whom the wish to do something...to make a difference, to support his friends, but in particular to support the mood of the entire nation, this was very, very typical of him. I saw that, and I valued those qualities of President Reagan. He was a wonderful man. He was an extraordinary person.

How amazing that after having such a close relationship with Reagan, Gorbachev would be talking to Larry during the funeral coverage. I will never forget Gorbachev looking at Reagan's coffin covered with an American flag at the rotunda in Washington. Two enemies who had turned into profound friends. What a lesson! What a moment!

❖

SHOULD YOU REALLY CARE WHO GETS THE CREDIT?

Even when no one gives you personal credit for what you did to make something a success, they know who you are. It always comes out eventually, even if someone else claims credit for what you did. More times than I can count, I worked my butt off on something and then someone took my ideas, put them in a memo, and claimed them. But the right people knew where the ideas came from, and these days, so do I.

That is why I loved this lesson so much, and why I kept Reagan's words on my desk in clear view. *I bet Reagan is right*, I thought to myself when I first saw it. People always find out who did the work. You just have to have a good attitude and not worry about getting credit, because even if it looks different than you expected, the end product is where you can derive your satisfaction.

CHAPTER 10

Be Grateful Every Day of Your Life

It's hard to believe that the terrorist attacks on the World Trade Center and the Pentagon on September 11, 2001, occurred nearly a decade ago. It still feels raw: the shock, the sorrow, and the disbelief as we watched thousands of innocent people lose their lives in an instant. As I consider this tragedy that forever changed the way we view life in the United States and the rest of the world, I see that those of us who lost loved ones can only feel grateful that we are here today, to speak up for those who were silenced forever.

Granted, this was the worst collective disaster that Americans ever experienced firsthand on our native soil. But the heart of the story is in the personal details, the smaller anecdotes of courage, compassion, and survival under fire that make this historical event come alive in its agonies and its triumphs. It seems that it takes a tragedy to bring out certain enviable human qualities. I'm talking about the kind of courage that makes us wonder, just before we drift off to sleep at night, what we would have done, faced with a similar situation.

Would we have measured up? Would we have been as selfless as some of the unsung heroes who rose to the occasion and sacrificed themselves to help others? How can we express our gratitude for still being here and being able to feel our sadness, give our opinions, and grieve our losses?

These kinds of pivotal, earth-shattering events imprint on people's minds so permanently, most of us remember exactly where we were, what we said, and what we were doing at the time. The attacks on September 11 were just such events that profoundly affected people all over the world. Whether or not we lost family and friends, no one was spared the emotional impact. Each of us turned on our television sets to view the now all too familiar images of ash-laden people, the lucky ones, who looked like ghosts, faces struck dumb in shock, stumbling away from a white cloud of destruction that seemed to be chasing them down the street. For a brief moment, most everyone in the world was looking at the same live pictures and holding our breaths to see what was coming next.

You had to be in a bubble not to know what was happening on September 11. This tragedy of epic proportions stunned the entire world, including those of us who were reporting the news. I was on the West Coast, in bed, asleep, when I got a call from Suzy. "Turn on the television right now," was all she said.

I ran into my office, dropped into my chair, and stared at the images of one of the tallest buildings in the world, One World Trade Center, on fire, spewing black smoke. At CNN Atlanta, anchor Carol Lin broke into a commercial at 8:49 a.m., EST, and said:

This just in. You are looking at obviously a very disturbing live shot there. That is the World Trade Center, and we have unconfirmed reports this morning that a plane has crashed into one of the towers of the World Trade Center. CNN Center right now is just beginning to work on this story, obviously calling our sources and trying to figure out exactly what happened, but clearly something relatively devastating is happening this morning there on the south end of the island of Manhattan. That is, once again, a picture of one of the towers of the World Trade Center.

My stomach churning, numb with disbelief, I watched the second plane slam into the next World Trade Center building. *This is not an accident*, I told myself as thoughts of terrorism escalated. When the giant structures crumbled to dust right in front of our eyes a short time later, my first thought was, *How many other planes are in the sky right now? Is it over or has it only just started?*

Every network and cable station, national and international, had their cameras set on what we would come to call Ground Zero, as we watched the planes slam into the building over and over again in a continuous tape loop, as if it were happening every three to five minutes. I scanned the monitors, trying to spot anything else in the sky, when I saw my friend, Jim Miklaszewski, Pentagon correspondent for NBC, come on the air. He started to give his report when a deafening crash sounded. Mik automatically ducked down, as if to protect himself from an invisible blow.

Now, on this monumental morning, Mik told his viewing audience that he needed to get off the air to see what had happened. We soon found out that he had been reacting to the deafening crash of the third plane slamming into the side of the Pentagon while he was on the air, a short distance away. Anchors Daryn Kagan and Leon Harris at CNN were live on the air just after 9 a.m., EST, as correspondent David Ensor reported that US officials had determined that "this is a terrorist attack." Aaron Brown, who had just come to CNN from ABC, anchored the day and night following the attacks. And I'm sure that anchor Paula Zahn will never forget this day, not only for the tragedy itself, but it just so happened that she was new to CNN, also, and September 11 was the day that she was slated to begin.

A little after 10 a.m., when the fourth plane crashed in Pennsylvania, my phone was ringing off the hook and thousands of e-mails were clogging my in-box. A colleague who managed to get through to me mentioned that Barbara Olson, a well-known conservative commentator and a friend of mine, might have been on the plane that slammed into the Pentagon. Both she and her husband, Ted Olson, then United States Solicitor General, had appeared on our show various times and I liked them both a lot.

Without thinking, I called Katie Couric, who was of course the host of the *Today* show at NBC, during her commercial break. After we said hello, we sat silently on the phone together, listening to each other breathe, taking a brief moment of comfort in the profound silence of a long friendship. Just before we hung up, I said, "Katie, I think Barbara Olson was on the plane that hit the Pentagon."

In a few minutes, Barbara's presence on the plane was confirmed as was her death, and Katie went on the air to report it. A few days later, the crawl beneath the television picture would run down the names of the dead, which seemed to go on and on. At that point, we had no idea how many people we had lost, but we knew the numbers were in the thousands.

The devastation hit me both personally and collectively. I was shattered by the tragedy, by the idea of terrorism on our soil, and the loss of someone I knew, but at the same time, I was Larry's executive producer and I had a responsibility to CNN to keep it together. As much as I felt the pull downward into the blackness of this tragic day, I needed to gather my wits about me and keep moving. My first responsibility was to book guests for the show that night who would help the public cope with their fear and learn more about what was actually happening. I was determined that our reporting would be a service to the nation, so I had to make sure we did everything right.

By the time *Larry King Live* aired on September 11, 2001, we had booked fifteen guests, including: New York Governor George Pataki; former Secretary of State James Baker; Senator John Warner from Virginia; Senator John Kerry from Massachusetts; Senator Dianne Feinstein from California; former Defense Secretary William Cohen; and four civilian eyewitnesses. It was established at airtime that approximately two hundred firemen and seventy-eight policemen were missing. An eyewitness, Bill Reitman, who worked in One World Trade Center on the eighty-first floor, said that when he was heading down the long flights of stairs, he saw firemen collapsing from smoke inhalation and the heavy loads they were carrying, including oxygen tanks and hoses. Rudy Giuliani, Mayor of New York, joined us toward the end of the show to report that both Chief Peter Ganci of the fire department and Ray Downey, the deputy commissioner, were missing. Later they were pronounced dead.

In the first few days, we showed footage of the immediate area where the tragedy had occurred, with people standing in the streets, forlorn and grief-stricken, clutching photographs of missing loved ones, holding them toward the cameras, pleading for news or sightings. "Have you seen my son?" "How about my wife? I forgot to kiss her good-bye this morning." Additional photos were tacked up on exterior walls as people entreated the camera crews to shine a light on the images.

Our journalists covered the grisly moment-to-moment unravelings of the terrorist attacks and we all were stretched beyond our limits whether we were in front of the camera or behind it. I recall a vague foglike pall surrounding me that was keeping my emotions separated from the horrific stories that were pouring in over the communication channels. I had dropped into my producer's chair early that morning with a phone glued to my ear and barely moved until after the show aired that night, thirteen grueling hours later. It felt like a year had passed, and at the same time an instant, when it was finally 7 p.m. and the show was finished. I pushed away from my desk, muttering, "I don't know if I should fall into bed and sleep or go to Starbuck's."

My daughter, Amaya, who was five at the time, looked me over. My hair was in complete disarray, my eyes were blood-shot, the circles under my eyes had circles, and I was so mentally exhausted I could barely speak. "If I were you," my precocious little five-year-old said, "I'd go to Starbuck's."

I smiled at her innocent wisdom. There was no way I could fall asleep right now, no matter how tired I was. I e-mailed Jim Miklaszewski at the Pentagon, using his nickname. "Mik, I love you," I wrote. I said "I love you" to a lot of people that day. Then I hit the closest Starbuck's for a tall latte and headed back home. I had never been so keenly aware of being grateful and lucky to be alive and wanting to reach out to my friends and family.

While the caffeine infiltrated my nervous system, my first personal call went out to Sarah Ferguson, the duchess of York, who had appeared on our show. She and I had become friends, and now, in 2001, she had office space at the top of the World Trade Center, within the suite of offices belonging to Cantor Fitzgerald. It was reported that almost the entire staff of Cantor Fitzgerald had been killed, and I dialed Sarah's number tentatively. I was deeply relieved when she picked up her cell phone. Speaking in a hushed, stunned voice, she said, "I'm okay, Wendy. I don't know why, but I didn't go in to the office this morning."

Sarah was lucky to still be alive to answer her phone. If only Barbara Olson had been so fortunate. The toughest call I made during that time was to Ted Olson, Barbara's husband, who was a major political figure at the time.

"She loved doing your show," Ted told me. "It made her happy."

What he told me next finally caused me to break down. Apparently, Barbara had been booked on a flight on September 10, 2001, one day earlier, to go from Washington's Dulles Airport to Los Angeles. But she had decided to stay behind so she could see her husband on his birthday, even if it was just to kiss him good-bye. That's how in love they were and how amazing their marriage was.

In a shaky voice, Ted told me that Barbara had called him from American Airlines Flight 77 and said, "We're being taken over. They have box cutters. What the hell is going on?"

Ted told her the truth without hesitation. "Two planes just crashed into the World Trade Center."

Now she knew she was going to die, and Ted was struggling with the fact that he had told her. "I think I did the right thing," he said, his voice crackling with emotion. That was when I lost it. The idea that he had respected his wife's courage enough to tell her the truth under the most devastating circumstances was more than I could bear without breaking down. Their relationship remains a role model for me when it comes to great marriages.

Courage under strain and grief was the theme of the aftermath of this terrible tragedy. Of all the survivors we had on the show during the four months following the terrorist attacks, Michael Hingson, a fifty-one-year-old blind man, and Roselle, his seeing eye dog, stand out. Hingson's gratitude and faith in the midst of this situation inspired everyone. We had Michael and Roselle on the show several times. Here are some excerpts from his interview one year after he survived the attacks.

KING: Roselle has been honored with a Congressional insert saluting her inspirational story, and Roselle is receiving the American Kennel Club's 2002 ACE Award as Service Dog of the Year. A big doggie deal, and Roselle deserves it all. How are you doing, Michael?

HINGSON: It's been a year of change...

KING: Can you describe briefly, on 9/11, what did you see, what did you hear? What happened?

HINGSON: When the airplane first struck the tower, I felt as much as heard a thud, just a big explosion. And then the building tilted...our guests at the office at the time were screaming and running toward the exit. I was in my office with a colleague, David Frank. He was the first to identify there was fire above us. I heard debris falling...I wasn't going to leave until they [our guests] were gone. David got them headed towards the stairs. I had attended lots of fire drills, so I knew not to take elevators. I told David to make sure they took the stairs. I called my wife while David was getting our guests out, to tell her that something happened, and then we left.

KING: How? Were you panicky?

HINGSON: No, I couldn't afford to be. Very consciously, I Felt a calming sense from God. I asked God what to do, and just had a feeling to stay calm. And so I did...I took Roselle's harness and gave her the appropriate command, such as to go forward, to go left and right and so on, to get where we needed to go. It was my responsibility to know how to get to the stairs, and her job to make sure we walked safely.

KING: Once you're in the stairs, you're hearing a lot of people around you? Screaming?

HINGSON: Not too much. It was tense, but people were calm. We had some burned victims pass us, but it was calm.

KING: You just followed them—followed *her* down the stairs?

HINGSON: Right. We [Roselle and I] work together, and I know we helped others go down the stairs. Roselle had a chance to flirt with some of the firemen...because as they came up, they would ask me if I were okay. Roselle gave lots of kisses and I know some of them petted Roselle.

KING: What happened when you got to ground?

HINGSON: We went to a parking lot across from Two World Trade Center. But before we got there, the building collapsed, so we literally turned and ran for our lives, and ran to a subway station to avoid some of the dust cloud. By that time, we inhaled a lot.

KING: How did you not run into things?

HINGSON: Roselle. Strictly following Roselle. I told Roselle to go forward. When we got to the end of the buildings, I could hear that we were at the end of the building. I knew we were at a street corner. I told her to go right, because that was away from the Trade Center. She turned and we went, and there were a lot of people running with us, and around us. So it was kind of a crowd mentality.

KING: At any time during all of this, were you scared?

HINGSON: Two times. Once when the building was hit. The other time, when the tower was coming down. I recall the second time, saying to God, how do you do this? You got us out of this building just for another one to collapse on us? Again, I was overwhelmed with a sense of calm and a sense of—don't worry about what you can't control. That's one of the things that I talk about in a lot of my speeches, is the concept of trust, and reminding people, don't worry about what you can't control. Worry about what you can.

Booking the show became methodical as we covered the stories surrounding the terrorist attacks, night after night, for four months straight. Each day, we sorted through the developments and gathered the appropriate images and people to report the next leg of the unfolding story. At some point early on, we decided to stop using the footage of the planes hitting the buildings over and over. I remember having some spirited debates with my colleagues at the time, about whether it was necessary to rerun these grief- and terror-provoking images. I didn't think it was.

Back in 1986, when the space shuttle *Challenger* exploded in clear sight of a viewing audience, we realized we did not need to see the devastating moment many times over to convey the agony. Now, in 2001, we took into consideration the influential voices of the 9/11 victims' families, who explained that each time they saw these unnerving images, they were forced to relive their grief as if it were happening for the very first time. In the end, there was no definitive decision among the networks to stop using the images. We each made our personal decisions and acted accordingly, doing our best to be sensitive to those who had lost their loved ones.

I thought for a moment. What if someone I loved had been

caught up in this? I felt a rush of gratitude flow through me that my family and I were spared. But what if we got up each day and felt grateful, above all other feelings, just to be alive on this day, no matter if something bad happened or not? What if gratitude were a lifestyle instead of an isolated incident? Why is it human nature to only feel gratitude in times of tragedy?

By December 2001, four months in, the earth was still smoking at Ground Zero and we were still doing shows about it. When a reporter asked me when I would stop, I remember shaking my head and saying, "When it feels right."

It felt right to stop the coverage on New Year's of 2002. I wanted a fresh start, so did everyone else, and it was somewhat of a relief to be moving on. The heartbreak would never go away, and there was no way to feel "good" about the shows we did, but I felt that we had done a thorough job of covering the attacks in a respectful way that honored both the fallen and their families. We had focused on telling the truth and allowing people to feel the depth of their pain. I was grateful to have survived this sudden attack with enough inner strength and fortitude to help communicate the depth and breadth of what we were all feeling.

Of course, there is no such thing as closure when you're dealing with such a far-reaching tragedy and with numerous pregnant women being left to fend for themselves and children being orphaned or raised by one parent instead of two. The stories of loss go on and on. But if I had to choose one story that personifies the odd serendipities that occurred surrounding this time, I would choose meeting up with someone in a most unlikely situation.

It was two years before the attacks and before Al Qaeda became a household term. I was at a fabulous designer sale in New York where women stood in line to get the latest name-brand clothing at slashed prices. It took place in a hotel suite where crowds of us grabbed amazing pieces and tried them on in a group. Modesty flew out the window as animated women tried on the finest clothing available at *almost* affordable prices. And there I was, in the group fitting room, connecting with a woman next to me.

Only women do this, as we try on clothes and become best friends in an instant, truthfully critiquing each other's outfits. "Hi, I'm Wendy," I said. "That skirt is fabulous on you but the top isn't quite right."

She smiled, told me her name was Christy, and we began to help each other choose some great new clothes. It turned out we were both in media, and when I finally left with my spoils, I was sorry we had not exchanged phone numbers. I just knew that we could have been friends.

Fast forward two years to the 9/11 tragedies. Two weeks after the attacks, I got a call from Maureen Orth, *Vanity Fair* writer and wife of beloved Tim Russert who has since passed away. "Do you remember a huge designer sale you went to a couple of years ago in New York?" she asked. "There was a woman there and the two of you hit it off?"

"Of course I remember," I said. "She was great. I wish I'd gotten her number."

"Well, her name is Christy Ferer," Maureen told me, "and her husband, Neil Levin, died in the World Trade Center on 9/11. He was the head of the Port Authority. I've known her a long time and she wants to contact Rosemary Altea, a British psychic who appeared on your show. Can you get them in touch?"

I did it right away, and now Christy and I have become friends. There was so little anyone could do for people who had lost their loved ones, I was happy to be able to offer someone a modicum of comfort. While we may be perfect strangers to people around us, we have connections that may only become apparent in times of crisis. Since we are all human, we can feel the gratitude and connectedness of being alive, right here, right now, and being there for someone else, when need be. The decision is up to us. We can choose to walk away from tragedy and repress our feelings of loss and grief. But they will rear their heads when we least expect it. Or we can choose to be grateful for each day as we join with others to say, "There but for the grace of God go I."

❖

BE GRATEFUL EVERY DAY OF YOUR LIFE

Being grateful for everything in life helps you focus on what's good and right, instead of what's bad and wrong. When I hear kids complaining about having a bad day, I would like to say, "No, the people in that Haitian earthquake had a bad day. You are having some aggravation in your life."

Remember the old cliché, Life is short. Why are you wasting time rehashing your problems when there is so much to be thankful for? The key here is that gratitude needs to become a habit. I have heard it said that it takes twenty-eight days of a new behavior to break a habit. So here again, make a list of all that you have to be grateful for and recite it each morning when you wake up. I've been doing this long before it was considered fashionable and before the self-help shelves in the bookstores were filled with books on gratitude. As a result, I can say from direct experience that it really does make a difference.

If you wake up in the morning with complaints and resentment, that is how your day will unfold. But when you remind yourself to focus on the good instead of the bad, then that is how you will direct your day. It's all about changing your mind-set and building new patterns that will help make your life more productive and satisfying.

Gratefulness can be contagious. Have you noticed how quick we are to tell someone when we're pissed off about something? But what about when someone does something nice for us? If somebody has changed the quality of your day from negative to positive, or if a child has behaved well, tell them. Give them the positive reinforcement that will encourage more of the same. It's a fine feeling to have someone say, "Hey, you made my day." In this way, you are setting a foundation of gratefulness.

Since being grateful opens your heart and shows you ways to comfort yourself and others, gratitude can help get you through some close to impossible situations. Let's act like this is the last day of our lives, and feel grateful for all the beauty that life has to offer. Crises will happen and so will loss. It is a part of the human experience. But so is being grateful. Give it a try. You'll like it.

CHAPTER 11

How Do You Want to Be Remembered?

I wonder if the Clintons considered this question when they moved into the White House in January 1993. Whatever they were thinking (or not thinking), they had a seriously shaky start with the press corps.

It is the prerogative of any new administration to target certain White House positions, fire the people who were hired under the previous administration, and fill the jobs with those who worked very hard to get the new president elected. This was the case when the Clintons first arrived at the White House in January 1993. Everyone understands that this is common practice and it occurs with each administration. But there are some positions, such as White House chef, various secretarial jobs, and certain nonpolitical and nonpartisan offices that work differently. The people who work in these positions serve whichever president is in office, and they remain in their jobs from administration to administration, no matter who is elected.

That was the case with the White House travel office. From the time I began work as CNN's White House producer,

I became attached to this group of highly skilled and caring guys who helped us in a major way during all of our trips, both domestic and international. I sometimes wondered what we would have done without them. In fact, they did such a great job for so long, I was completely stunned and upset when I got a call from Billy Dale, director of the travel office who had been there since the Kennedy administration. "We've been fired," he told me.

"Who was fired?" I asked.

"The whole travel office," he said. "All seven of us. They fired us and asked us to clean out our desks."

I could hardly believe my ears. These people had worked as hard as any of us, sacrificing holidays with their families and flying halfway across the world with us to make sure we had everything we needed when we traveled. Over the years, the press corps and the travel office had come to know each other's names and families, and we considered each other friends. Barney Brasseaux, one of the travel guys, had come to my wedding, I was so close to him.

Now, the Clintons were set on replacing this experienced, hardworking, egoless staff who had served us loyally for many years, with friends of theirs whom they thought would do a better job. When we balked at these firings, the people in charge inferred that maybe we didn't get the whole story and how much more efficiently things could be run.

The truth was that the Clinton White House didn't understand the press corps' relationship with the long-standing travel office staff. This was not like firing a group of anonymous people whom we barely knew. Quite the opposite. We had dealt with these wonderful people on a steady basis for many years as they arranged our international as well as our domestic travel, including chartering press planes, buses, booking last minute hotels and conference rooms, and anything else we needed. They knew all of our idiosyncrasies and they always did their best to make us as comfortable as possible. This was particularly important for me because I was not what you would call a great traveler. I absolutely detested flying and my suitcase was so big, they called it "the suitcase from hell."

This group also took a lot of abuse when things went wrong. If a plane was delayed or a bus didn't get through on time and someone missed a deadline, these men bore the brunt of that. But time after time, they kept their heads down and weathered the rage and criticism without complaining. They just took it and moved on. Now, instead of being respected or even rewarded for a hard job well done for many years, they were being replaced. On top of that, since they were not going quietly, it appeared that the administration was leveling charges against them, focusing on Billy Dale, the director of the travel office.

Billy and his staff of six men were accustomed to booking what we needed, and then billing the costs back to the networks. This is where Billy and I worked very closely. For example, I would call him, give him the particulars of an upcoming trip, and ask him, "How much do you think this will cost?"

"Let's see," he would say, "first you head to New York, which will cost this much, and then it's on to Paris, which will cost this much"—and so on. He had extreme patience with me because he kept in mind that CNN had less money and had to justify the expense of each trip.

One time, NBC reporter Andrea Mitchell said to me, "Wendy, you're so lucky you don't have an evening news deadline every night like we do."

I looked at her, amazed, and said, "CNN doesn't have an evening news deadline like yours because every minute is a deadline. We have them all day long and all night."

In order to meet those deadlines, we had depended on Billy Dale's travel office to make it all work, which required Billy to keep a large amount of petty cash on hand, to tip the drivers and pay people along the way to do their jobs. For example, if we suddenly needed to leave Budapest in the middle of the night, Billy would pay the appropriate people to make sure we had a plane on the tarmac, ready to go.

But the Clinton administration was leveling charges that Billy had been skimming off the top in order to fund a lake house he was building for his family. The fact that he had been saving for this house for many years did nothing to convince them of his innocence. One of the main problems was that although Billy kept meticulous notes, he wrote them in pencil and entered them into a ledger. No electronic data had been entered because Billy kept his files the old-fashioned way that had always worked for him in the past.

In the midst of this turmoil dubbed Travelgate, in a related crisis, President Clinton was faced with the undoing of his White House counsel and old friend from Arkansas, Vince Foster. Because Foster was defending Hillary in the travel office scandal, he had been the target of several hostile *Wall Street Journal* editorials, and he was quite upset over the entire matter. A stickler for integrity, in early May 1993, Vince Foster had given a commencement address at his alma mater, the University of Arkansas Law School. He said:

The reputation you develop for intellectual and ethical integrity will be your greatest asset or your worst enemy. You will be judged by your judgment... There is no victory, no advantage, no fee, no favor, which is worth even a blemish on your reputation for intellect and integrity... Dents to [your] reputation are irreparable.

Now, he feared being asked to testify at a Congressional hearing because he so disliked the public spotlight. Dedicated to maintaining his personal integrity, he had considered resigning his position as White House counsel, but he feared facing humiliation if he returned to Arkansas.

Now, a few months later, Larry landed an interview with President Clinton, which would be shot live in the library of the White House. I rushed around doing my usual job as White House producer, doubly anxious to make the show run smoothly. I had yet to become Larry's executive producer, but I knew the job was coming available, I had my sights set on it, and I wanted to make a good impression on him.

It was 9:10 p.m. on July 20, 1993, and I was watching the show on a monitor in a room across the hall from the library. All was going fine until I glanced down the hall and noticed that some of the president's aides, George Stephanopoulos, Dee Dee Myers, and Mack McLarty, were whispering among themselves. I caught Mack's eye and he motioned for me to come and join them. As soon as I got there, Mack said quietly, "We have to end the show right now."

"Why?" I asked.

"Off the record," Dee Dee told me in a whisper, "we believe that Vince Foster just committed suicide. He was found dead off the George Washington Parkway in Virginia. We can't have you telling anyone else yet. We're afraid someone will call in and tell the president about Vince. That's not how we want him to find out."

George began to tell me who Vince Foster was, when Mack stopped him. "She knows who Vince is," he said. "They're neighbors."

I could not have been more shocked. Since our marriage, I'd been living with my husband in his town house in

Georgetown, and Vince Foster had lived across the street from us. The three of us had met at a White House dinner, and we had struck up a neighborly conversation and had talked about getting together. That would never happen now. I knew that Bill and Hillary had been close friends with Vince, and the idea of the president finding out about his friend's death on the air from a live caller was unacceptable. But it was also unacceptable to stop the show ten minutes in. If that wasn't a clear sign to the general public that an emergency had occurred, I couldn't imagine what was.

"We don't have to stop the show," I said. "I can prevent the president from finding out on the air by screening calls. If we only take overseas calls and skip the domestic ones, no one will find out until the show is over."

I asked Dee Dee to go to the production truck with me and I spoke to the producer of the show. "Something very serious just happened," I told him. "We can't report it yet, but the president's aides want to stop the show. I talked them into continuing, but we have to make very sure that the president doesn't hear this piece of news from anyone before we tell him."

He understood. But as I was walking back to the monitor in the control room, I heard Larry tell his viewing audience, "Well, you've heard it now. The president has just decided to stay on for an hour and a half. We'll have an extra half hour with President Clinton."

I literally ran back to tell George, Mack, and Dee Dee, who had not heard Larry's announcement about the president staying on for an extra half hour.

"He can't do that," George said. At the next break, George and I went into the library and George said, "I'm sorry, Mr. President, but you can't stay on for the extra half hour."

"Why not?" he asked. "Larry just announced it." The truth

was that President Clinton would have stayed on for two more hours if they would let him. He loved doing interviews.

"I know Larry just announced it," said George, "but you can't do it tonight. You can take a rain check. Just not tonight."

The president looked at George more closely and said, "Oh, you know something I don't. Right?"

"Well," George said, "we have some things we have to do after the show."

When they went back on the air, Larry announced that they would not be doing the extra half hour. "The president has something to do at ten," he explained, "but he'll come back again."

The White House press room was full of reporters covering the president's appearance on *Larry King Live*. When they heard the announcement that the extra half hour was being canceled, they knew something was up. When the show was finally over, President Clinton stood up and said, "C'mon Larry, get your whole gang and we'll give them a tour. Has everyone seen the Lincoln bedroom? Let's go upstairs and take some pictures."

George stepped in and said, "We can't do that tonight. Really sorry," and he whisked the president away. I called my husband, Ralph, to say I'd be late and then I got ready for a long night of work. But fifteen minutes later, Ralph called me at the White House. "What's going on, Wendy?" he asked me. "I think the president is on our block. There are all these unmarked cars at Vince's house. Something's happening."

While Ralph walked across the street in his sweats to see what was up, I let him know what had happened since Dee Dee was about to announce it. By now, I was in the press room with all the other reporters. Several of them asked me, "Something is going on. What is it?"

I confirmed their suspicions by saying, "If I were you, I'd stay right where you are. If you leave and go home, you'll just have to turn right around and come back."

Eventually, Dee Dee came to the press room to tell the reporters that the President's special counsel and friend from Arkansas had taken his own life. Apparently, Vince had been diagnosed with clinical depression months earlier, and it was obvious how much the Travelgate scandal was taking out of him, a man who was a stickler for integrity. It was clearly more than he could bear, and the police found a draft of a resignation letter doubling as a suicide note, torn into twenty-seven pieces. The authorities also found a list of complaints in Foster's briefcase, including a note that said,

> The *Wall Street Journal* editors lie without conse-
> quence...I was not meant for the job or the spotlight of
> public life in Washington. Here, ruining people is consid-
> ered sport.

Vince Foster's death, piled on top of Travelgate, was weighing down the Clintons. Their integrity was in question, and many believed it signified the end of optimism among much of the White House staff. Not much had been resolved in Travelgate when, on November 7, 1995 (I was working with Larry by then), an article appeared in the *Washington Post* by journalist Toni Locy. Here are excerpts:

> Some of the people from whom Billy R. Dale allegedly
> stole $68,000 testified yesterday in his defense, saying they
> trusted him when he ran the White House travel office and
> still trust him today. Dale, 57, is charged with embezzling
> money the news media paid to cover costs of traveling

with the president from 1988 to 1993 by putting it into his personal bank account.

"It doesn't surprise me," said Wendy Walker Whitworth, a vice president for CNN and senior executive producer of "Larry King Live" who formerly was assigned to the White House. "Billy is not an e-mail kind of guy. He doesn't have a lot to do with computers. If he was doing this, he was doing it to run the kind of operation he had to run [as] efficiently [as he could]."

The defense is expected to call other journalists, including Sam Donaldson of ABC, to give similar testimony... Whitworth testified that Dale's job was not easy, especially when presidents decided to travel on short notice, a frequent occurrence...

On December 7, 1994, I was distressed to learn that Billy Dale had been formally indicted by a federal grand jury on two counts of embezzlement and criminal conversion. He was charged with wrongfully depositing into his own bank account the sum of $68,000 in checks from media organizations, while traveling with the president between 1988 and 1991. If convicted, he could serve up to twenty years in prison. But Billy's attorneys insisted that he had used the deposited monies for substantial tips and off-the-book payments that the job required, especially when we traveled to foreign countries.

The trial lasted thirteen days during the latter part of October and the beginning of November 1995, and a group of us testified. ABC's Sam Donaldson and *LA Times* reporter Jack Nelson both appeared as character witnesses for Billy, as did I. We knew that all these gentlemen, particularly Billy, were honest and their function had been critical to the well-being of the entire press corps. I was glad for the opportunity to stand up for Billy and there was a moment when my testimony proved pivotal in this terrible ordeal.

Here is an excerpt from the transcript during my direct examination:

Q: Does the fact that he [Billy Dale] put those fifty-five checks into his personal bank account cause you to change the opinion that you have developed over the ten years that you have dealt with him?

A: No.

Q: Why not?

A: Because it doesn't surprise me if that were the case. I mean it wouldn't—Billy is not an e-mail kind of guy. He doesn't know a lot—he doesn't do—he doesn't have a lot of computers or things like that in his office. He—if he was doing this, it is probably something that he was doing for a long time.

At this point, there was an objection from opposing counsel that was overruled. A few minutes later, during cross-examination, I gave the following testimony:

Q: Ms. Walker, did you ever put checks that belonged to CNN into your personal account?

A: Yes.

Q: And those belonged to CNN?

A: Yes.

Q: The money belonged to CNN, and you used it for your personal purposes?

There was an objection made that was sustained, but I had made my point.

We went on:

Q: The travel office didn't ask you to come in and look at those [documents], and you never asked to look at them, did you?

A: No.

Q: You trusted the travel office employees, didn't you?

A: That is right.

Q: You said that the fact that these checks were in Mr. Dale's personal account wouldn't change your opinion about them, right?

A: Right.

Q: You are aware that this case involved charges of embezzlement, right?

A: I am aware that is the charge, yes.

Now everyone knew that both he and I kept a large amount of cash on hand, and while we didn't do the same job, we both had to be prepared for any kind of emergency. Like Billy, I had deposited certain CNN checks into my account for easy access. Billy's accounting was harder to track than mine, though, because of his old-fashioned bookkeeping practices.

When the jury went out, they deliberated for less than two hours before they acquitted Billy on all charges on November 16, 1995. The other suspects were acquitted as well, and on January 16, 1996, Larry had the seven travel office officials on the show. Here are some excerpts:

DALE: I would like for her [Mrs. Clinton] or for anyone at the White House to prove that I mismanaged one dollar of funds. If she wants to look at mismanagement, let's look at the Energy Department, those were government funds. I want to make it clear to the American people right now, not one dollar of government funds are we talking about. This is money that I collected from the press corps and paid out on their behalf.

KING: Did you spend your own funds on your defense?

DALE: I have spent $105,000 of my own funds. All my life savings.

KING: Gary Wright, you are the assistant former deputy director. Mrs. Clinton has stated that there was expressed concern over financial mismanagement. Was that fiction?

WRIGHT: As far as I am concerned it was fiction. I'd like to know who she heard it from. I believe that the people that she was hearing it from perhaps had an agenda of their own, or a reason for taking over the White House travel office, that was giving her this information. At no time, before or after the Clintons took office, did they ever send any top level senior administrative types to our office to ask us what our job was, how we did it.

KING: Barney Brasseaux, are you saying that Mr. Watkins, Vince Foster, none of them ever came to see you?

BRASSEAUX: They never came to see me. You may want to check with Billy, because I know Billy made several attempts to meet with some of the staff there at the White House just to discuss how he ran his office and what they expected of him and his office.

KING: Billy?

DALE: That's correct. The day after the inauguration I went to George Stephanopoulos's office, who I assumed was the press spokesman, that was my understanding, and it was tradition for us to introduce ourselves to the people that we were going to be working closest with. I was told by his assistant that they would get back to me as soon as they could arrange an appointment. In the next few days, in three attempts to see him with no success, I turned to Dee Dee Myers and I met with the same luck there. So, up until the time that we were fired, I never had the pleasure of meeting George Stephanopoulos or Dee Dee Myers.

The travel people were all acquitted, but the wounds had cut deep. No one got their jobs back, and since Billy was close to retirement age, he retired early, a sad ending to a bad experience. It remains something to ponder: When integrity is called into question, how do you want to be remembered?

❖

HOW DO YOU WANT TO BE REMEMBERED?

There are people in this world with great attributes, they contribute to charities and help elderly women, but they are not necessarily people of integrity. Are you? Ask yourself the following questions:

- If you could get away with stealing a million dollars and nobody would ever find out, would you do it?
- If you could get away with cheating on your spouse and he or she would never know, would you do it?
- If you could tell people that you graduated with honors from Harvard and nobody would ever know you went to Middle Nowhere State, would you do it?

If you answered yes to any of the above questions, ask yourself, "What if my children found out? Would that be okay with me? What if my husband or wife knew? And then, would my boss be impressed to know who I really am?"

All we can really count on is our integrity in this life, and what you do in your professional life bleeds over into your personal life as well. Think Tiger Woods who, unfortunately for him, became the poster child for lack of integrity. So did Bernie Madoff when his billion-dollar scam became public.

You can be a really good president or the best golfer in the world, but if you have no integrity, that is what people will remember about you. Tiger Woods may be able to repair his golf game, but his reputation is forever soiled. You just can't get that back. He should have kept in mind that no matter how subtly you sacrifice your integrity, it will come back to haunt you. Someone will find out, and the world at large will discover who you truly are from the inside out.

CHAPTER 12

Opposites Attract

Larry King is a true icon who is known the world over. He is instantly recognizable by his face and his voice, and I feel privileged to be an integral part of his life and his extraordinary career. He just makes it look so easy. No matter whom we put on the show, no matter how Larry feels personally about someone, he is masterful at setting aside his feelings so his guests always get a fair shake during the hour.

One of his most impressive qualities, arguably the backbone of his success, is that when the spotlight starts to shine on him, he immediately brings the attention back to his current guest. This is a rare quality in a talk-show host. Larry *never* tries to skew the show to be about him as he asks direct questions, he listens to the answers, and he doesn't judge. He really is an egoless interviewer who gets right to the point. When there's a breaking news story, if we have five inroads by which to cover it, Larry tackles the topic with gusto, and together we figure out which road to take. He eats these challenges up, he always has, something I saw in him when we first met seventeen years ago.

The White House producer job had been my dream, and it had taken me all over the world for a decade. During this time, I met a number of world leaders and I stood beside President Reagan in the Far East when he visited the Great Wall of China. I saw and heard him exhort Mikhail Gorbachev to tear down the Berlin Wall. I accompanied President George H. W. Bush when he ate Thanksgiving dinner with the troops in the Persian Gulf. I saw Clinton elected, I testified in court, and I was on call twenty-four hours a day, seven days a week, for a decade. When it was time to meet Larry to talk about being his executive producer, I was ready to make a change. Actually, I'd been on alert for the right opportunity for some time, since my White House job would be a hard act to follow.

While I waited for the proposed meeting between Larry and me, I understood that interviewing a baseball great every night would have been his dream come true. Since Larry describes himself quite simply as "a Jewish guy who loves sports," he had his heart set on filling the empty producing spot with another "Jewish guy who loves sports." He had even found someone he was considering, so it's a good thing Larry didn't know how disconnected from baseball I really was.

Several years earlier, in 1983, I had been Dean Reynolds's White House producer when he was CNN White House correspondent.

Dean, a baseball freak like Larry, took me to a game in Baltimore where we were sitting with a load of VIPs. Clearly in his element, Dean was very excited, and at one point, he asked me if I wanted a hot dog.

"Thanks," I said, "but I think I'll wait until halftime."

He looked around to see if anyone else had heard my ignorant comment and then he looked at me like he had no idea who I was. At that moment, I realized that he and I would never make it as a couple because I had no idea that baseball had a seventh-inning stretch instead of a halftime. Believe me, I have never told Larry that story (until now), because there is no way he would get the humor in it. Rather, he might see it as violation of his chosen religion—baseball.

But I didn't let my baseball-challenged personality deter me. It was obvious Larry and I were polar opposites, which could work in our favor. If he and I were exactly alike, I reasoned, the show's topics could get boring and so could our relationship. As opposites, we would bring different things to the table and it would never get humdrum.

When the big meeting was approaching, I knew Larry was only seeing me to placate Tom Johnson (then CNN boss), but I also knew that I was far more qualified for the job than his other pick. Since I loved a good challenge and I really wanted the job, I kicked in and made a concerted push.

Before the meeting, I contacted some of the most influential people in my life so far, such as Ethel Kennedy, financier T. Boone Pickens, and George Bush, Sr., to name a few. I asked them to write recommendation letters for me and send them to Larry. They all complied. Gail Evans, who was head of CNN's central booking unit at the time, touted me to Tom Johnson who was already pulling for me, so I had a lot of allies. Still, as a blonde WASP female with little to no interest in baseball, I knew I had to overcome the "Jewish sports guy."

"I already have someone I want," Larry told me immediately when we sat down for coffee at Duke's Restaurant for the very first time.

"Okay," I said, not appearing concerned. I was ready for him.

"But I did get your letters of recommendation," he added.

"Oh, good," I said. "What did you think?"

"I was impressed with the number of influential people you know and how they feel about you," he said.

"Would you like more?" I asked him.

He looked deeply impressed as I went on to explain to him how much I wanted this job, what I was willing to put into it, and how much I disliked losing anything. He sat back, smiled broadly, and said, "I don't need any more letters. I just made up my mind. The job is yours."

Larry swears to this day that when I offered more endorsements, that did it for him. I believe he gave me the job when he saw how badly I wanted it and how competitive I truly was. And my contacts didn't hurt a bit, either. When a host of a show is shopping for an executive producer, he and his pick are entering into a sort of marriage, in which they agree to talk several times a day every day, to make decisions, and to work out compromises together. The host needs to know that the producer is loyal, something that can only be proven with time, but he also needs her to be effective on the phone and to be on top of whatever is going on at any given moment. Basically, a host needs to know that his executive producer can pull off whatever she needs to, has all the right contacts, and always has his best interests at heart. I think Larry realized on that day that not only could I do these things but that I was eager, I had a healthy competitive edge, and I was ready to go forward right away. And did I have contacts!

As I began my new job, two things were foremost in my mind. The first was getting to know Larry, since he was so different from me. I needed for us to build trust, and I worked on balancing the two distinct parts of my job that sometimes clashed: doing what was right for the network and doing what was right for Larry. Today, I'm one of the few people who can say pretty much anything to Larry without offending him.

He trusts me totally because he has learned that my criticisms come from a good place. And I always make sure he remembers how much I admire his work. That's easy because I don't think anybody else can do what he does, and I respect him for his ability to show up every night and give it all he's got. People are eager to criticize him, because when he slips up, he does it publicly. But how many people do you know who could do a live show for an hour, five nights a week, for twenty-five years? Actually, no one. In fact, Larry just made *Guinness World Records* for the longest-running show with the same host in the same time slot on the same network!

Second only to getting to know my new boss was finding great guests for the show. Fate was in my corner, since two of my closest friends in the world are Palestinians named Sabih and Hani Masri, part of a famous Palestinian family who are as wealthy and influential as the Kennedys are in the United States. It just so happened that the Masris were close to Yasser Arafat, Palestinian leader and chairman of the Palestinian Liberation Organization. Arafat was labeled a terrorist in America, and I wondered what Larry would think if I got him an interview with Yasser Arafat himself? He never did interviews, but I had an in.

I had always considered Arafat to be one of the bad guys, and now I had the unique opportunity to hear about Israeli-Palestinian issues from a different perspective. I learned a great deal about those issues from the inside.

As we began to negotiate the terms to have Yasser Arafat as a guest on *Larry King Live*, I became privy to the security machinations that were necessary to keep this man safe. He feared assassination most of the time, so it was not uncommon for him to be moved from one place to the next several times during a night. I recall being at Hani's Washington home where Arafat was staying. We had a Zen moment when we saw his outfit with his red headpiece folded on the bed, ready for a quick exit to the next place. Needless to say, his security detail was so rigid that it was difficult to get him to agree to an interview.

We got him, though, and Larry was excited. I could actually say that Larry was thrilled since all the other networks wanted this interview so much. I impressed Larry with this fantastic "get," and we were off and running.

Everyone agrees that Larry and I are an interesting team, mainly because we are so different. But we have enough mutual respect to get along with each other and hear what the other has to say. There are days that Larry would prefer not to do a certain interview and I have to explain to him why I booked it. Ninety-nine percent of the time, at the end of such a show, he tells me, "Now I get why you booked that guest." We usually see eye to eye in the end, we talk several times every day, and we tell each other that we love each other nearly every time we talk.

What most people don't know about Larry is that he can feel anxious when he's off the air. Imagine walking down the street and a perfect stranger calls out, "Hey, do you think the Lakers are going to win?" Everyone thinks they know Larry, and he tries to accommodate them by being kind and giving them an answer. But it does create stress that he has to combat. When he's on the air, though, something overtakes him. It's as if a miracle happens and he is endlessly patient, he sits still with no problem, and he feels and looks utterly comfortable in his own skin—characteristics of a true professional.

Of course, there are many times when Larry and I don't agree. And there are times when we tease each other. He may call and say, "Wendy, we're doing a show about Manny Ramirez tonight, right?"

"No, Larry," I'll answer. "We're working on getting the octomom."

"You're kidding," he'll say.

"Yes, I'm kidding," I'll answer.

Our shared sense of humor, one of the few things about us that is similar, keeps us laughing at each other and ourselves. I remember a party at Larry's house when, out of the blue, Don Rickles said Larry looked like a "Jew Buick." Larry and I laughed our heads off.

Today, when I think about our long and enduring friendship and business partnership, I believe that our diversity is the secret to our success. It's been working for years and years, and Larry and I both acknowledge that we are each other's longest relationship (without sex) to date.

Over the many years we've worked together, we've gone through a great many personal changes and we've always been there for each other. He was thrilled when my children came into my life, and I was there when Larry got engaged a couple of times and finally when he married his wonderful wife, Shawn Southwick, who gave him his two youngest boys. In fact, I was in the room with Shawn and Larry when they were born, which went way beyond my job description!

When Larry got interested in Shawn initially, he came on very strong in his usual fashion. He had known her a short time when he called me one day and said, "Wendy, I'm so crazy about this girl. Would you call and tell her that all the stories about my marriages are exaggerated? Tell her I was only married four times instead of seven."

I knew Shawn, I liked her, I considered her an intelligent

woman, and I had no interest in lying to her. At the same time, I needed to placate Larry, so I got her on the phone at 4 a.m., Pacific time. "Shawn," I said, "I'm really sorry to be doing this, but I'm supposed to tell you that Larry has only been married four times."

"Oh, my God," she said with a laugh.

"Well," I said, "I'm just the messenger."

From the moment I met Shawn, I had a good feeling about her. I recall early on, when she and I were sitting in a limo together, facing each other. Shawn, an absolutely beautiful woman, was touching up her makeup with some blemish concealer. I was wearing a pair of sandals when she suddenly reached over without missing a beat in our conversation and applied some concealer to a scar I have on my second toe. A moment later, she stopped and said, "Oh, my God, I just did that without asking you or thinking."

"I know," I said as we both burst out laughing. She is a girl's girl and it was instinctual in her to take care of me, too, while she was doing the finishing touches on her own makeup. We bonded over my toe and we laugh about it to this day.

Despite the number of his previous marriages, Shawn, thirty-seven, and Larry, sixty-three, were engaged in record time and the wedding was planned for September 4, 1997. It was going to be a lavish affair at a friend's luxurious home, but while we were in Los Angeles preparing for the wedding, Larry woke up one morning and didn't feel well.

Ever since his open-heart surgery about a decade prior, Larry had been in close touch with his body and he knew when something was wrong. That morning, I went to his LA doctor with him, who agreed that something was off with Larry's heart. But when he suggested a second open-heart surgery, Larry was hoping for something less invasive. Since he had another set of doctors in New York who had performed his original open-heart surgery, he also called them.

His brilliant surgeon, Dr. Wayne Isom, a man missing a thumb, was a calming force in Larry's life. I recall a great story that Larry tells in his biography about the night before his first surgery, in New York. When Dr. Isom showed up and began tapping his chest, Larry noticed that this man, who had operated on David Letterman and Walter Cronkite, had a stub for a right thumb.

Larry said, "Dr. Isom, I've had this peculiar habit all my life and I can't explain it. But when I meet people, I count their fingers…and with you I get to nine."

When the New York doctors heard Larry's prognosis, they got so worried, they flew all night to see Larry for themselves. So while they examined him and reviewed his medical history, I had to cancel the wedding. The Beverly Wilshire Hotel gave me a banquet room which I dubbed Wedding Central. They filled the room with phones, and a few other people and I began to make the calls to let people know that the wedding was off for now. By the end of the day, when I was through with my calls, the doctors told me that the next day, they would medevac Larry to New York to perform an angioplasty, because open-heart surgery was not necessary. Needless to say, we were nervous about the upcoming operation, but we were also relieved that the surgery would be less invasive, which meant fewer things could go wrong. There had been another consideration, which was how long Larry would be off the show. Open-heart surgery would take a long stretch of recovery time. After an angioplasty, he could be back on the air in days, which meant a great deal to him.

Early the next morning, as many as thirty people gathered in Larry's hospital room in Los Angeles, including two sets of doctors and Larry's and Shawn's family and friends. Determined to get married anyway, Shawn showed up that morning in a gorgeous lavender Chanel dress to make her wedding vows with Larry in his hospital room. Before the minister started, Larry looked up at me and said, "How do I look?"

Everything happened so spontaneously that nothing was recorded as the minister stood beside Larry, who was lying in his bed, with Shawn standing beside him. This was before texting and phones with video capabilities. I had to record everything the old-fashioned way, so there I stood at the foot of the bed, with a yellow legal pad, writing everything down since I would have to put out some kind of press release after the marriage. I listed every person who was there, and I framed my notes and gave them to Larry and Shawn since there was no way they would ever have remembered who had attended their hospital-room wedding.

When the ceremony was over, Larry was flown to New York for his surgery. It was successful, and once he was back in Los Angeles, he and Shawn had a second wedding ceremony, a great celebration, with Ted Turner as best man. Ted's wife, Jane Fonda, was a bridesmaid. Toward the end of the ceremony, Al Pacino read a passage for them, which elevated the cool factor that already was high as a kite.

While I am a constant participant in Larry's personal life, for Larry and me, our focus is first and foremost on the show. Over the years we have learned to anticipate each other and understand how the other person ticks, but it took some time to get there, especially for me to get accustomed to the way Larry did things and how he viewed them. Little did I know that the following story, as bizarre as it seems, was and still is quintessential Larry.

When I had just begun working with him, Larry was living

in an apartment that overlooked the Potomac River in Washington. I was having a hard time getting him to make certain phone calls that might bring in some of the bigger guests. He said he just didn't feel like doing it, but I was determined that he would get over his reluctance. I called him one morning and said, "Larry, I'm picking up bagels and I'm coming over. You need to call Barbra Streisand and see if she'll do the show. I'd do it, but it won't work unless you make the call yourself."

I arrived as promised, bagels in hand, and said, "You need to get this booking. When you get her on the phone, if she says no, you can't just hang up immediately. See if you can talk her into it." Larry has such a short attention span, he was capable of hanging up the phone in ten seconds if someone refused his offer.

I dialed the phone in one room and I yelled to Larry in the other room, "It's ringing. Pick it up."

He picked it up and I heard that amazing voice on the other end of the line, saying, "Hello?"

It was *Barbra*! I became mesmerized and kept listening. I just had to hear the conversation for history's sake!! But after she said, "Hello?" it went downhill from there.

"Barbra," Larry said, "good to talk to you. Hey, I need you to do the show. I'd really love you to do it."

"I'd like to, Larry," she said, "but I really can't right now. Thanks for thinking of me."

"Oh, Barbra," Larry coaxed, "you can do half the show. Or how about ten minutes? I just want you on my show."

"It doesn't matter if I do ten minutes or an hour," she said. "It takes the same kind of preparation. I love you madly, Larry, but I really can't do the show. Thank you anyway."

Larry persisted. "C'mon, Barbra. Jew to Jew. As a personal favah."

She sighed and repeated, "Once again, I love you, but I can't do the show. I'm not ready to do the show right now. Luv you, Lar."

"Well, just think about it," he said.

They said good-bye and I walked back into the room. He had stayed on the phone and really tried, so maybe next time. I was ready to console him when he said, "Okay, she'll do it. Call her agent!"

I was perplexed. But I learned that day that Larry is a glass half-full kind of guy. Needless to say, Ms. Streisand did not appear on our show at that particular point in time. When she did come on the show a few years later, in 1995, Larry took the opportunity to remind her that she had played hard to get. We learned during that interview that an icon like Barbra Streisand was also a normal human being with stage fright and fear of public speaking.

KING: We began this program with the standing ovation at Harvard [for Barbra] and your closing remarks. And let's trace back a little bit. First, why did you agree to speak there [at Harvard]? How did that come about?

STREISAND: They asked me.

KING: But we asked you. How many times did we ask you? Twenty times.

STREISAND: Well, I was supposed to do the Harvard speech in April, before my tour started in London. I thought that was interesting, because I've always had strong feelings about the artist as citizen, the artist constantly getting denigrated in society. I heard an interesting story the other day about Molière. On his deathbed, they wouldn't give him his last rites unless he denounced his profession. So this thing goes back a long way, you know?

KING: So, did you agree to speak, with trepidation, or with forthrightness?

STREISAND: With both. But I was so consumed with rehearsals for my show that I had to cancel it. I thought maybe they'd let me off the hook after the tour. But they said, "No, no, we still would like you to come and speak." And so that's why I did it this last February.

KING: Can you tell us why so public a person is so stage frightened or nervous?

STREISAND: First of all, I think I'm, like…95 percent of the population who would have stage fright standing up to speak publicly. You know, I'm like everybody else.

When Larry asked her about an interview she had done with Mike Wallace, she said:

STREISAND: Well, as when I asked him afterwards, "Why were you so cruel to me?" He said, "Well, you wouldn't want me to do another show like Barbara Walters did, you know, where she was so nice to you and everything." Probably thinks you're too nice to me, too.

KING: I just ask questions. I don't know about nice or not nice. I'm just curious.

STREISAND: You're a nice person.

We have never been at a loss for interesting people and topics. For example, it was thrilling to find myself on a ferry to Ellis Island with Larry and Governor Mario Cuomo, who were both being honored as sons of immigrants. Cuomo gave an extraordinary speech in which he asked us to look at the walls around us and remember the history, since everyone had their start right there.

Then he said something like, "Imagine Mrs. Zeiger, Larry's mother, and Mrs. Cuomo, my mother, sitting here on this bench a long time ago. Mrs. Cuomo says, 'Someday, my son is going to be the governor of New York.' And Mrs. Zeiger says, 'Someday, my son is going to become an international communicator, and he will be famous all over the world. The most famous interviewer in the world.'"

It was one of those moments when I realized how amazing it was that these men had made so much of themselves. Their parents had arrived at Ellis Island, and they truly were living the dream. Now, with my current position, I was helping to bring those images to the American public and the world at large.

Today, I find it a bit ironic that as much as Larry prefers interviewing sports figures, his favorite interview of all times, he says, was with Frank Sinatra. I met Sinatra once at the 1984 Republican National Convention in Texas, where Reagan was nominated. I remember running around the convention, busy as usual, when a beautiful-looking man walked up to me. His face was familiar: It was Old Blue Eyes himself, and he was with a gorgeous blonde woman, Barbara, his wife.

"Where is the main event?" he asked me. He knew I was working there because I had a press pass hanging around my neck.

Omigod! It's Frank Sinatra, I thought. "Let me take you there," I said as the three of us walked in silence to the main event. Too bad I couldn't have said to him, "In nine years, I'm going to become the executive producer of your friend Larry King's show."

The following excerpt is from Larry's favorite show in 1988, on the eve of Mr. Sinatra's eighty-fourth birthday:

KING: Is it still a kick when the man says, and now, ladies and gentlemen—

SINATRA: Oh, it's a kick. Absolutely. And I swear on my mother's soul, the first four or five seconds I tremble every time I take the step and I walk out of the wing onto the stage. Because I keep thinking to myself, I wonder if it will be there? When I go for the first sounds that I have to make, will it be there? I was talking about it just the other night at Carnegie Hall at the Irving Berlin thing. I said, even just going out and looking at the audience, I was terrified for about four seconds and then it goes away.

KING: How do you explain that?

SINATRA: I don't know. I can't explain it. I always had it. Will you remember the lyrics? Is your tie right? Will you use your hands right? Will you look pleasant to the audience? You have to be on the ball from the minute you step out into that spotlight. You have to know exactly what you're doing every second on that stage. Otherwise, the act goes right into the bathroom. It's all over. Good night.

KING: Fame—let's say we're in Washington, you and I. We go into Duke Zeibert's restaurant, popular restaurant. You're aware when you walk in at lunch, let's say everybody recognizes you. Everybody knows you. Everybody is looking at you. What's that like to feel that? Very few people have felt that in their lives.

SINATRA: I think it's an honor...but I have imaginary blinders in a sense. I look around and if somebody smiles at me I smile, hello, how are you whatever, talk to me. But it's not unlike anybody else in our world. They walk into restaurants or a theater. The only time I felt like I was causing a problem was, if I go to the theater in New York. As you come down to go to your seat, people get up and look around and they buzz—it's sweet. It's wonderful. But you want to run and hide a little bit and between acts, you go out and get a smoke or get a drink next door in the bar. It happens again. Then you got to walk down there again is what takes place. But it's a nice thing, though, the recognition is really quite nice.

KING: We're out of time, Francis. Thank you so much.

SINATRA: I had a good time. I enjoyed it. Anytime, just call me and I'll come running.

Larry has never really understood what a big deal it is for people to be around him. I guess in his own mind, he's still little Larry Zeiger, the son of Jewish immigrants with no patience whatsoever. Changing his last name to King didn't change him on the inside, which is one of his greatest charms. But it is also one of his greatest challenges. And mine!

For example, Larry and I were scheduled to have lunch with Nancy Reagan in Beverly Hills one day, years after she had left the White House. As we entered the restaurant and I saw Mrs. Reagan flanked by her Secret Service detail, I became a little nervous. I knew what Larry was capable of and I admonished him, "You have to stay for the whole lunch. Do not leave early. Mrs. Reagan doesn't want to have lunch with *me*. She wants to have lunch with *you*."

Larry was on his best behavior for at least thirty minutes while we ate a lovely meal and chatted. But the minute he finished his chopped salad with tomatoes and no dressing, he stood and said, "I have to go to the dentist now." He kissed both Mrs. Reagan and me and he was gone. As I watched him disappear out the door, I realized that we could have been with anyone (with the exception of Jackie Robinson), and he would have done exactly the same thing.

Mrs. Reagan was surprised to say the least, but I was accustomed to his behavior by now. I looked at her calmly, smiled a little, and said, "Would you like some coffee, Mrs. Reagan?" At least she knew me, since I had covered her husband's presidency for years.

In the final analysis, a wonderful and whimsical story comes to mind that defines Larry's and my complicated relationship, to a tee. I have what I can only call a *fabulous* handbag collection, which was photographed for *Vogue* magazine. A fashion enthusiast for most of my life and obsessed with all kinds of purses, I was thrilled when the *Vogue* crew actually came to my house to photograph my handbags with several Chanel and Valentino outfits for me to wear. Of course, my daughter always bursts my bubble when I say I was in *Vogue*. Amaya reminds me, "Mom, it was only for your purses, not for your clothes."

To this day, I see this *Vogue* shoot as one of the biggest and most surprising events that ever happened to me. And as usual, Larry was a part of it. It all began when one day, he asked me to make a particularly awkward phone call to get him out of an event he had agreed to attend. "Please make the call for me, Wendy. This is so damned uncomfortable," he practically begged. "Please do me this favor."

"Okay," I agreed, "I'll make the call, but it'll cost you."

"What will it cost me?" he asked.

"My first authentic Chanel handbag," I said.

When I was traveling the world as White House producer, I visited a shopping area in South Korea where I got a number of knockoff bags such as Gucci and Prada. They were gorgeous and looked authentic, but now I wanted the real thing.

"Done," Larry said, "it's a deal."

I made the call, got Larry out of his dreaded commitment, and he took me to Chanel on Rodeo Drive in Beverly Hills. I chose a gorgeous classic black bouclé handbag that cost him a lot. He feigned upset at the price tag and teased me like crazy. But now that he knew how much I love them, for each special occasion, Larry buys me a gorgeous handbag and he always includes a note that says, "Dear Wendy, F— you. Larry."

I've framed every F— you card he ever sent me, and I hang them in my closet with a piece of tape covering the four-letter word so my kids can't see it. Maybe when they're old enough, I'll decorate my bathroom with a load of F— you cards from Larry King, one of my dearest friends in all the world.

❖

OPPOSITES ATTRACT

As magnificent as Larry is on the air, he could never be his own producer. And I could never be on-the-air talent on a steady basis. It's all about teamwork, and as opposite as we are, Larry and I make a perfect team. I have often found that combining two opposite talents makes a successful and exciting end product. After all, if we were all the same, imagine how boring life could get.

When you take a good look at Larry and me, I'm sure no one would necessarily have chosen us as a match. Quite the opposite. We could not possibly be more different, but we share two things that cement our foundation for a successful business partnership: our sense of humor and our work ethic. We love to laugh and we love to do it right. And so, it's not as if we decided that we were so alike, we needed to work together. It was more like, we're so *different*, we need to work together. And we have been going strong ever since! I just can't imagine my life without Larry Zeiger.

Look at your own life and find people who are very different from you, but you still complement each other. Some of the best marriages are set up that way, so when you meet someone you might work with, your differences might be at the foundation of your success.

CHAPTER 13

The Love You Take Is Equal to the Love You Make

Certain stories become an integral part of our pop culture, partly for their shock value, and partly for the intrinsic lessons that we learn from them. Included in the short list of pop culture stunners we have covered on our show are the Scott Peterson trial, the JonBenét Ramsey tragedy, the homicide of Michael Jackson, and of course, the infamous and never-ending saga of OJ Simpson and the double murder case.

It was called the trial of the century for good reason. The effects of this nine-month-long public trial and OJ's subsequent acquittal affected the American lifestyle at its core as people sat in their living rooms and got to follow, step by step, the inner machinations of the US judicial system. There was the double murder, the Bronco car chase, the arrest, the stunning acquittal, the civil trial, and then, there was the aftermath years later, in which the ex-football trophy-winning hero landed in jail anyway, proving that karma is real and it *will* get you.

It was June 17, 1994, and I was in the control room in Washington, just like any other night. It was a little after 9 p.m., EST, and Larry was interviewing Cyndy Garvey, wife of baseball star and notorious womanizer Steve Garvey. She was on the show, however, not to talk about her husband, but rather to discuss OJ Simpson. It seemed that he was missing.

On June 13, four days earlier, Nicole Brown Simpson, OJ's ex-wife and mother of his children, and her friend Ronald Goldman had been found dead, lying in a bloodbath outside Nicole's condominium in West Los Angeles. OJ had been questioned and released, but he was still a person of interest. Now, Cyndy was talking about the fact that OJ was missing, when I caught sight of a white car on a highway on a monitor feed that was coming from Los Angeles.

I picked up a line to Atlanta and asked, "What's going on with that car?" pointing to the monitor directly in front of me. There was an image of a 1993 white Ford Bronco, slowly making its way down the Interstate 5 freeway. It was heading south (incidentally, the direction of Mexico), and a number of police cars were following the Bronco, driving slowly and keeping a controlled distance away.

"We think it's OJ Simpson," said a voice from the Atlanta control room.

Was OJ trying to make a getaway? It certainly looked like it as the Bronco exited the freeway suddenly, the police cars still on its tail, a good distance back. Then it drove along the on-ramp to the northbound Santa Ana freeway, changing direction and heading back toward Santa Ana.

We kept our eyes glued to the monitor and Larry began to follow it while he continued to interview Cyndy Garvey.

KING: Aren't you shocked by this?
GARVEY: Not a bit. Not a bit...A psychopath...is a person who leads their lives often doing acts without any sense

of remorse or feeling that maybe you and I would have. If I hurt someone, if I do something wrong, I'm saying I'm sorry until I'm blue in the face. Psychopaths tend to walk amongst us, and, because of their charm, maybe their added talent, and their acumen to garner public acclaim, they are given what's called celebrity license to misbehave. If I hear one more time how people are sorry for OJ Simpson, I don't know what I'm going to do. Why don't they show a picture of Nicole Brown and Ron Goldman? They have no options. They're taken out. They're slaughtered.

KING: Didn't you like OJ Simpson?

GARVEY: I have to tell you, I kind of figured out OJ and many people like OJ and Steve Garvey early on, because they treat everyone about the same in the public, then, when that camera, which I call the public eye, is off, you see the true person, if you're still around. Many times, I was still around.

KING: Cyndy...do you think OJ—and this would just be a layman's guess—may have taken his life?

GARVEY: I have two thoughts on this, Larry. I think men that beat on women and have a history of abuse are too cowardly to commit suicide. That could be one. You might think I'm coldhearted. I am not. I don't think he will commit suicide...I don't know what he did there that night, in front of Nicole's house. But, whatever came down there, it's pretty heavily weighted that he was involved.

While the slow-speed chase continued, producer, CNN vice president, and friend Rick Davis brought a copy of an LA map onto our DC set so Larry could track where the SUV was heading. We were getting affiliate reports that Simpson's friend A. C. Cowlings was driving. It was his Bronco, in fact, and OJ was holding a gun to his own head.

This is the 911 call from Al Cowlings:

911 DISPATCHER: 911, what are you reporting?

COWLINGS: This is A.C. I have OJ in the car, OK.

DISPATCHER: OK, where are you?

COWLINGS: I'm coming up the 5 freeway.

DISPATCHER: OK.

COWLINGS: Right now, we're OK, but you've got to tell the police to just back off. He's still alive but he's got a gun to his head.

DISPATCHER: OK, hold on a minute…

COWLINGS: He just wants to see his mother. Let me get to the house [unintelligible] right now is OK, Officer. Everything is OK. He wants me to get him to see his mom. He wants to get to his house.

911 DISPATCHER: OK.

COWLINGS: All I—that's all we ask. He's got a gun to his head.

The Bronco finally pulled up in front of OJ's house and he exited the car where the police were waiting to handcuff and arrest him. As we watched the onset of the unfolding of a true American tragedy, how could we ever know how huge it would become?

The first indication came when the network asked us to stay on the air after our usual sixty minutes. We'd been following the Bronco chase and it was another two hours before I drove home, so mentally exhausted I almost fell asleep on the road. But I was also disturbed. OJ had been caught trying to flee with money and his passport. He had held a gun to his own head, and then he was arrested and booked. The idea that OJ Simpson, a celebrated American football hero, sportscaster, and actor, could be under suspicion for two brutal murders was impossible to believe. Doubly disturbing was the fact that this family man with so much talent and so many opportunities could very well be guilty.

During the months leading up to the trial, in which the prosecutors announced they would seek a life sentence with no possibility of parole rather than the death penalty, the world was watching. On January 23, 1995, with OJ languishing in jail, the trial began with opening statements by the prosecution and the defense. Since the judge had granted television privileges throughout the entire trial, an unprecedented decision, the networks were on high alert at all times.

As Larry's producer, this was the first time I was faced with covering the same topic night after night. But while it was grueling in its own right, I found it easier than I had expected. Each time a friend said, "You must be so busy with the OJ trial," I smiled to myself. They had no idea what "busy" really was. Try being a White House producer. Imagine falling asleep at night and being awakened three hours later with a call that you have to go to the White House right then. That kind of thing was business as usual back then. I could be on vacation, at a wedding, at the gym, or in bed with ice packs on my face after dental surgery, and the call inevitably came. I was in all of these positions at different times when I was roused in the middle of the night and ended up outside in the dark, hailing a cab to the White House. Or worse, at a moment's notice, I would find myself half asleep, getting on a plane to God only knew where. It was no wonder I had come to hate flying so much.

A moment on March 6, 1991, stands out in my mind. I had worked all day and I was at the gym exercising when my pager went off. I called in to find that President Bush was going to address the nation and I needed to go directly to the

White House. My hair was wet, I had on my pink sweats, and I rushed over to the White House. I still have a picture on my wall of a group of us standing in the Oval Office with George H. W. Bush, with me still in my gym clothes.

Years earlier, in 1983, when the Beirut bombing occurred, 241 service members were killed, including 220 Marines. I'd just had four wisdom teeth extracted and I was in bed doped up with cold packs on my face, when the news of the bombing hit the airwaves. I dragged myself out of bed and made my way to the White House, looking like someone had hit me in the face repeatedly since my cheeks were swollen, I was in a lot of pain, and my voice wasn't working very well.

Dean Reynolds, the first person I saw, was mortified when he looked at me, his producer. "Why the hell are you here?" he asked me. "You look terrible."

Dean and I had seen each other at our worst. Back in 1983, I had been Dean's White House producer when he was CNN White House correspondent and he had been demonstrating some irritable behavior. When I got a call that day that my father had had a stroke, Dean met me outside the White House to talk. "I've been a little tough on you lately," he said. "I just wanted you to know that my dad is sick, too, and I haven't told anybody. I've been under a lot of pressure and I'm really sorry."

My father was in the hospital recovering from the stroke when I had a bad feeling some days later. I picked up the phone in the White House where I was working and called my father's hospital room. My mom answered and said in a shaky voice, "Dad just died." He was sixty-eight, which we considered old at the time.

I hung up the phone and before I could figure out what to do next, Dean called the CNN bureau and said, "Wendy's dad just died. I want to leave the White House and take her home."

A producer said, "But your story will be late."

Dean said quite calmly, "I just told you that Wendy's father died. I'm taking her home right now."

He drove me home, and later that day I got a flight back home to Jackson, Michigan, to attend the funeral and be with my mom and my sisters. Ironically, Dean's father, Frank, died a few days later. When I got back to Washington a little bit earlier than planned so I could attend the Reynolds wake, Dean was very glad to see me. "I can't believe you made it back, Wendy," he said. "Thank you so much for being here."

I stared at Dean and then at the casket. "Dean," I said, "we got the exact same casket for my father." That was kind of eerie. Contrary to my father's modest funeral service, however, Frank Reynolds's funeral was a huge affair.

Back to the present, as my face was swollen almost beyond recognition. I mumbled an answer to Dean, unable to speak clearly, and I ordered clear soup for lunch because I couldn't eat. A reporter, I don't recall who, called me Face that day, and the name stuck. We remained in the newsroom until someone announced that it was all over and we could go home. Especially Face. They wanted me out of there and I don't blame them.

With my new job, however, all that was over. I figured it would be easier than what I had just come from, and it was, even when I woke up in the morning with no idea who or what would be on the show that evening. Now, with the OJ debacle, it was a lot easier because that same story went on and on. But it had its own difficulty level as well. It's like learning to play golf. When you first swing a club and you manage to hit the ball, you think, *Hey, this isn't so hard.* But the more you learn about golf—stand just so, concentrate, hold the club a certain way, and all the rest of it—the more complicated it becomes. The same was true with my new job. But with OJ, at least I had a clear direction.

Each morning when I got up during the trial, I already knew where I was headed and with whom we needed to speak. I based it on what happened yesterday during the trial, and what was scheduled for today. I once heard Larry say, "I do infotainment," and I was incredibly turned off. But during the trial, I understood what he meant. The whole idea is that people have to *want* to watch us. In my opinion, the extraordinary length of this trial marked the beginning of reality television, which offers the audience real information that is entertaining. The OJ trial fit that description to a tee since each evening, reality met entertainment on our show. For the first time, the public at large was watching a criminal trial from start to finish during the daytime. Then, at night on *Larry King Live*, we would discuss the threefold topics that were triggered: our judicial system, domestic abuse, and racial prejudice.

We booked some terrific guests for the show who continually reported on the ongoing trial, including slow-talking cowboy defense lawyer Gerry Spence, a judge who looked particularly unassuming, and a couple of pundits. Each day, my staff would contact the trial principals to try to get interviews, but booking them was unreliable because so many venues were vying for them. We got Kato Kaelin (whom I took to a restaurant in Washington one night and everyone was all over him), OJ's maid Rosa Lopez, who made a big splash during the trial, and once in a while we got one of Simpson's primary defense attorneys. But we relied on our loyal panel who appeared most nights to cover what had occurred that day and to discuss what it all meant and where it appeared to be heading. People responded to our core group, and I would duplicate that format when future stories became extended for weeks or months on end.

We were at the bureau in Washington when Larry and I heard that F. Lee Bailey (of Patty Hearst kidnapping fame) was going to be part of the defense team that had been nicknamed the "dream team." It consisted of Johnnie Cochran, Robert Shapiro, and now, F. Lee Bailey was joining the ranks.

"Larry," I said, "you know Lee. He's a good old friend of yours. Why don't you give him a call and see if he'll come on the show tonight?"

"I don't have his phone number," Larry said.

I called Miami information to discover that Lee Bailey's phone number was unlisted. When I told Larry I couldn't get his number, he picked up the phone himself and called information in Miami.

"Can I help you?" said the operator.

"Hi, there," said Larry in his raspy New York accent. "Larry King here. What's your name?"

"Laurie," she said. She knew it was really Larry because no one else has a voice that remotely sounds like his.

"Well, Laurie," Larry went on, "here's how you can help me. F. Lee Bailey is a good friend of mine and I need to talk to him. But his phone number is unlisted. Laurie, can you please give me his number?"

She did it. In the next moment, Larry was talking to F. Lee Bailey. "Hey," Larry said, "how are you going to do this? OJ doesn't have a prayer."

"Doesn't have a prayer?" repeated Bailey. "He was set up. This is a racial situation. It's gonna be a piece of cake. He'll be fine."

F. Lee Bailey called in to our show that night. By now, we had become so involved with this trial, we were considered OJ

Central, and Larry and I were traveling between LA and Washington regularly. For example, during a midmorning break in court a few days later, Larry and I were ushered toward the back of the courtroom, down the hall, and into Judge Ito's chambers. Larry and the judge chatted, Ito seemed to be really enjoying himself, and I could hardly believe I was sitting opposite the most controversial judge in the country. He became so well known, by the way, that this many years later, there is no name plaque outside his office because people keep stealing it, so he stopped replacing it.

The recess had gone long over the proposed fifteen minutes—almost forty minutes—when Larry said, "Don't you have to get back to work?"

Judge Ito stood reluctantly, it seemed, and said his good-byes. Larry stood, too, but to my dismay, he followed the judge through the rear door into the well of the courtroom. He was going the wrong way. I tried to guide him in the opposite direction, but when OJ spotted him, he yelled out, "Larry!" He stood to shake Larry's hand until the bailiffs quickly returned OJ to his seat. "Thanks for being so fair," OJ called out. I cringed. All we needed was for the courtroom to think we were being partial. I just had to get Larry out of there.

Before I could guide him away, however, Robert Shapiro stood and gave Larry a bear hug. Next, Larry shook hands with F. Lee Bailey. I groaned when Suzanne Childs, part of the prosecution team, rushed to Larry's side and led him over to the prosecution table. "I watch you all the time," Marcia Clark said.

I reached for a door, any door, to get Larry the hell out of there and into another room when a bailiff said to me, "That's the door to the lockup. Most people try to stay out of there."

Jeffrey Toobin, reporter, senior analyst for CNN, and writer for *The New Yorker*, wrote a definitive book in 1996 called *The Run of His Life: The People v. O. J. Simpson*. Toobin says:

> By far the most important experience for me came on Monday night, July 18, when I traveled to Washington to be the first guest on that night's *Larry King Live*. King would come to occupy an unusual niche in the Simpson case. By the time of the trial, King had decided to devote the bulk of his program to the case, and he even moved his base of operations to Los Angeles for long periods. I eventually made several dozen appearances on the show, and King's CNN studio on Sunset Boulevard came to resemble a sort of Hyde Park Corner for the Simpson case. On any given day that I appeared, I was likely to find a defense lawyer, an expert witness, or some other witness or peripheral figure lingering in the makeup room. For me, a reporter who was actually covering the case, the visits amounted to priceless opportunities to chat with these people in a quiet and intimate setting. So many people involved with the case developed relationships with King that he became a quasi-participant himself.

I finally got Larry away and I could exhale. When I look back now, I believe that OJ did for domestic abuse what Rock Hudson did for AIDS by putting it on the map with a face and a real-life situation. And we at the *Larry King Live* show helped that along. How horrific was it that a beautiful and educated woman like Nicole Brown was so frightened of her ex-husband that she had pictures of her beaten, swollen face locked away in a safety deposit box, just in case? And still she got murdered.

Larry and I had just arrived at the Beverly Wilshire Hotel on

October 2. Larry was working out and I was at the bar, meeting with a source who was close to Nicole, when I glanced up at the TV screen. The OJ jury had reached a verdict. *What? How could that be?* I thought. They had only deliberated for four hours after the lengthiest trial anyone could remember, and they were ready to read the verdict in court the next morning. What did it mean?

I left the bar and rushed into the gym area to tell Larry they had reached a verdict, which they would read in the morning. He was as shocked as I was. That evening, I went to dinner with Jo-Ellen Demetrius, a jury selection consultant who had helped the defense team choose jurors who might be sympathetic to OJ. She had been rooting for an acquittal and she was really down in the dumps. "This is not good for us," she said. "They're probably going to bring in a guilty verdict because it came so fast. I feel sick to my stomach."

I awakened in anxious anticipation the next morning, believing that this was OJ's last day of freedom. At about 9 a.m., I called Larry and said, "I need to come to your room and watch the verdict with you." I gave him no choice, I just hung up the phone and ran over to his room. But I was so nervous while we watched, I suddenly blurted out, "Larry, can we hold hands?"

Larry stared at me. "Huh, why?" he said.

"I don't know why," I answered, "I just need to hold your hand."

I grabbed his hand, squeezed hard, and held my breath.

"Not guilty," the foreman said.

I dropped Larry's hand and said nothing. All I could think was: *Where is the karma? Is he getting away with double murder?*

I was in utter disbelief when several of my colleagues and I attended a celebratory party that was given by OJ's group at a bar that night. We went to observe and there was much patting on backs and celebratory toasts. When we went on the air the next night, Larry interviewed Johnnie Cochran to discuss his victory. But no one was more stunned than I when the show was nearly over and a screener told me that OJ, himself, was calling in. He wanted to talk to Larry.

We have an 800 number for the general public to call in with questions or comments, and they may or may not get on the air. But we also have an "invited caller" number system where we ask an invited guest to join us on the phone. They are given a password along with a private number so we can separate a real caller from an impostor.

"Are you sure it's really him?" I asked.

"He called on the right number and gave us the password."

It was OJ. I was about to put him on when a producer from Atlanta called me to say hurriedly, "Wendy, Larry has to stop exactly at ten. We have a great taped show all about OJ Simpson."

"Well," I answered, "I have him live on the phone." OJ live on the phone or a taped show about him? There was no decision to make as we put OJ on. Here is an excerpt from that call:

KING: We're back on *Larry King Live*…For the benefit of our radio listeners, we will be extending this program… because with us on the phone now is OJ Simpson. How are you?

VOICE OF SIMPSON: I am doing fine. I want to thank you a lot, because so many of my friends told me that you have been fair in hosting your show and bringing the points of view from both sides…most of all, I want to thank that man, Mr.

Johnnie Cochran, for believing from the beginning, listening, and putting his heart and soul on the line to send me home and spend time with my kids.

 . . . I've been watching your show, and I don't really have a lot to say now. Pretty soon I will have enough to say to everybody and hopefully answer everyone's questions, but one of your callers . . . asked the question about a "shadowy figure . . . running down the driveway and across the lawn and into the front door." That's one of the problems I am having today, with people who have followed this trial, they have not listened to the evidence . . . Throughout this case, it's been this misrepresentation time and time again. People come home from work and they hear the pundits elaborating on these misrepresentations. Listen to what the witness says, listen to what their testimony is, and not what Marcia Clark told you. And not what Darden told you . . . Fortunately for me, the jury listened to what the witnesses said, and not Marcia Clark's or Darden's or anyone else's rendition of what they said.

KING: OJ, how would you describe yourself, as relieved, angry, what?

VOICE OF SIMPSON: A little bit of everything. I think my basic anger, and this is the last thing I am going to say before I leave, my basic anger is these misconceptions . . . People I've heard that followed the case, heard experts say this was the testimony today . . . and that wasn't the testimony today. There were so many times I went back to my cell and I watched TV, I go to my attorney room, I talk to my attorneys and some witnesses, and we say, "Were these experts looking at the same . . . were they in the same courtroom that we were in today? Did they hear the testimony today?" Because what they were reporting on the news . . .

on these various shows, was not what the witnesses were saying. And, once again, that lady who called in, look at the testimony. Marcia Clark told you that...

KING: A couple of quick things, and I will let you go.

VOICE OF SIMPSON: No, I've got to go.

KING: All right, can you just tell—

VOICE OF SIMPSON: I'm sorry, I've really got to go.

KING: What was it like with the kids today?

VOICE OF SIMPSON: Thank you.

KING: What was it like with the kids?

VOICE OF SIMPSON: It's been—it's been great. It's been great. Thank you. Soon—and I appreciate what—how fair you have been.

KING: Thank you. And—

VOICE OF SIMPSON: Thank you.

Getting that call was a terrific coup for us, but now all the networks were vying for the "money interview"—the first live television interview with OJ following the verdict. After much wheeling and dealing, Larry and I lost the big interview to Katie Couric and Tom Brokaw at NBC. It was a huge disappointment, but I called Katie to congratulate her. Larry and I both got on the phone and I told Katie how proud I was of her. Larry congratulated her as well, since this truly was a great "get." Katie would be flying from New York to LA for the interview.

But overnight, everything changed. Much of the television viewing audience were incensed that any network would carry this interview. People wanted to know how NBC could dare to put this man on their network, a pariah who they thought had gotten away with double murder. The protests got so loud, NBC canceled the show altogether. In essence, this interview that we had all fought so hard to get, disappeared in a couple of hours. The only positive outcome was that Katie had all of her congratulatory flowers sent to my hotel room since her trip was canceled!

In pondering how anyone could do what OJ did, I can only turn to the definition of a sociopath. Sociopaths, a psychological title under which this man clearly falls, have selective memories and believe only what they want to believe. OJ must have believed that he was justified in what he did, or perhaps he has no memory of it at all. I would tend to go with the justification explanation.

Either way, though, OJ sits in jail right now, not for the murders of his wife and her friend, but rather for an armed kidnapping in Las Vegas in October 2008. It seems that however much we try to be who we are not, or as much as we try to "get away with murder," we eventually seek our own level.

I guess OJ was destined to go to jail, for one reason or another. I can think of two really good reasons, offhand. Today, he is sentenced to thirty-three years behind bars, with eligibility for parole after less than a third of that term. This is one of those times in life that can only be described by one word: "karma." And OJ is living his.

❖

THE LOVE YOU TAKE IS EQUAL TO THE LOVE YOU MAKE

More and more people are looking within these days to find a mind/body/spirit kind of spirituality. This means living a life in which you feel good about yourself, and the logical way to do this is to put into life what you would like to get from it. This is karma as I understand it, or the Golden Rule, where you do unto others as you would have them do unto you.

When someone hurts you, it's a normal human reaction to think, *I want them to feel the same pain I'm feeling. They don't deserve happiness.* But contrary to how you might feel, the best thing you can do for yourself is to forgive that person. If you don't, the anger festers inside of you and permeates your life. On the other hand, when you release it, it leaves your system and you can heal your heart and walk away from the misery. In this way, forgiveness is for *you*, not for the person you are trying to forgive. Doesn't that make forgiving seem a little more palatable?

When you have been disappointed by someone and wish them harm, if you take a good look at that person, you will see that they are already suffering with no help from you. Look at the person who has upset you and ask yourself the following questions:

- Is she happy?
- Would you like to be him?
- Do you think she's living a good life?
- Do you think your life is healthier than his?

If you really look at someone who hurt you, you probably don't want to be connected to him. The more you can put yourself in a bright light and feel good about yourself and let your anger go, the more you release negative connections. In fact, if you can't or won't forgive someone, no matter what they did, it's like taking poison and wishing the other person would die. Not too smart.

I have developed a habit of forgiving people first thing in the morning when I wake up. It would be beneficial for you to make a list of those whom you need to forgive because forgiveness is not a one-time thing. It is not something you aspire to, reach, and then consider it done. Forgiveness, just like faith, needs to be renewed each and every day.

It's like a 12-step program. You take it one day at a time. You need to forgive that person today and then do it again tomorrow. Someone once told me that the word "forgive" means thank you "for giving" me this experience. It's all about learning who you are and how you want to live your life. When I found a way to forgive, something I do every day, people asked me why I looked so well. It was because I was learning to forgive, gradually and consistently.

When you hold a grudge, you are actually holding on to a memory. It is no longer a tangible thing, but rather a thought that keeps repeating itself over and over in your mind. It is not a book or a tree or any other object. It is a memory, and each time you go there, you will feel the sadness all over again. You have to get strong enough to remind yourself, "I'm feeling the effects of a memory. It isn't real. I don't have to go here again. It's time to move on."

My dear friend JZ Knight (who channels an entity called Ramtha) says we become addicted to our emotions. If the emotions are sadness and pain, we go there for comfort and we feel all of our sadness and pain. But if we are addicted to feeling calm and happy, well, that's a much better place to be.

So don't be concerned if you feel forgiveness one day and have trouble with it the next. There will be times when you fall back into the negativity, but you can keep reminding yourself to forgive, not for the other person but for yourself. It may take prayer, meditation, or a one-on-one meeting. Whatever it takes, it's worth it to clear your own heart and soul.

CHAPTER 14

Read People Like You'd Read a Roadmap

On December 24, 2002, a twenty-seven-year-old woman named Laci Peterson went missing from her home in Modesto, California. The fact that she was eight months pregnant only added to the urgency of finding her. On the day after Christmas, police searched the home that she shared with her husband, Scott, who had supposedly been out on his boat on Christmas Eve, fishing. The story unfolded over the next several months and on April 13, 2003, the remains of a male infant were discovered on the shoreline of the San Francisco Bay.

The next day, all hopes of finding Laci alive were dashed when a decapitated female body washed up on the shore. Soon afterward, the remains of both mother and child were positively identified as Laci Peterson and Conner, her unborn son. When Scott Peterson was arrested in San Diego as the prime suspect for what they were calling a double murder, the case was splashed all over the media. Scott's disinterest in helping the police and his flat emotional affect following the discoveries of the bodies contributed to a heavy pall of suspicion hanging over him.

The fact that, after the murders, he was found with multiple credit cards belonging to family members and enough cash and supplies for a long getaway only added to the suspicion, as did dyeing his hair and goatee blond. Then, with the discovery of a major extramarital affair, Scott seemed to be displaying the behavior of a sociopath and the media erupted into a feeding frenzy.

At *Larry King Live*, we were the first to grab the story and run with what I thought was the most gripping murder case since the OJ Simpson double murder trial about eight years prior. But as compelling as the ins and outs of the OJ trial were, in many ways, I found the Scott Peterson case even more peculiar and confounding.

There were several reasons for that. While OJ Simpson was an aggressive sports jock, a football star with a powerful attitude and body to match, Scott Peterson was a soft-spoken, unassuming gentleman, a cute guy, a fertilizer salesman who liked fishing and was everybody's darling. While OJ boasted winning the Heisman Trophy and being touted around the world as a champion, Scott Peterson was a regular kid who went to a public school in a small town in California, the same school my kids attended, where he smiled pleasantly and opened doors for older women. In fact, when he and Laci wed, she was considered to have married up in the social world. They had a nice life, they were pregnant, the grandparents all around were happy, and Scott could not have appeared more clean-cut and polite. Too bad no one guessed what evil was brewing under all that grooming, manners, and courteous behavior.

The Peterson case made compelling television for many of the reasons listed above, but something else was driving me in a personal way toward this case at this particular time. I was in the painful process of a divorce and I needed a diversion that was compelling enough to hold my attention. I turned to the weirdness of the Scott Peterson case, initially relieved to have something dramatic in which to bury myself. But as time went on and more of the facts came to light in this odd case, it took on a life of its own, and I was not the only one who couldn't get enough. The one thing that everyone agreed upon was that Scott Peterson looked like the most clean-cut, well-groomed murder suspect anyone had ever seen.

We did many shows during this time, discussing Scott Peterson's affair with massage therapist Amber Frey, and who on earth could have killed lovely, smiling Laci, who was nearly nine months pregnant? People thought Scott had acted strangely after the killings, they became aware of his comings and goings, and everyone wanted to put in their two cents. The panel discussions on our show were thoughtful and informative as we turned to experts in the field of criminal law. I booked a number of experts who weighed in on the mystery, which was how attorney Mark Geragos ended up being on our show a number of times before he became Scott Peterson's defense attorney.

The consensus opinion among our experts and callers was that Scott Peterson was probably guilty, no matter how handsome he looked. At that time, even Mark didn't have anything substantial to say in Scott Peterson's favor. This is an excerpt from a conversation on our show on April 18, 2003, between Larry and Mark.

KING: Mark Geragos, is this case kind of plea-bargainable, or will they not go for that?

GERAGOS: I can't imagine...unless something comes up that I'm not aware of, that any prosecutor's going to plea bargain this. This case, from a prosecution's standpoint...

KING: Is it a slam dunk?

GERAGOS: ...even though it's a circumstantial evidence case, the most damning piece of circumstantial evidence comes out of his own mouth and his own hands, when he hands the police that receipt from the very location where two miles away, she's found. I mean, that is just a devastating thing. If you believe that he's the one who, for whatever reason, got into it with her, killed her, put her in a tarp, put her in the boat, did all of that...they'll try him [for first degree murder] with special circumstances. I'll be shocked if they don't.

...as I've said, it's a damning, circumstantial case—the man is a sociopath if he did this crime. I mean, there's no other way to put it. This is his wife, his unborn baby boy. If he's the one who took the two of them up there and put concrete around them and threw them into the ocean and concocted this story and went out onto Diane Sawyer and gave that impassioned plea with the tears—I mean, that's not somebody that generally you're going to want to give a manslaughter [charge]...There's apparently information on the tides and currents on his computer when they did the search, that is some pretty compelling evidence.

Mark's statements on our show that night apparently angered Scott's parents so much, they called him afterward to say they basically believed their innocent son was being convicted and sentenced on the air before he even went to trial. They asked Mark how he dared do such a thing, adding that it was people like him who got innocent and good people like their son wrongly arrested and convicted.

The upshot of the phone call was that Mark paid a visit to the Petersons' home at their request. "I was completely taken by Jackie, Scott's mom," Mark told me. "She's really an incredible woman. I remember when she came in, she was wearing an oxygen tank. When I asked her what was the matter, she said, 'I've had this lung condition that they say is terminal.'"

"How long do they give you?" he had asked, genuinely concerned.

"The doctors give me two years," she had answered, "so every two years, I change doctors."

"With an attitude like that," Mark added, "how could I not love her?"

The next thing we knew, Mark had agreed to visit Scott in jail, with the intention of possibly representing him. "I just felt like it was the right thing to do," Mark said. "When you become a defense attorney, you take an oath, just like a doctor takes the Hippocratic Oath, to help your clients. We are not supposed to refuse a client because public opinion has denigrated him. I had to at least meet him and see who he was."

On April 30, 2002, Mark appeared on our show again.

KING: Where do we stand with you and the Petersons?
GERAGOS: I've met with them. I've talked to Scott, and I'm going to make a decision...very shortly. I've met with the parents on a couple of occasions. They've called me up, and I've talked to them, and we've had some in-depth discussions. And I can tell you that Scott's mother especially is a very compelling advocate for her son. I've met with Scott, and I've talked with the public defenders. I was up in Modesto yesterday. And I'm going to sleep on it and make a decision.
KING: What can you give us? Just a couple things, Mark. Can you give us what are the balancing points, what's for, what's against?

GERAGOS: I think he's already universally been convicted in the court of public opinion. I don't think there's anybody that you can talk to that doesn't just assume his guilt, and… that's a part of what presents a challenge…Part of why people go into criminal defense is to defend the underdog and to try to make it a truly adversarial system. And that is definitely intriguing in this case.

KING: So what's on the downside?

GERAGOS: The downside is that it's a monumental undertaking, in terms of time, number one, and effort, and, as well, the other clients and the impact to the other lawyers in my practice. There are other people that I have to think about, and I suppose that's weighed by the fact that—here's somebody who is truly up against it, in terms of public opinion, if you will. And there's a whole lot of factors, others that I won't even get into, at least on the air.

KING: Knowing you, Mark, would you say you're leaning toward helping him?

GERAGOS: Yes, I would definitely say I'm leaning toward helping him.

On May 1, 2003, Nancy Grace, our guest host that night, took an enraged phone call from Lee Peterson, Scott's father.

PETERSON: You are speculating on these facts as much as I am.

GRACE: (Peterson continues, but Grace talks over his comments) And you are believing what your son is telling you."

PETERSON: Please don't interrupt me. You've had your say here for months and you've crucified my son on national media. And he's a wonderful man. You have no idea of his background and what a wonderful son and wonderful man he is. You have no knowledge of that and you sit there as a judge and jury, I guess, you're convicting him on national media. And you should absolutely be ashamed of that.

GRACE: I think who should be ashamed of themselves is who-ever is responsible for the death of Laci Peterson. And lashing out at me, I completely understand where you are coming from. I'm simply stating what has been leaked or what has been put in formal documents. If you find them disturbing, I suggest you ask your son about some of them, sir.

PETERSON: There you go, Nancy, look at this look on Nancy's face. You absolutely hate my son. I don't know what it is. (Grace begins speaking again) Does he remind you of someone?

GRACE: No, no I don't hate your son. But I hate what happened to Laci.

Mark called me at home during that time to discuss whether he should represent Scott. Since our show was focused so intently on the case, Mark wanted my opinion as to whether he should take this high-profile case with a suspect who looked like your favorite neighbor on the block. "What do you think, Wendy?" he asked me.

"I don't think you should do it," I said. I just couldn't see this working in Mark's favor. My son, Walker, who was four at the time, agreed. He grabbed the phone and in his baby voice, he chimed in with, "Don't do it, Mark. Don't do it."

This article came out in *People* magazine on May 19, 2003:

Curiously, this is the same Mark Geragos who, days before, while analyzing Peterson's prospects on a TV talk show, had concluded that the accused didn't have much of a chance. In the interview he declared that the circumstantial

evidence—including the fact that Peterson had been having an affair, that the bodies washed up near where he
said he had gone fishing and that he had tide charts of the
area—was almost "overwhelming." "You combine all that
together," said Geragos, 45, "there's a lot of guys sitting in
state prison on a lot less evidence."

Now the lawyer says that a visit with Peterson's mother,
Jackie, changed his mind. "I heard things that I had never
heard before that had not been out in the press," says
Geragos. Among his colleagues, Geragos is considered
especially adept at deflecting negative p.r., which should
come in handy with Peterson, given that polls show a large
majority of those surveyed believe he is guilty. One of the
first things that Geragos did was mount a vigorous effort
to make sure that the arrest and search warrants remained
sealed, thus preventing any more prejudicial information
from leaking out. Says Steven Cron, a criminal-defense
lawyer in L.A.: "Peterson needs someone like Mark, who
knows how to deal with the media."

On April 21, 2003, Scott Peterson was charged in Stanis-
laus County Superior Court before Judge Nancy Ashley with
two felony counts of murder with premeditation and special
circumstances. He pleaded not guilty, and Mark took the case
on May 2, 2003, but he also took a lot of heat for agreeing to
defend Scott.

"People say I took it for the publicity," Mark says. "That, I
find to be ironic, because we were instantly put under a gag
order so I couldn't say anything. I could have literally had any
one of three different networks write me a very large check to
be an exclusive commentator the day before. So it wasn't like I
needed the aggravation of a death penalty trial in that firestorm

to get publicity and be on TV. In fact, it was the opposite. It took me off TV."

Mark accepted the case, he obeyed the gag order and stopped appearing on our show. Once they did opening arguments on June 1, 2004, I traveled to San Mateo a number of times and sat in on this extraordinary trial. I must have been there about twenty-five days in all and I was riveted. I took a great liking to Jackie Peterson, just like Mark had, and I invited her and her daughter-in-law to my home for lunch since they lived close by. When a grieving Jackie Peterson left my house, oxygen tank in tow, my heart went out to this woman who had lost everything—her son, her daughter-in-law, and her grandson to be. At the same time, she truly loved her son, worried about his health, and considered him incapable of murder. This was when I understood how Scott's actions had not only destroyed his wife and son. They had destroyed his entire family and would continue to do so.

Perhaps the most remarkable part of the trial was seeing Scott himself sitting there quietly, day after day, looking like a sweet man, while the truth about him was making itself known. In the courtroom, he was not allowed to talk to his parents, but I saw him give his mother a nod and a smile when she walked in each day. He was such a good-looking guy and he was nice to his mother. *What the hell was going on?* was all I could think. I remembered Jackie had told me she was worried that Scott was not getting the proper nutrition. "He isn't getting any fruit in jail," she told me, clearly distressed.

She was right. Throughout the course of the trial, I watched Scott's coloring change from a normal skin tone to a gray pallor, caused by lack of good food, fresh air, and sunshine. And still, he never looked like someone capable of ruining the lives of everyone around him by murdering his pregnant wife.

Time, however, was the great equalizer, as the truth began to emerge in this grisly ordeal that no one wanted to believe had happened. After all, the evidence the district attorney was presenting against Scott was circumstantial. In the OJ case, there had been solid, physical evidence, like a glove, blood, and DNA. With Scott, on the other hand, no matter how much we believed he had done this terrible thing, there was no DNA, he had pasted a photo of Laci on the wall of his jail cell, and no physical evidence ever emerged. To this day, while Scott maintains his innocence, I have no idea *how* he did it. And neither does anyone else. For this reason alone, I thought at the time that Geragos might win his case.

On November 13, 2004, the principals were called to the courthouse in San Mateo to hear the verdict. But Mark Geragos was in Los Angeles. "The jury had been out for several days," explains Mark. "I lived in LA and the case was up north, in Redwood City in San Mateo, a good three to four hundred miles from home. I got accustomed to shuttling back and forth, but most of the time, I just stayed in San Mateo. On this particular Wednesday, a couple of jurors had gotten into a fight and the judge had replaced a juror. That meant that the new juror would need to get briefed on what had come before, which meant they would virtually be starting deliberations all over again.

"I figured there was no way there could be a verdict until the following week since the next day, Thursday, was a court holiday," recalls Mark. "All they had was Friday, and it would take that long to get the new juror up to speed. I approached the judge. 'With your permission, your honor,' I said, 'I'd like to go to Los Angeles and do a hearing on Friday, if that's okay with you.'"

"I just put in a new juror," the judge said, "and they can't possibly come to a verdict on Friday. Just be back here on Monday."

"I left my associate Pat Harris up there," says Mark, "just in case and I headed south to Los Angeles. Pat had been there with me for three months, now, and he had been present every day at court, so he was completely up-to-date and I felt secure."

No one was more surprised than Mark when the jury came to their verdict on that very Friday. When Mark heard about it in Los Angeles, there was no way he could scramble around and get on a plane in time. The fact that close to five thousand people had turned up in the street in San Mateo when they heard that the verdict was in only made it more impossible for Mark to get to the courthouse, which was completely surrounded.

"I watched the guilty verdict on television," Mark said, "and I couldn't believe the way bystanders were screaming for blood and hurling things at Scott's mom, Jackie. It reminded me of a Jim Crow trial."

When I heard that a verdict had been reached, I called Mark immediately. He was terribly upset. He truly had believed the jury would hang, because all the evidence had been circumstantial. "There were two jurors I call 'stealth jurors,'" he said, "because they had an agenda against Scott and lied to get on the jury. We would never turn them around, and it was pretty apparent by the fifth day of deliberations that the jury was hung. But the judge refused to call a mistrial. Instead, he removed the foreperson, which was a disaster for the defense. On top of that, two other jurors were removed for fighting. In my experience, when you have a struggling jury with a presumption of guilt, you basically engineer a guilty verdict by removing jurors. I thought it was unfair and just awful."

Mark made his peace by realizing he had represented the

underdog as best he could, which was part of the reason he was an attorney in the first place. When a panel discussed the outcome of the trial on *Larry King Live*, I asked criminal attorney Michael Cardoza, "How did this happen? How could this cute-looking guy have killed his own wife?"

Michael's answer chilled me to the bone. "With a sociopath like Scott," he said, "killing Laci was like killing a moth. It held no more significance for him. Sociopaths feel that nothing is their fault, they are able to justify everything, and they have no remorse and basically no feelings whatsoever."

So that was why Scott looked so cool and collected. Maybe he really believed he was innocent. But I wondered why Laci had chosen a husband who was incapable of real feelings. Spouses lie to each other from time to time, but what woman would ever think that the very man who impregnated her would kill her and his own unborn child?

A month following the verdict, the jury sentenced Scott to death by lethal injection. He now lives on death row in San Quentin Prison, where after a requisite number of appeals, they will eventually end his life.

Larry did a show at San Quentin after Scott had been placed on death row there. Our show was about a group of men who had made a significant enough mistake in their lives to be sentenced to prison for life without the possibility of parole. We were interested in their stories and it made a very provocative show. But when he inquired about Scott, Larry was not allowed to visit him since no one can visit the death row building. The other prisoners told us that death row inmates were treated like animals, as they were chained and shackled before they could go anywhere in the building. What a life for a guy like Scott who looks like anybody's older brother, next-door neighbor, or kind uncle.

While I have absolutely no doubt about Scott's guilt, I still feel uncomfortable about his being sentenced to death because there was no real evidence and so many questions remain unanswered. No one saw him making the weights that held Laci underwater, no one knows where he killed her, and no one knows how he got her body into the truck and, subsequently, into the bay. But he was found guilty, despite his looks, the things he said, and his constant claims of innocence. It took some time, but his character revealed itself like a roadmap, and now we all know who he is.

Perhaps the final irony is that Scott's San Quentin jail cell overlooks San Francisco Bay where he dumped his wife's pregnant body. Now, he has all the time in the world up to the day that he dies to decide whether or not it was worth it.

❖

READ PEOPLE LIKE YOU'D READ A ROADMAP

You can cover up for people and sugarcoat things they say and do, or you can look past the outer trappings to see someone's true character. I suggest you keep your antenna up so you won't end up missing the signs that you are facing someone with no integrity.

If you're the type of person who likes to see others through rose-colored glasses, ask yourself these questions about a potential friend, business partner, or romantic partner:

- Does he talk about himself all the time?
- Is she concerned about you?
- Is he loud and intrusive?

- Did you catch her in a lie?
- Is he controlling?
- Does she have a temper?
- Is he a liar?
- Does she say one thing and do another?

The answers to these questions should clue you in about someone's character. Don't make up excuses for another person, such as, "Oh, she's having a bad day." Most likely, she was like this yesterday and the day before. It's all out there to be seen. All you have to do is open your eyes, follow the roadmap, and learn the truth about someone's character. The signs are always there. In hindsight, ask Amber Frey, Scott Peterson's lover, who was duped by him. I bet she can come up with a ton of signs she overlooked when she was smitten with a bad guy.

This is where you have to really hone your intuition. It's all about how someone else makes you feel. Their attitude can affect your mood and your decisions. So if you see signs of poor character in someone, move on. Who wants someone with bad character and negative energy hanging around? Just look for the signs. They are always there.

CHAPTER 15

Extraordinary Things Happen
When You Least Expect Them

It was 1990, and I was in Prague in the wee hours of a dark morning. I had just finished a long day of work and was standing at the front desk to get my key (it was one of those big old keys that didn't fit into my purse), when someone caught my attention. It was summit time, and I was so exhausted, I could barely keep my eyes open. I glanced over at a circular seat in the middle of the lobby of one of those dark Eastern European hotels to see ballet dancer Rudolf Nureyev sitting there. He was slumped over, he had his hands in the pockets of his long trench coat, and he looked ill. But it was Nureyev. There was no doubt about it.

When I was twelve, our one local movie theater in Dubuque was showing a documentary on a Saturday afternoon about the life and ballet roles of Rudolf Nureyev, the Russian star who had famously defected from the Soviet Union. My sister Mary and I were ballet buffs, so we went to see the documentary together. There, we ate popcorn and marveled as this gazelle masquerading as a human being leapt up in the air and seemed to hover a moment before he came back down to earth again.

Now, here he was, a few steps from me. I wanted to run over to him and tell him how much I loved his dancing over the years, but he looked like he was not in the mood to be bothered. I was surprised by how ill he looked. I didn't know he would die of AIDS a few years later, at fifty-seven, but then, no one knew because he kept it a secret. I just watched him from afar and marveled at the miracles and surprises that my job brought me.

My life has continually been filled with rewards beyond anything I could imagine. And they usually happened when I least expected it. Take Jerry Lewis, for example. I was in Washington DC, on the set of *Larry King Live*. We had booked Jerry Lewis, circa 1994, on the show and I was excited since I had grown up laughing at his jokes and antics. I think the reason I get so excited when I meet comedians is that my dream job would be getting hired as a cast member on *Saturday Night Live*. But for some reason, Lorne Michaels and Marci Klein haven't called.

When I stepped onto the set, a little weak in the knees, Larry and Jerry were already standing there together, talking. I caught my breath and instructed myself to stay cool, when Larry told Jerry, "Hey, I'd like you to meet Wendy, my producer."

I stuck out my hand to shake his, and said quite loudly, "Hi, I'm Jerry Lewis."

He looked at me and said, "You are, darling?"

I turned bright pink and walked away. After all, this was not a president or someone who has just won the Nobel Peace Prize. It was the Nutty Professor. And I was acting like a schoolgirl. And then years later, it happened all over again, this time with another comedian. It started with an unusual call from Larry. "Wendy," he said in a grave voice, "I'm really upset about our director. There are some issues here that I don't want to discuss on the phone. I need to see you tomorrow, on the set."

That's weird, I thought. *Larry usually says what's on his mind right away.* When I showed up midmorning the next day at the bureau, Larry grabbed my hand and said, "Let's find a quiet place to talk. How about the green room?"

There was no one in there so we sat down to talk. But in the next moment, the door opened and in walked Jim Carrey. Larry and my staff had surprised me, and I was embarrassed and thrilled at the same time when Larry said, "Thanks for coming in, Jim. This is my producer, Wendy, and she really loves you."

My face got redder by the second as Jim Carrey flashed his white teeth and gathered me up for a hug. When I realized he was in on the surprise, too, I was completely mortified. Here I was, the mother of two children, having a majorly cuckoo moment with Jim Carrey. My staff and Larry had done this for me, since they knew that Jim Carrey was my dream guest and my comic mentor. And now, they were about to tape a show. What a gift!

And then there was the state dinner under the George H. W. Bush administration to which I was invited in August of 2002. I really liked this president but I thought I was much too low on the totem pole to be invited to a state dinner. When the invitation arrived, I accepted, of course, and I brought an escort. When I walked into the East Room where the dinner would be held, the only people I knew were the camera crews and the Secret Service agents. They all waved and nodded at me, I waved back, and I went to get my table assignment. I'd expected to be delegated to the back of the room, right next to the kitchen, but that was not the case.

This particular state dinner was being given for Poland's president, Lech Walesa, so many famous Polish Americans were there. I found my friend Jim Miklaszewski, a man of Polish American descent, who was at NBC. He had the seating arrangements in front of him and he said something to me like, "Lucky you, Wendy, you're at the president's table."

I stopped a moment and said, "Excuse me, but there has to be a mistake. My last name is Walker and I think they must have mixed me up with the Walkers in the president's family. You know, George Herbert *Walker* Bush."

"No, you're at the president's table," Mik said. "There's no mistake. Go sit down."

It turned out that the president liked having an eclectic mix of people around him, and we had a great time eating and bantering. I remember chatting with TV host Pat Sajak, some famous football player wearing one of those huge Super Bowl rings, and the president of Coca-Cola, who turned out to be a very interesting man. I'm sure he was impressed when I told him that Diet Coke was my drink of choice.

And still, with all these unexpected and amazing rewards, nothing compares with the day I turned fifty. Joining the half-century club is a landmark in anyone's life, even though it's often something we would rather ignore. I thought I might forget about my fiftieth, but you know what they say about the best-laid plans. In fact, not only was it impossible for me to ignore crossing over the half-century mark. It turned out that my fiftieth birthday became a story in newspapers all over the world.

The upside? There's nothing like having your fiftieth become your fifteen minutes of fame! Just when life feels mundane or boring, there is nothing like a surprise boost from somewhere unexpected.

The downside? I can never lie about my age.

When my fiftieth birthday rolled around, I'd have been satisfied to go out for a quiet dinner with my family and friends and have done with it. After all, fifty is a daunting age and most women do not welcome it with open arms. But my husband told me he wanted to throw me a party at a local restaurant, and I could invite some people who were close to me. It sounded okay, and since my family and friends wanted to help me celebrate a landmark birthday, I went along with it.

I made out my guest list, which included my family, some local friends, people from Washington, and a few others from out of town with whom I felt particularly close. I ended up with about a hundred people, a conservative number considering how many people Ralph and I knew. But I wasn't into making a big deal out of this birthday. And I didn't know how many friends I was going to disappoint when my birthday party became an international story and they hadn't been invited.

My husband always did things in a big way, that was his style, so I expected he would go over the top when he told me he wanted to hire some entertainment. Since he knew I loved soul music, I figured he would hire someone like James Brown or the Temptations. I kept asking him who was doing the music, but he said it was a secret. Apparently, he didn't tell anyone else, either, because I tried to pry the information out of a friend or two, but no one knew whom he had booked.

It was the afternoon of the party, February 22, 2003, the day before my actual birthday, when my curiosity got the better of me. The center of town is one small block, so I went out to do a random errand and "casually" drove past the restaurant Delicias, where the party was being held. I expected it to be relatively quiet, but I was surprised to see several huge production trucks parked outside. I stopped my car in front of the restaurant to stare at the activity, when a woman in a security uniform walked toward me and stood by my open window. "Who are you," she said, "and what are you doing here?"

I smiled and told her, "I'm Wendy. This is my party."

"You need to go away right now," she said. "You really have to leave."

I did as I was told and I went home to get ready for the party. I picked out a white leather skirt and gold boots, trying to look kind of wild and crazy, but Ralph took one look at me and said, "No, that's not the right look for tonight."

Without hesitation, I changed into a black leather skirt and top. "How's this?" I asked him.

"Yeah, that's better," he said in a serious tone.

At about 7 p.m., when I arrived at the restaurant and went in, they had done a terrific job of turning the place into a nightclub atmosphere with low lighting and an open bar. I went to compliment my husband and wondered why he was so revved up. But as I proceeded to greet my friends and family who were arriving, little did I know the saga of what had been going on behind my back.

Ralph had contacted Kevin Mabbutt, owner of Delicias, a few weeks earlier, to see if he could rent out the restaurant for the party. We had been frequenting Kevin's restaurant for years; it was one of our favorite spots. We knew Kevin's family and he was happy to help Ralph out.

"Ralph said he was booking blues singer B. B. King," says Kevin. "He wondered if I could handle a hundred fifty to two hundred guests. I said okay, happy he had gone with my intimate restaurant instead of a much larger one, but when I found out who he ended up booking, I was stunned. It was the next day when he called to tell me that he had passed on B. B. King because he had landed a much more famous and charismatic performer—Paul McCartney himself."

Ralph and I had met Paul and his girlfriend Heather Mills (they weren't married yet) when they appeared on Larry's show to talk about her foundation for the eradication of land mines. I was thrilled beyond belief to meet them and so was Ralph whom I brought with me.

When the interview was over, Paul and Heather were leaving the set when Paul said to Ralph, "I'm really glad we got to promote our land mine foundation. But if you're serious about putting your money where your mouth is, why don't you buy a table at our land mine dinner?"

Paul had mistaken Ralph for a CNN executive, but Ralph didn't miss a beat. "How much is a table?" he asked.

"Fifty thousand," said Paul as Ralph whipped out his checkbook and wrote out a check, right then and there, for $50,000. When Paul and Heather realized later that Ralph was my husband, not a CNN executive, they apologized for soliciting us for a donation. But we were happy to donate and we ended up chairing the dinner the very next year, of which we were very proud. Our name—the Whitworths—was next to the Annenbergs, both of us having given $50,000. That was funny.

Now it was about a year later and my fiftieth birthday had nearly arrived when Ralph got Paul's number from my staff. He called him directly and said, "I have a proposition for you. It's Wendy's birthday in a few weeks. If you come to our town and play for her private party, I'll write you a million-dollar check for your foundation."

Heather was thrilled, she was all for it, and according to her, it took Paul a moment to agree. He shied away from doing private concerts because of the security nightmare they inevitably caused. Besides, he didn't have to do private parties, but he eventually said, "Okay, Ralph, I'll do this for you and Wendy. We're about to go on tour and my band and I need some practice." The last time Paul had agreed to do a private party was back in the sixties, but now, he was determined to help Heather raise money for her charity so he considered it a trade.

"Paul's security people arrived a few days later," says Kevin, "to look over my restaurant and ask questions. When they were about to leave, they told me that if even one person found out about this beforehand, they would have to call the whole thing off. They would have no choice because they would never be able to handle the throngs that would arrive if they knew what was going on. This only escalated the immense pressure we were under. Now we had to do all of our planning, from the look of the interior, to the hors d'oeuvres, the food and beverages, and the sound system, without letting anyone know who was performing—not my wife or my staff."

I learned later that in order to give the restaurant a nightclub vibe, Kevin had agreed to let Ralph's people change the entire place around, which included moving a huge, extremely fragile, and very expensive Lalique table in the dining room that had held large arrangements of flowers for the past fifteen years. It was dismantled under Kevin's watchful eye, which involved removing and saving close to a hundred delicate screws that held the table together. All in secret.

"We were up late into the night," recalls Kevin, "moving things out of the restaurant. I held my breath when they moved the table. Then early the next morning, the designers arrived to begin their preparations. When locals looked in to see what was going on, we just told them we were doing a birthday party for someone who lived in town—which was true. Being a Brit, I loved the Beatles as much as anyone and it was totally exciting for me.

"Then, on the afternoon of the event, security escalated and keeping the secret was getting harder and harder," he recalls. "Paul's band needed to rehearse and to do a sound check at four thirty, and I had loads of staff members scurrying around, preparing to serve dinner and entertain a large group of people by seven p.m. I had kept them all in the dark about the entertainment and they were amazed when I gave the directive, 'Okay, everybody out.' They couldn't believe I was sending them out in the midst of setting up, but I had to.

"When my staff left, I pulled the blinds, closed the curtains, and Paul and his band stepped in to do a sound check. I heard later that people in the street figured they were hearing a Paul McCartney impersonator, and they walked on by. No one imagined that, in their little town just outside of San Diego, one of the Beatles and his band were rehearsing to entertain at a private party."

I got excited when my friends began arriving at the restaurant. It was so good to see everyone, especially Larry and Katie, who had agreed to share the emcee duties. After sipping champagne and greeting our guests, Ralph headed up on stage to get everyone's attention. At that precise moment, Kennedy, the husband of Sara, one of my college roommates, who was a real rock and roll fan, suddenly said, "That's Paul McCartney's guitar."

"Yeah, right. Like Paul McCartney is about to play for this private party!" Sara told her husband as Paul and the band members were sneaking down the back alley and entering the restaurant by the service door.

"You know," Ralph told the crowd, "we were going to do a

little R&B tonight. But I decided it would be better to have a little rock and roll. So without further ado, ladies and gentlemen…"

Ralph jumped down off the stage and, suddenly, everyone began to scream, men and women alike. Paul McCartney was in the house and he jumped onstage wearing a bright red T-shirt. He smiled (at me!) and picked up his guitar. Then he opened his mouth and sang, "You say good-bye and I say hello. I don't know why…"

I did not believe what I was seeing and hearing. It wasn't possible. I had a flashback to the fifth grade in 1963, in Dubuque, Iowa, when I gave up my bedroom to my grandmother one winter. I was relegated to a tiny room in our house that was the size of the width of a double bed. It was the year the Beatles came to America, and there were magazines entirely devoted to them that cost 35 cents at the grocery store. Since Paul and Ringo were my favorites, I bought a bunch of magazines, tore their pictures out, and wallpapered the entire room with photos of my two most adored Beatles. I recently found all of those photos that had graced my walls when I was young and I gave them to my teenage daughter to put on her wall.

Now, Paul McCartney was standing on the stage, in person, amid our screams of joy and shock. And not only was he playing his famous guitar. He was dedicating his songs to me on my birthday. I was in shock, wondering for an instant if this was actually a tribute band. But I knew it was unmistakably Paul when he looked directly at me and said, "Hey, Wendy baby!"

If I still had any doubts, there was Heather, glowing, in a pair of jeans and a white top, rocking out to her husband's music. We found out later that she was pregnant but only Paul and she knew at the time. To add to the excitement, Paul's entire band backed him up as he went through a playlist that would bring the totally shocked guests to their knees.

How can I describe the faces of my friends as they rocked out to the live music of Paul McCartney? As I danced to the music, I thought I had some pretty good moves. I smiled when I thought about how embarrassed Walker got every time I danced. I didn't care. The entire room stood up and danced, singing along with Paul for almost two hours. What if I had said no to the party? I would never know what I had missed. Now, all of us in that room had experienced something that would bond us together forever.

When Paul finished his rendition of "Hello, Goodbye," he went on to the next song. By the time he was finished, the playlist, believe it or not, had gone as follows:

Hello, Goodbye
Coming Up
Let Me Roll It
Your Loving Flame
Live and Let Die
Freedom
Blackbird
We Can Work It Out
Here Today
Eleanor Rigby
Calico Skies
Here, There and Everywhere
Michelle
Back in the U.S.S.R.
She's Leaving Home
Maybe I'm Amazed
Lady Madonna

Let It Be
Yesterday
Birthday
Hey Jude
I Saw Her Standing There

We all knew the words, we all sang along, and each of us had our personal experience of what the song had meant to us in the past. The entire evening felt elevated as if we had traveled to some magical sphere in the past where everything was exactly as we had left it.

As the decibel levels of the music escalated, however, so did the screaming, and Kevin got a call from the local sheriff's office. He had warned them about the party, that there might be some noise, but they had not expected it to be so loud or for it to go on for so long. The sheriff asked Kevin, "Can you just tone it down? People are complaining."

But when Kevin told him it was Paul McCartney, the sheriff backed off completely. The mention of the Beatle's name was enough for the police and it was apparently enough for the neighbors, too. When they were told who was there, instead of complaining further, they all came out into the street to listen.

Back inside, when Paul began to play the chords of "You Say It's Your Birthday," all eyes turned to me as he called me up to the stage. He continued to play, directing his famous lyrics to me, and when he pulled me in for a dance, I understood the meaning of the expression, "Now I can die happy." When it was over, Paul reached out to me, hugged me in front of everyone, and whispered in my ear, "Hey, baby, happy birthday." *Paul McCartney just called me "baby,"* I thought to myself. *Nobody has a better life than I do.*

When the night was nearly over, Kevin was approached by a

security guard. "We have a problem," the guard told Kevin. "In the last hour, television and radio trucks are parked in the street and a huge crowd has gathered outside. The networks are setting up cameras and we have to keep Paul away from all this."

Kevin was ready with a solution. "Tell the people out there that the concert is about to end. Keep the red carpet out front for a while and assure them that Paul will walk down that carpet in fifteen to twenty minutes. Tell them everyone will get their shot."

In the next moment, in a move reminiscent of the Beatles' movie *A Hard Day's Night*, when they spent so much energy ducking their fans, Paul, Heather, and company snuck out the back alley and into a waiting car that shuttled them all away. They left a load of disappointed people out front who eventually wandered home and went to bed.

The next day, I held a luncheon for my out-of-town guests and everyone was still shocked and amazed. A call came in on my cell phone shortly after noon from a CNN reporter. "This is really weird, Wendy," he said, "but there's a rumor circulating that Paul McCartney played live music at your private birthday party last night. Is it true?"

"How on earth did you find out?" I asked.

The man at the other end of the phone laughed. "How could we miss it? It's an international story. It's on the wires."

It was true. Reports of the party had shown up in local newspapers in larger cities, and were as far reaching as London and Reykjavik. Eventually, my birthday party was covered in *Rolling Stone* and *People* magazine. Now everyone in the world knew I was fifty. But I also got some irate calls from friends. "How could you have Paul McCartney playing at your party and not invite me?"

I passed the buck to Ralph, since he had kept it a secret.

I saw the wisdom in that. If he had told me, I probably would have invited so many people from all over the country, they would never have fit into the restaurant. But I have friends who are still taking me to task for leaving them out. And as fate would have it, it was the gift that kept on giving, since Paul and I were destined to meet again, some years later, in August 2007.

It started with a call from Larry right after breakfast one morning. "Wendy," he said, "you need to call David Saltz right away. He has a great idea for us to go to Vegas. Promise you'll call. He said it's huge."

I'm glad Larry didn't see me roll my eyes. I considered Vegas to be very ho-hum, and I couldn't imagine what on earth would make us go there. But there it was again. What seemed like an ordinary and mundane request would become another extraordinary day in my life. When I called David Saltz, a highly successful music producer and friend, as a courtesy to Larry, was I ever excited when he said, "The Beatles are celebrating the one-year anniversary of their hit Cirque du Soleil show *Love*. If you're interested, I can get you an exclusive interview with Paul, Ringo, Yoko, and Olivia Harrison before the show."

"You have to be kidding," I said.

"I'm dead serious, but you have to set it up right now," he said.

Were we interested? What do you think? I hung up and started the wheels rolling. Within ten days, we were in Vegas, ready to do an interview before *Love* started. Just before our show began, I walked into the green room, where Paul and I spotted each other. He gave me a hug and we were both commiserating about our divorces when someone walked in behind us and said in a very familiar voice, "Hey, bloke." It was Ringo.

Paul smiled at him and said, "Ringo, I'd like you to meet my friend Wendy."

My friend Wendy. As I shook hands with my other favorite Beatle, I flashed back to my little room that had been wallpapered floor to ceiling with photos of these two rock stars. If someone had told me back then that, one day, Beatle Paul would call me a friend and introduce me to Ringo, I would have said, "Yeah, right!"

❖

EXTRAORDINARY THINGS HAPPEN WHEN YOU LEAST EXPECT THEM

When I was onstage dancing with Paul McCartney, my childhood idol, I was that little kid again, buying 35-cent magazines and pasting pictures on my wall. I could never have predicted that, much later in my life, I would dance with Paul McCartney on the extraordinary evening when I turned fifty.

I walked into Amaya's room recently to find that she had removed the pretty pictures and objects of art with which I had decorated her room. In their place, she had plastered the walls of her room with pictures of her favorite rock stars. Just like I had done.

I looked from poster to poster, wondering, Which of these idols will she end up meeting someday when she is older? The truth was that she already had met one of them, since he's a neighbor and friend. Tom DeLonge, our rock star friend from the group Blink-182 and Angels & Airwaves, is Amaya's version of Paul McCartney. He is my daughter's inspiration for her love of music. So, if my life went full circle from pictures on the wall to meeting Paul, why couldn't hers go the same way?

I have to say, I'm grateful that both of my children have a great passion in their lives. For Amaya, it's music, and her vibrant walls tell the story. Walker, on the other hand, is passionate about his dreams, which he turns into amazing stories after he wakes up. I have roused him in the morning, only to have him say, "Please come back in five minutes so I can finish my dream." When I come back, he gets out of bed, starts pacing, and says, "Just listen to this before I forget it." Then he tells me an intricate and amazing story with a beginning, a middle, and an end, each with its individual and fascinating plot. He is now writing chapter 13 of his book of dreams.

The thing is, you never know what's coming down the path. All you can do is go about your life and when things seem dull and mundane, never give up hope. Since nothing ever stays the same, if things are predictable today, something spectacular is bound to be on its way. The key is in remaining open, having a great attitude, and believing that miraculous things are just around the corner. Because they are.

CHAPTER 16

Everything Happens for a Reason

Ten months after the extraordinary birthday party that my husband threw for me, he and I separated. I've been through some pretty tough times in my life, and I can say without hesitation that separating from and divorcing my husband of eleven years was the most difficult thing I have ever done. In fact, it still hurts to this day, although I understand how everything happens for a reason.

During the OJ trial, Larry and I had spent a lot of time on the West Coast. Now it was over and we were settling back in Washington. But in 1997, Larry admitted to me that he missed Los Angeles. He had met Shawn a year prior in LA and she also missed it. They wanted to move, he told me. I was surprised, but as luck would have it, my husband had been suggesting that we move to the West Coast, too, since his business partner lived in San Diego.

Although I was initially leery, the idea began to grow on me. There were several reasons for the move that seemed to make sense. First of all, if Larry was going there, I needed to be near him. There was also the benefit that Ralph could travel a great deal less and be with us more. That would be good for our family since we wanted another child. And then there was the idea of having a real life. While our show aired on the East Coast from 9 to 10 p.m., in the West it was over by 7 p.m. That meant that when the show signed off, I would have a full night ahead of me to be with my daughter or go out with my husband.

But what would Tom Johnson, CNN president, think about this? He had believed in me enough to give me my big break when he touted me for Larry's producer job. Now, since Larry was instigating the move out West, I was counting on Tom's faith in me. When he arrived at Ralph's and my home in McLean, Virginia, where I was about to sign my new contract, I broke it to him.

"There's good and bad news here, Tom," I said. "Larry wants to move to California, and so do Ralph and I. That's the good news. The bad news is that while Larry wants to live in Los Angeles, we want to move near San Diego, about two hours south of LA."

"What about the set? How is that going to work?" asked Tom, looking distressed.

"You know what, Tom?" I said. "It'll work the same way it works here in Washington. All we have to do is build the identical set in Los Angeles and one in New York, while we're at it. Don Hewitt (executive producer of *60 Minutes* who has since passed away) calls it the most recognizable set on television. We can build it anywhere."

Tom did not look confident when he said, "Look Wendy, I really can't have you doing that. You have to be with Larry."

"Tom," I countered, "as far as Larry goes, no matter where I am, I'm on the phone with him and various members of my staff as soon as I get up. I stay on the phone in the grocery store, in the bathroom, the bathtub, at the movies, the doctor's, and in the car. You name a place, I'm on the phone there. Since my job is to decide who is on the show every day, that's what drives the show. I can do it from anywhere. And if it doesn't work," I assured him, "I'll be the first person to admit it. You know me well enough by now. Just let me give it a try."

He believed in me and let us go forward, albeit a bit reluctantly. So, in the fall of 1998, I signed my new contract with CNN while Ralph and I packed up our Virginia home, our daughter, and our four-month-old son, and we moved to the West Coast. We initially rented in La Jolla, a beach town twelve miles north of downtown San Diego, while we were waiting for our house to be built. Five months later, we made a final move to a larger home on the outskirts of San Diego, where I originally had my office in the basement. All was going well with my work. I never had to discuss the move with Tom Johnson again, and soon I had satellite dishes on my roof and fourteen monitors in my office, which I made into a virtual newsroom. I had the computers, the faxes, all the technology that allowed me to talk to Larry while he was on the air.

The drawback was that my home, previously my sanctuary, became a miniversion of CNN, with overhead pages calling me to my desk. To this day, I have a load of computers and complicated phone systems that I can't get away from, which makes it easy to get cabin fever since I'm stuck in one place all day long. No matter how beautiful my surroundings are. But from the time we decided to move, the benefits outweighed the obstacles and they still do.

Things have a way of turning upside down, however, with no rhyme or reason in sight. I separated from my husband and I was totally devastated. I had watched friends and colleagues get divorced and I was aware that it was extremely painful. I was compassionate, but I never really appreciated how debilitating and soul-shattering a divorce can be until I went through it myself. In some ways, I think it's harder than a death because you are constantly reminded that the person you loved is still around but not with you anymore.

I thought I had taken enough time deciding to get married, that I would pretty much know what was in store. I recall in 1981 when former President Richard M. Nixon was booked on a CNN weekend news show. It was noon on a Saturday and a group of CNNers were gathered in our original small newsroom in Georgetown. And there stood Richard Nixon, in a corner of the room all alone, in his famous hunched-over Nixon stance. Nobody was approaching him because those big hangdog jowls made his face look like a "I am not a crook" Halloween mask, but I was there expressly to see him. I had brought with me the newspaper clipping of him holding me in my fat coat when I was three. I wanted him to autograph it for me, and I made my way over to him.

"Excuse me, President Nixon," I said, "my name is Wendy Walker and I'd like to show you something." I took out the picture and he looked closely at it.

"Where was this taken?" he asked in his odd, slow voice.

"Johnstown, Pennsylvania," I said. "It was 1956."

"I did a lot of campaigning in Pennsylvania," he said. "Let me sign this for you." He signed his name and wrote, "1956–1981." When he handed it back to me, he asked, "Are you married?"

"No, sir," I said, "not yet."

"I hear there aren't a lot of good men to go around these days," he said slowly, "so take your time. Don't rush into it."

"I won't," I promised him.

I had heeded Richard Nixon's advice and not rushed into anything, since I was nearly forty when I got married. And so, it was with great disappointment that my husband and I parted in January of 2004. This would be the worst and the best period of my life, as the severe upset of my disintegrating marriage sent me careening into a downward spiral of sadness. Really, it was the saddest I had ever felt. That was the worst part.

The best part was that I entered a new phase that forced me to go deeper inside than ever before, which resulted in a spiritual awakening of sorts. I was about to find out that things happen for a reason, even if you can't see it at the time.

One of the best things that came out of my marriage was meeting my close friend Mary Heckmann. I still remember my reaction when Ralph called me from work one day and said, "We need to have a business dinner with a fellow from my work, Dick Heckmann, and his wife, Mary."

I was not thrilled. I imagined a boring, humorless couple coming over whom I would have to entertain after a long day of work, but did I ever have a surprise waiting! The doorbell rang, I walked a bit reluctantly to open the door, and in front of me stood Dick Heckmann and his beautiful wife, Mary, who was smiling warmly.

I found out quickly that night that her extraordinary outer beauty was only a hint of what was inside. And we had a lot in common. Dick and Mary had five children, she was just finishing her PhD in English, and she had a great spirit. We talked incessantly, we became fast friends, and we remain so to this day.

"I saw Wendy as someone who thought outside the box," recalls Mary, "and I was drawn to her creativity and how much she loved her children. We connected in those areas. When she separated from her husband, she was so distressed, I sometimes came over in the evenings, climbed in bed with her to commiserate, and we would fall asleep. It looked like the life was flowing out of her and I was very concerned."

I needed some help, that was for sure, when Shawn King told me about a psychic named Char Margolis. I had been open to metaphysics and psychic phenomena for most of my life, and my belief was strengthened by a childhood experience that had haunted me for many years.

Maura, a neighborhood friend, and I grew up together in Dubuque. We were so close, we used to tie a long string between two tin cans and try to talk to each other from our bedrooms. When I was about to come home for summer vacation at the end of my freshman year at Hollins, in 1972, I was so looking forward to spending time with Maura. But I got a shocking phone call from my mother. Maura had gone to an end-of-the-year party at her college, she had gone out on a boat ride with a boy, and neither of them had come back. Maura had drowned at age eighteen.

From then on, I had a recurring dream that I was staring at Maura's house, which was completely dark except for her reflection in the upstairs window. When I knocked on the front door, I could see her inside but her mother said, "Maura can't come out of the house."

The dream continued to haunt me and about ten years later, a friend who lived in India sent me a letter out of the blue that said, "You have to let Maura go. She's trying to go but she's still with you."

How could she know that I was still having my Maura dreams? It was so many years later. I visited a male psychic at the time, who asked me almost immediately, "Do you know someone who drowned?"

"Yes," I said, my voice unsteady. I had not told him about Maura.

"She needs to leave but she keeps coming to you in your dreams," he said.

He put his arms around me and began cradling me, rocking me back and forth while he spoke to Maura as if she were standing there. He told her in a gentle, firm voice that it was okay to leave now, that I was letting her go. After that experience, I never had that dream again, and it cemented my spiritual beliefs even more firmly.

Now, in the wake of my divorce, I turned to the spiritual part of my life to find healing and I quickly began to understand the meaning of good and bad energy in the people around me. I sought out people who were not interested in being negative but were there to support me and to help me rebuild myself. My self-esteem had never been so low, and I consider myself really lucky to have met Char who calls herself a psychic intuitive. In my opinion, she is that and so much more.

I have always relied on my intuition to get me through life's ups and downs and to make important decisions. I can feel an energy presence when people are around me. My daughter has that gift, too, and I began to view my healing process not so much as spiritual, but rather as science—quantum physics, to be exact. We know that we can transfer energy to others and we know that when we are around people with a great deal of negativity, we begin to feel negative, too. The same is true of positive energy, so after getting two recommendations from people I respected, I went to see Char. I wanted a new and positive perspective on my life and what was happening to me. I wanted to believe that what was happening was more than bad luck. I *needed* there to be a reason for it and I wanted to find out what it was.

"Wendy had almost no self-esteem when I met her," says Char. "I could tell right away that she was the kind of woman who was serious about her commitments, and her divorce threw her for a loop. She was in shock when I met her, her sense of humor was gone, and she needed a lot of emotional support."

I had countless conversations with Char, who encouraged me to take a good long look at myself. She said, "There is an unspoken force that is around us. We all have our own energy thumbprints and our energy is constantly progressing all the time. Quite simply, positive energy attracts more positive energy, just like negative energy attracts more of the same. I'm glad you've grown tired of the negativity. And I believe that your children can be instrumental as a motivation to seek out goodness in your life from now on."

Char basically encouraged me to use my intuition when it came to choosing my friends. "We are all intuitive," she assured me, "but you have to *practice* using your intuition. It's like any other muscle in your body. You need to use it so it doesn't weaken and disappear."

When I thought about it, I had been using my intuition all my life. I always had let my instincts guide me, especially in my work where I was required to make decisions all day long that seemed so random. My intuition had never let me down. Why couldn't I use that same instinctual understanding to choose the people who would be most beneficial to my healing process?

Even more important was the question of how to accept my loss. Since my husband had not died, my task was to find forgiveness. And to find forgiveness, I needed to understand my inner patterns while I was grappling with the idea of real love. I had a few examples of people in love who had really affected me. Larry and I had had lunch with Nancy Reagan when her husband was ill but still alive. Larry had looked at Nancy with great compassion and gently asked her, "Do you ever wish he would just peacefully move on?"

"No," she said, "because then I wouldn't be able to kiss him good night."

Now that was a love to emulate, a role model for the way a husband and wife could be with each other, even in the most difficult of circumstances. And then there's Jenny Craig, weight-loss guru and philanthropist. She and her husband, Sid, were like a second family to me and they had the kind of love affair that dreams are made of. When Sid died in 2008 at the age of seventy-six, Jenny wrote the following letter and read it at his funeral.

Remember when our love was in its infancy? Because of work commitments we lived in two separate cities. We wrote letters expressing our desire to one day be together. You later reminded me that you saved each letter as a treasured keepsake...so I write you my last letter.

My darling Sid,

I can't remember the very moment that I fell in love with you. It was as though it had always been. From the start, I knew it was God's plan for us to share a life...and what a life he had designed for us. Whether at business, watching our horses cross the finish line or dancing to our favorite songs...each day was like a trip to the Winner's Circle. Was it your flashing smile, your sparkling eyes, your intelligent wit or the kindness in your heart that made me know from the start that it was you I wanted to spend the rest of my life with? How do I begin to thank you for the happiness you brought to each day...each hour...each moment that we were together? How do I begin to summarize the many celebrations of achievement as each year brought us more and more blessings from God? Sid, together we created a family and lifestyle that most people only dream about. How soon you were taken away from me. Was that all part of God's master plan? If so . . . then he must have needed another angel in heaven. I will always cherish our years together . . . the midnight talks . . . the love-filled moments when I thought I heard God whisper, "Until death do you part" and now the time has come . . . the time when we must say good-bye. I will be with you again in heaven one day and until that time . . . rest in the knowledge that my love for you is undying and will grow stronger with each day until we're together for all eternity.

Rest in peace, my love . . . and once in a while wink at me from Heaven . . . I promise I'll be watching.

With all my love forever,
Jenny

I remember when my father died, my mother said life was like drinking champagne without the bubbles. I was lucky to have had parents who were so in love with each other.

And so, with the help of some really great friends, like Char, Mary, George, Ken, John, Michelle, Cindy, Jenny, Katie, and so many more, I realized that I *could* rise above it, but it was a process rather than something you did and then it was over. I needed to find forgiveness newly, every day. And then the next day and the day after that. Blame only made the pain hurt more and I needed to find a way to release it and move on. When it was gone, I'd have a chance to see the higher purpose for the pain in the first place.

During this challenging period, I consulted my friend, spiritualist Deepak Chopra, who asked me an intriguing question. "What do you really want for yourself?"

I thought for a few minutes. Then I said, "I want good

health. I want to enjoy my life and my children and I want to live for the future, not the past. I want to find someone who truly loves me and it would feel so good to be a family again."

He listened carefully and said, "Here's how you get what you want. You need to be ruthless, cunning, patient, and sweet."

That was some food for thought. I had so much to consider, but the turning point came for me when I finally realized that I had loved my husband completely, as much as I possibly could. When I finally realized that, I started to heal. I found some peace in that recognition and enough personal forgiveness to move forward and embrace my new life as a single woman, once again.

Another turning point came when I took a good long look at my friends. Being in crisis really shows you who your friends are, what they believe, and how much they care about you. Char says, "I got to watch Wendy transform into the person she always was. I could see traces of her emotional scars fading through time and she became herself again and found some new and wonderful friends. Life is a school and we are here to learn lessons."

Char taught me that our lives unfold according to the choices we make. And there is a reason why things happen. She told me that she uses her psychic work to prevent problems and achieve goals. "When we combine logic, common sense, and intuition, we get our best answers."

I recall a night during my divorce when Char and two new friends of mine, John Assaraf and Ian, were at my house for dinner. We were just finishing our main course when John said, "Let's go around the table and say one thing we're grateful for."

While the others were talking, I thought about my divorce, the children, the upheaval in our lives, and the loss of a dream of a tightly knit family who were there for one another. I thought about our menagerie of animals—our three dogs, the cat, nine fish, and a bearded dragon. When Walker wanted yet another pet, I recalled telling him I would get him anything he wanted—as long as it didn't breathe. I thought of gorgeous, successful women like Halle Berry and Reese Witherspoon who were disappointed when their relationships fell apart. And they had found the strength to move on. It was true that I had lost the fairy tale of happily ever after, but I had gained the people who were smiling at me and making me feel loved. And I had gained myself. That was a good enough reason for anyone.

When my turn came, I said, "I'm grateful for having met each one of you. I can see why this happened. If I hadn't divorced, none of you would be sitting at this table."

I have come to realize that in order to forgive, I can say, "Thank you for giving me this experience." I also understand that when I relinquish my desire to impose my will on the future, the path to happiness becomes clear.

❖

EVERYTHING HAPPENS FOR A REASON

This might be the most important and most difficult lesson of all. Life is full of both wonder and excitement. In an attempt to see the glass half full, let's list our accomplishments for the year. There are plenty, and the list keeps getting longer, the more you think about it.

Now, list your disappointments that have happened throughout your life. Put them all down and take a look. When I did this, I was amazed to find that the things

that had most upset me in life had all been gateways
to something better. *Oh, now I understand*, I thought to
myself, *it's all in the perception.*

My list included my father dying early in my life as a
terrible disappointment. As a young woman, I had no
male figure on whom to lean and who would take care
of me. But now I can see that the loss of my father was
a pivotal reason for my success. Since I had no one to
fall back on and no one to make my decisions for me, I
had to do it all myself.

Then there was my divorce, during which I opened
myself up to a spiritual part of life that I never fully
understood. I began a search for the light and positive
energy in people and in situations that I had previously
overlooked. And I found what I was looking for.

You just have to let go. If you can take your list of disappointments and understand the good that came out
of them and how they helped you change for the better,
that will help you deal with future disappointments. For
each difficulty along the path, there is a really good reason that it happened, whether you get to see it now, a
year from now, three years from now, or even thirty. You
just need to keep your faith, believe in yourself, cultivate
patience and goodwill, and surround yourself with positive people. Then the rest will take care of itself.

CHAPTER 17

Treat All People like the "Big People"

Marlon Brando had been on our *Larry King Live* wish list forever, but we didn't have a lot of hope. We'd tried many times, but rumor and conventional wisdom told us that legendary Marlon Brando had become a recluse. Few people ever saw him, and although we knew he lived in Los Angeles, he reputedly was hugely overweight and rarely left his home.

During the OJ Simpson trial in 1994, I was booking a show featuring some of the principals when I heard an overhead page in the CNN newsroom in Los Angeles. "Wendy," a voice called out, "you have a call on line one."

I picked up the closest phone to talk to one of my bookers who could hardly contain her excitement. "Wendy," she said, "are you sitting down? You're not going to believe this. We just got one of the top people we really wanted. They called us. Guess who it is."

"Is it Michael Jackson?" I asked hopefully. Larry had once interviewed him when he was twelve but never as an adult. He had been on our wish list for a long time.

"Nope," she said, "better. It's Marlon Brando."

"You're kidding me, right?" I said.

"No, I'm not," she assured me.

I could hardly believe our luck. Generally, with someone as legendary as Marlon Brando, it takes forever to do the negotiations, to come to terms, and to finalize the interview, if it ever happens at all. You see, no matter who it is, we never offer to pay for an interview. While other news shows find ways around this by perhaps paying large sums for photos, we make no exceptions to this rule. Not even for the Marlon Brandos of the world, the people who are not only uninterested in publicity but generally run from it like the plague. So why was he offering to come on the show? I wanted to know.

Apparently, someone had written a kiss-and-tell biography about Brando that had really made him angry. He had decided to write his own book and tell his own story but he hadn't read the small print in his contract with Random House, stating that he was required to do one publicity appearance to promote his book—any one he chose. While he preferred to do nothing, rather than breach his contract, he had decided to appear on *Larry King Live*. So instead of our having to work with his people to try to nail this rare interview, his rep had picked up a phone and offered him as a guest—with one caveat. He wanted to meet Larry in person first. Right away.

I've seldom heard Larry sound more excited than when I told him Marlon Brando wanted to appear on the show. "But he wants to meet you beforehand," I told Larry.

"When?" Larry asked.

"Actually," I said, "he's in his car right now on his way to our hotel. He wants to pick you up and take you for a drive."

We were staying at our usual LA spot, the Beverly Wilshire Hotel in Beverly Hills, and in less than ten minutes, Larry and

I were standing in the hotel breezeway as this larger than life man came driving up in a great big white Chevy. He waved, so did we, Larry jumped into the passenger seat, and they zoomed off. I stood there, dumbstruck. He was bigger than life. I mean huge, so I had expected someone else to be driving. But it was Marlon himself at the wheel of the car. What kind of trouble would these two men get into?

I had no idea where they were going or how long they'd be gone. Neither did Larry. But in a couple of hours I got a call from Larry that they were returning. When I headed back down to the breezeway to greet them, they were sitting as close as they could manage in the front seat of Marlon's car, their arms around each other, hugging, singing songs, and having a great time. Clearly, the interview was on.

As I saw them reluctant to leave each other, I had an idea that this kind of intimacy would thrive in a more homey atmosphere than the CNN studio. Larry and I were of one mind about this when he happily told me, "He'll do it but he wants to do it at his house on Mulholland Drive."

That was where Marlon felt the most comfortable, so I called Atlanta to speak to Tom Johnson, then president. "You're not going to believe this," I said, "but we have an interview booked for a few days from now with Marlon Brando. We have him for the whole hour and he wants to do it at his house. I'd like ninety minutes. What do you say?"

It was an unequivocal yes. In fact, it was all systems go as I kicked into high gear and gathered the production team to head up to Marlon Brando's house for a site survey. When I walked through the front door, I thought I had entered a time warp. Everything in this bachelor pad–type bungalow felt like it was straight out of the sixties and relatively small compared to what I had expected.

A few days later, I arrived at the house around midafternoon once again, this time to prepare for the upcoming live interview. But time was going by and as our crew was setting up, I wondered when the great man himself would come out and show his face. As we approached 6 p.m., the start of the show, I wondered if Mr. Brando intended on coming out at all. But just when we had less than fifteen minutes to airtime and we were all in terror that he might have changed his mind, he wandered out from a back room, barefoot, with a coffee cup in his hand. But there had to be more in that cup than just coffee! Still, I have to say, I have rarely seen a man act more graciously before a show. He was determined to show no favorites as he stood at the entryway of the room.

After a quick look around, the legendary Mr. Brando did not greet Larry first, which surprised everyone. He also did not greet me. Instead, he went around the entire room, shaking hands with every technician, truck operator, soundman, camera operator—anyone doing anything of a technical nature. He personally introduced himself to each person, saying, "Hi, I'm Marlon. Welcome to my home."

I was in awe that this extraordinarily unusual man was not acting arrogantly or rudely, as his reputation dictated. Instead, he was making everyone in the room feel comfortable as he walked around with no shoes. And in my opinion, he was badly in need of a pedicure! To add to that, he had applied his own makeup, he looked pretty rough around the edges, and I made an unusual decision to leave him exactly the way he was. If it were anyone else, I would have made sure his feet were covered and that he looked reasonably well groomed, but in this case, I decided to just let it be. Marlon Brando was Marlon Brando, with no help required from me.

In the end, I believe that one of the reasons this ninety-minute show was so appealing was because it was so real. I gave no directives to "lose the cup" or "fix his makeup" or "straighten his pants" or shoot from a different direction to eliminate a crotch shot. If Marlon Brando was willing to let it all hang out, so was I, a decision that gratefully worked in our favor.

The interview began when Marlon said to Larry, "You can't see my feet, can you? I forgot to put my shoes on."

Larry answered, "That's okay, that's all right."

From there it progressed into a mutual admiration exchange.

KING: Explain what you did, don't put me on, Marlon, you put your own makeup on today?

BRANDO: I did because I wanted to look exactly like you and... This was my goal, that's right.

KING: And you believed...

BRANDO: I wore some red suspenders in your honor. I did everything I could and then I've received some criticism from these people [the makeup people] then.

KING: They wanted to do you themselves?

BRANDO: They wanted to do it.

KING: I'm honored. Do you see my eyebrows that dark and that way and that sort of stark look?

BRANDO: Yes, a little of the, what do you call it, who was that famous Italian guy, the big lover that played the Sheik, what was his name?

KING: Valentino.

A few minutes later, Larry asked Marlon a provocative question.

KING: Why don't you like being interviewed?

BRANDO: Because I don't like the idea of selling yourself for money. I—

KING: You don't like to go on to sell a book?

BRANDO: I don't.

KING: Or sell a movie?

BRANDO: I don't. I've never sold a movie and this is the first time I've ever been beating the drum for some product. In this case, it's Random House's book.

KING: Because you promised them you would do one?

BRANDO: It was unbeknownst to me that it was part of the contract and if I didn't [do an interview], I would be in breach of contract. But aside from that I've had pleasure talking to you. I'm fascinated with people, especially the kind of people—I wouldn't lump you with others because you are exceptional.

As the show went on, I watched them becoming more intimate in a way that Larry rarely allows. Some wonderful things came out of that interview that surprised all of us. Mainly, we all learned that Marlon Brando did not act for the art of it alone. One thinks of him as one of the most iconic actors who ever lived in such roles as Terry Malloy in *On the Waterfront,* or as Stanley Kowalski in *A Streetcar Named Desire.* Surely acting was under his skin and he did it for the art, not the money. But he had something different to say about that.

KING: Why did you choose acting as a career? Why did you choose to be other people?

BRANDO: It's useful to make an observation that everybody here in this room is an actor. You're an actor and the best performances I've ever seen is when the director says, "CUT," and the director says, "That was great." That was wonderful. That was good. But they said we had a little lighting problem. Let's do it again. What he's thinking is, Jesus Christ, that's so fucked—excuse me…It wasn't done well, so we've got to do it over but everybody tried to handle it.

When you say, how do you do, how are you, you look fine, you're doing two things at once. You're reading the person's real intention. You're trying to feel who he is and making an assessment and trying to ignore the mythology.

KING: So when the director says, "Cut, but I didn't like the lighting," he's acting…You chose it as a profession.

BRANDO: Because there isn't anything that pays you as much money as acting while you are deciding what the hell you're going to do with yourself.

KING: So wait a minute, are you saying you're still deciding?

BRANDO: It took me a long time to decide. You know people who have never decided. I mean, most people—if you ask them what their dreams are—give this guy a Kleenex.

The interview carried on from there as Brando ribbed Larry about perspiring too much. He called him a "darling man" and then continued to discuss the art of acting and making money. He insisted that regrets were not part of his life, that they belonged to the past. And then he asked once again if his bare feet would show up in the shot.

At the end of the interview, which had covered sundry topics including acting and his life in Tahiti, with mostly unexpected answers from Brando, I watched Larry and his new best friend put their arms around each other and start singing. Brando's crotch was directly in the face of the camera, his legs and bare feet hanging out, a big bulge visible in the front of his pants, and I did nothing. I gave the camera crew no directives and just watched as these two men, arms locked around each other, turned face-to-face, staring into each other's eyes while they sang. I was convinced there was a whole lot more than coffee in Brando's cup by the end of that ninety minutes as the two of them seemed to become lost in each other.

Just before we wrapped the interview, they leaned in and kissed on the lips. In my opinion, it seemed almost normal, as if it would have been weird if they hadn't kissed, they were so close. But apparently, my boss in Atlanta did not agree. The moment the interview was over, I got a call from Tom Johnson saying, "Wendy, why did you let them kiss? How could you let that happen?"

I said coolly, "Tom, you know, I actually forgot to tell them not to kiss. I forgot to say, 'Oh, by the way, guys, at the end of the interview when you feel like kissing each other on the lips, just don't do it.'" That moment had made television history.

I hung up the phone, thinking that the interview had been magical. It seemed that Mr. Brando was quite happy about it, too, as he proceeded to bring out several iced bottles of fine champagne and some chicken salad sandwiches. And then, once again, he skipped over Larry and the producers as he personally handed every crew member a glass of champagne and toasted with them. He posed for pictures with the cable people, the sound crew, and the camera crew, while Larry and I watched. It seemed that although he was a well-established recluse at this point in his life, Mr. Brando had enjoyed the experience a great deal and he was making sure everyone could feel his appreciation.

He made his way around the room, and although he posed for pictures with anyone who wanted them, he stopped short of signing autographs. He didn't believe in it. But he looked sincerely happy to have been on the show, once he got into it, and he was not shy about expressing his gratitude. At the same time, it was clear that he was interested in taking care of the people behind the scenes first. If someone didn't like it, well, he obviously didn't care.

When the entire crew had sipped champagne and it was our turn, he walked over to Larry and me to toast with us. "That was quite a kiss," Larry said to Marlon. "Kiss my producer like you just kissed me."

I stared at him for a moment and closed my eyes as Marlon Brando took me in his arms. As he placed his lips on mine, gone were bare feet, dirty toes, coffee cups, overweight bellies, and perspiration. It was Stanley Kowalski, Terry Malloy, Fletcher Christian, you name it. It was *that* man kissing me like I had never been kissed before.

For weeks afterward, Larry walked around the set saying, "You know, after I kissed Marlon Brando, I just can't stop thinking about him."

I silently nodded my head. He wasn't the only one.

❖

TREAT ALL PEOPLE LIKE THE "BIG PEOPLE"

Al Gore was on our set recently, and I watched him walk from one side of the room to the other, shaking hands and greeting each and every person there, from the highest level executives to the entry-level secretary. Just like Marlon Brando did. And on the other side of the coin, we recently had a huge guest who was a severe disappointment. He and his publicist were so disrespectful to the entire crew, we all felt very let down.

Treating everyone the same says so much about who you are in your heart. Have you ever been with someone who was rude to the waiter, nasty to the grocery checker, or impatient with the sales clerk? How does it make you feel about your friend? Maybe he or she is not the great person you thought they were.

Treating others like you want to be treated is a universal spiritual concept because, in spiritual terms, we are all connected. It's that simple. It's not about making someone else like you or say nice things about you. It's all about how you feel on the inside and how much respect and love you radiate to the people around you. Energy is constantly moving, and we live in a universe where "what goes around, comes around," and "you reap what you sow." Regardless of how you say it, when you act negatively toward someone else and disrespect them, the bad karma will come back to you, just like a boomerang!

Some of the most profound lessons in life are extremely simple and are not at all new or revolutionary. Treating everyone as an equal is one of those simple lessons. I will always remember Jackie Onassis's habit of looking me in the eye when she spoke with me, a private secretary to one of her family members. You just never know who these wonderful people will be, the ones who walk into a room and treat everyone the same. Just because someone gets paid a higher salary or has more power in their field does not make them a better human being.

Being kind to others is the same Golden Rule that we learned from our grandmothers, our mothers, and now we are passing it on to the next generation. If everyone treated people the way they wanted to be treated, there would be no violence or wars. I am not suggesting you become a doormat or a yes-man, but there is usually a kinder and gentler way of stating what you want that includes considering the feelings and desires of the other person.

People who treat everyone with respect know that we are all equal, that we were all born naked, and we will all die the same. No matter who we are. So if you are in a higher position than someone else and you take the time to treat them with respect, it will absolutely make their day! And it will make yours.

CHAPTER 18

Know When to Hang Up Your
Nightly Suspenders

On Monday, June 28, 2010, I called Bill Maher's office and spoke to his assistant. "Sarah," I said, "I need to speak to Bill privately. I'm sorry I can't tell you what it's about, but it's very important."

Now, Bill is not a guy who's just sitting around waiting for people to call him. In fact, he's very hard to book on the show because he's so incredibly busy with his own show, his books, his stand-ups, his documentaries—his everything. And he prepares endlessly before he comes on *Larry King Live* because, at heart, he is a perfectionist. That makes it tough to get him to commit to a specific date for our show. So I really wasn't sure he would call me back since I couldn't leave a detailed message.

But an hour later, when I was in the car driving to Los Angeles and stressing, my cell phone rang. The voice at the other end said, "Hi, Wendy, it's Bill Maher."

"Thanks so much for calling me back," I said. "I have to share something with you that only a handful of people know about. My staff doesn't even know yet, but I'm taking you into my confidence. I need you to say not a word. Pinky promise?"

Pinky promise? I couldn't believe those words just came out of my mouth, and I was mortified. But I moved on as if my stupid twin had said that. "Tomorrow night," I continued, "Larry is going to make a very important announcement, and I want him to be with someone who really cares about him. That would be you. I know this is really short notice, but is there any way you'd consider doing this for him?"

"I take it this has something to do with his future?" asked Bill.

"Yes, but no one knows that."

"Well, I'm supposed to be shooting a pilot for a show tomorrow night. I don't think I can do it, but let me see. I just doubt I can move everything around."

"Thanks for even considering it," I said, resigning myself to the fact that Bill couldn't do it.

I met Larry at Spago Restaurant in Beverly Hills that night, just the two of us. He had decided to leave his nightly show in the fall, and we were meeting to talk about it. I could understand why it was time. Consider that *Larry King Live* airs 365 days a year. Each week, we do five new shows, and on the weekends, we repeat the best of the week, unless there's breaking news, and then we all come in and create a brand-new show. Going from that to doing four specials a year on CNN (what Larry was going to do next) would certainly give him a chance to breathe, to spend time with his beautiful family, and to do some things he always wanted to do—like interviewing more athletes and working for Major League Baseball. Things like that.

At dinner, Larry told me, "During this twenty-fifth anniversary week, I just interviewed the biggest business man, the biggest music phenomenon, the biggest head of state, and the biggest athlete: Gates, Gaga, Obama, and LeBron James. It doesn't get any better than that. Let's leave on a high."

We didn't say much else at dinner, but because of what was about to happen, I had a good excuse to eat a pizza of my own and eat half of Larry's, too, before the evening was through. This was going to be a huge change and I could hardly take it all in.

The next morning, I woke up to find a voice mail message on my cell phone. It was from Bill Maher. "I'm on the set of my pilot and I'm still moving things around. I'm hopeful I can make it to the studio by the start of the show. I just have one more major thing to move. I'll give you an update in a few hours."

I could hardly believe it. How cool was Bill Maher? But we still had to book an alternate show in case he didn't show up. Remember, my staff knew nothing about Larry's decision and they didn't understand why I was freelancing and calling Bill Maher to do the show. I said nothing but I kept my fingers crossed. I knew Bill was really trying to make this happen and he understood that Larry really needed him.

I waited to hear from Bill, but in the meantime, Larry and I had a difficult day ahead. Our first stop was to meet with Bert Fields, Larry's longtime attorney, and Rick Rosen, Larry's agent, who brought Christian Muirhead with him to consult. Together we all prepared the statement that Larry would read on the air that night. It was important to him that he relay his sentiments accurately and in his own words. I came up with a suggestion. "How about if you say, 'It's time to hang up my nightly suspenders.'"

Larry liked that a lot and we got to work crafting the rest of the message. When we were through, our next stop was lunch with CNN president Jon Klein at the Grill, a noisy, fun place in Los Angeles where you can feel the buzz of people brainstorming and making deals. Larry and I got there first and when Jon walked in, he said to me, "Wendy, you look great."

Larry said deadpan, "You don't have to tell her that anymore, Jon."

It got a laugh. Then, while we were eating, I got *the* call. "Hi, it's Bill. I'll be there."

How could I possibly thank him? I could only imagine what kind of juggling it had taken to pull this off for Larry. Bill hadn't moved a mountain; he had moved a pilot—which is a lot bigger. And he didn't want a thing from us. Most of all, he didn't want us to make a fuss over him. "It may not be the best show, though," he warned me, "because I've had no time to prepare." ·

I didn't care if he talked about gardening for the hour. Just knowing that Larry would not be sitting there all alone to make his important announcement was all I wanted. I called Allison Marsh who is in charge of booking and said, "Cancel all the other guests. Bill will do the hour."

Larry, Jon, and I went over the plan for the announcement. Now I had to tell the staff before Larry went on the air—the hardest part. Larry's staff is loyal, skilled, and very accomplished. I know it sounds like a cliché but we've been a family for years, and there's been very little turnover because everyone loves working on the show. Just like there was only one Johnny Carson, there is only one Larry King. The staff, Larry, and I have gone through everything together: marriages, births, deaths, surgeries—all the ups and all the downs. Telling the staff would be the toughest part.

When I arrived at the CNN bureau in Los Angeles, I closed my office door and called in my second in charge, Carrie

Stevenson, who'd been with the show longer than I had. When I took the job in 1993, she was already interning there, and sixteen years later, I'd never had a bad day with Carrie. She never lost her cool, she was always "up," and she worked so hard. When she was in charge, you knew she would always pull it off beautifully.

When I told her the news, I felt instantly better because it was unlike me to keep any information from Carrie or from the rest of the staff. I'd been dreading this moment, but now that I'd told Carrie, I was ready to tell my other direct reports, the people who reported to me on a daily basis. No one had been told formally as yet, but the Los Angeles staff was getting the drift that something was up because Barbara Levin, a lovely woman from Public Relations in New York, was there, and so was Jon Klein.

I got on a conference call with my direct reports: Carrie; John Gilmore, an impressive journalist in Washington; Allison Marsh, my arm in charge of booking; and Greg Christensen, a funny and solid producer who is in charge of the Los Angeles staff. As I explained what was happening, it felt like I was breaking up with them. It was a day that we all knew would come at some point, and at the same time, we never really thought it would. But as Carrie got the entire staff to call in to our conference line, they knew something was going on. Once our staff members across the country were conferenced in from Washington DC, New York, Denver, Atlanta, and San Diego, I told them all, "Hi, everyone, Larry wants to speak to you before the show starts."

In his softest and most heartfelt voice, Larry said, "I've been giving this a lot of thought and I decided the fall will be a good time to end the nightly show. I'll still be doing specials on CNN, but this will give me time to do other things I've always wanted to do, especially spending more time with the family."

Choking back tears, I said, "Well, Larry, I know I speak for everyone on the staff when I say we're all really proud of you. You're an icon, we love you, and it's been an honor working on the show."

"I never had to do anything like this before," Larry said. Everyone was sniffling when John Gilmore in Washington spoke up in his beautiful Irish brogue, "Larry, we love you and it's been a privilege to work on the show." Larry started to sniffle along with the rest of us. In the end, the staff took the news like I knew they would as they put aside their sorrow and turned their undivided attention toward the evening's show. Larry went on his Twitter account and tweeted a message that he was ending the show, while Jon Klein put out a statement to the entire CNN network.

Of course, the news spread quickly and it became breaking news on CNN before we even went on the air. Larry put on his suspenders and prepared for the show that night, later telling a reporter that his announcement call to the staff was one of the saddest ten minutes of his life. We left the offices and walked into the makeup room beside the studio and I nearly cried when I saw Bill Maher getting ready. I held back my tears, though, as I looked into Bill's eyes, and said, "Thank you. It's so perfect that you're here."

He smiled at me. It was showtime.

KING: Good evening. Before I start the show tonight, I want to share some personal news with you. Twenty-five years ago, I sat across this table from New York Governor Mario Cuomo for the first broadcast ever of *Larry King Live*. And now, decades later, I talked to the guys here at CNN and I told them I'd like to end *Larry King Live*, the nightly show, this fall. CNN has gracefully accepted and agreed, giving me more time for my wife and me to get to the kids' little league games.

I'll still be part of the CNN family. I'll be hosting several Larry King specials on major national and international subjects, and we will be here until a replacement is found. We'll be here into the fall. Tomorrow night, in fact, Elizabeth Edwards is our special guest.

I'm incredibly proud that we recently made *Guinness World Records* for having the longest-running show with the same host in the same time slot on the same network. With that chapter closing, I'm looking forward to the future, what my next chapter will bring.

But for now, for here, it's time to hang up the nightly suspenders. Until then, we've got more shows to do, and who knows what the future's going to bring.

Bill Maher is the Emmy-nominated host of *Real Time with Bill Maher* on HBO, stand-up comic, best-selling author. We called him in today in view of this announcement and asked him if he'd come on as an old friend. Thank you, Bill.

MAHER: I'm honored you would ask me to take over the desk, Larry. Thank you so much. I'm ready to step in at a moment's notice. Do you want to finish the hour or would you like me to take over right now, Larry?

I am reminded of what my father, who was a broadcaster, said the day Mickey Mantle retired. "Say it isn't so," he began the broadcast.

KING: You put me in that class?

MAHER: Mickey Mantle? You are the Mickey Mantle of broad-
casters. Mickey Mantle played eighteen seasons. You played
more than that.

KING: I did the twenty-fifth anniversary week. We had Lady
Gaga. We had Bill Gates. We had President Obama. We
had LeBron James. I'm flying home from that week and
I'm thinking to myself, I've done fifty thousand interviews.
I'm never going to top this. I want to move on. I want new
horizons. I want to try other things.

MAHER: Well, I think I speak for a lot of people in America
who say, I will miss you terribly at this hour. I mean, there
is nobody who does what you do, because you had a mini-
malist style that is gone from television and you are taking
it with you, Larry.

The phones were lighting up. Everyone wanted to call in
and talk to Larry. E-mails started flashing on the screen that
read: "Diane Sawyer is trying to call into the control room."
"Regis is calling!" "So is Nancy Reagan!"

NANCY REAGAN: I couldn't let you do this without my calling
you. You didn't call and ask my permission.

REGIS: Larry, I am totally surprised by this. For some reason,
I feel very badly about it...There has always been a Larry
King. All of a sudden, I can't believe that we are not going to
see you on during the week at night in the fall...I feel like
leaving the same time you do at this point. But I think Bill
Maher is totally responsible for this...I'm going to miss you
terribly, Larry. Because, frankly, you are one of a kind.

DIANE SAWYER: I just want to say, Larry, what a monument of
vitality you have built for all of us. And I cannot wait to
see your specials, because everybody in the world wants to

talk to you and to see you do them in a concentrated way. When you choose to do them, it's going to be a thrill... And again, we love you.

Ryan Seacrest tweeted from his vacation, using Larry's Twitter name: "You are a legend @kingsthings. One of a kind."

When Anderson Cooper did his usual nightly cut-in on our show to promote his show, Bill asked him, "Anderson, did you engineer this coup?"

Big laugh!

Anderson said, "I just heard the news that you are scaling back at CNN and hanging up your suspenders, as you said. I am stunned and I am sad."

The last thing Bill said on the show that night was, "Larry. Don't go, Larry."

That's why he was the perfect person to sit with Larry. A brilliant performer with a brilliant intellect, Bill really understands what Larry means to our culture. So thank you again, Bill, for making Larry's tough night a celebration. In fact, when Larry left the set, he actually felt good. Mission accomplished!

The e-mails came streaming in faster than I could read them.

Sanjay Gupta: "Oh, boy..."

Mark Geragos: "What does this mean for you, Wendy?"

My answer: "That I won't have to work as hard?"

Jeff Zucker: "You doing okay?"

Miko Brando, Marlon's son, called producer Nancy Baker who told us, "Miko said to tell Larry that his dad would have been so proud of him and wish him the best."

My friend Sabih Masri, from Amman, Jordan: "What are you planning to do now?"

Christiane Amanpour in London: "Larry is part of our common modern global history... Whenever I think of him my mind automatically free-associates with the first Gulf War. I always picture myself at the end of an ifb from Dhahran, listening to the real-time diplomacy being conducted on LKL between Washington, New York, Geneva, Moscow, the Middle East...trying to resolve Saddam's aggression before it led to war. And of course the thousands of other important moments on his program. An era passes."

Haim Saban: "Call me. Just found out. I am surrounded by fifteen people in the board room."

Suze Orman: "I am here for you all, anytime you want."

Candy Crowley: "He carried it off with great style. You OK?"

Chelsea Handler: "How are you?"

Jeff Probst: "I hope you are OK with this news."

Lisa Ling: "I imagine it is chaos over there. I am in Colombia at the moment on a shoot but aware of the news. U OK?"

Dr. Dean Ornish: "Please let me know if there is anything I can do to be supportive."

Ryan Seacrest: "I know today has been a hard and tough emotional day for you."

Ryan, a great friend of ours, had left for vacation that day. Larry had shared the news with him earlier, after his radio show, so he wouldn't hear it on the air. I e-mailed Ryan back, "It has been tough but it went as well as could be expected. Larry keeps telling people when asked that you would be his pick for a successor. He said it on the air and to reporters."

"Suggesting me as successor is a great honor," Ryan told me. But in order for him to ever seriously consider the suggestion, he would have to clone himself, since his workday already consists of twenty-five hours. I don't know a busier guy!

I e-mailed Bill, thanking him for a perfect show, and he wrote back, "I was happy to do it for Larry, you, and everyone at the show who has been so good to me. I've considered LKL a second home on television for a long time, and it was an honor to be chosen to hear Larry's confession that I would not have missed for the world, so I thank you for asking."

After the show, Larry and I had dinner with a great friend, Haim Saban, a mega media mogul and worldwide leader in the entertainment industry. It was a terrific celebration and we relaxed as we went over the day's events. Haim congratulated Larry on his body of work and said, "There's only one of you, my friend." He celebrated Larry's brand and counted off many things that he could do with his name and reputation. Larry even had a few sips of red wine. (He's never liked to drink.) At the end of the evening when we were all hugging good night, Larry took the written statement out of his pocket and gave it to Haim. "Here's a souvenir for you." Haim smiled and put it in his pocket.

That night, the price of Larry's suspenders went way up on eBay. With more than fifty thousand interviews in fifty-three years under his belt? Yes, I guess it was time.

❖

KNOW WHEN TO HANG UP YOUR NIGHTLY SUSPENDERS

In life, you know when it is time—to speak up, to move on, to share, to go to ground, to live, and finally, to die. This was Larry's time to hang up his nightly suspenders, a decision he made with grace, humility, and humor. When he announced his intention to end his nightly show, he was at the top of his game and he left everyone in his life and the entire world wanting more—including me.

A Final Thought:
Be True to Yourself

I'd like to leave you with a final lesson that lies beneath all that I've written before. No matter who you are, where you live, or what your gender, race, or religion, you know in your heart what is right and you know what is wrong. After all, you live with yourself every day. When you take a look in the mirror, you won't see happiness looking back at you if you feel bad about the choices you've made.

A wise friend of mine once told me a wonderful story that sums it all up. A single dad, the time came when he had to have the "sex talk" with his teenage daughter. Girls don't want to hear about this, especially from their dads, but he sat her down and said, "There are only two things I want to say about sex. First, if you're about to do it, make sure you're doing it for you, not for the boy. Second, think about how you'll feel five minutes after you do it."

When his daughter eventually married and had children of her own, she told her dad that she never forgot that talk. It was all about being true to herself, and she considers it one of his greatest gifts to her.

We can apply this gift to any area of our life:

- How will you feel after you hurt someone?
- How will you feel if you don't take the chance?
- How will you feel five minutes after you tell someone that you love them?
- How will you feel if you let a friendship drift away?
- How will you feel if a friend died today? Do you have unfinished business?

To me, being true to yourself is the only way to go. That is the best that anyone can ever do.

ACKNOWLEDGMENTS

I could not have written this book had it not been for all the amazing experiences I've had in my life and all the good energy that has surrounded me. There are many people who are responsible for my happiness, so I'll attempt to say thank you and how much I appreciate everything all of you have done for me.

First, I would like to acknowledge and thank the staff of *Larry King Live*. I honestly believe this is one of the most amazing and talented group of people in the television news industry. They know what it takes when we are asked to stay live for two more hours after we have planned for only one. They know what it takes to work around the clock during a breaking news story. They know what it takes to put on a telethon to raise money for a natural or national disaster, when that is not in our job description. Or just the everyday battle of changing the show five times before we go on the air. I am so proud of all of them and want them to know that this book would never have been written had it not been for them. Thank you so much, you are all the best.

Thank you, Benjamin Alden, Nancy Baker, Andrea Beaumont, Barbara Berti, Erika Birkholm, Quinn Brown, Carol

Buckland, Carmelina Castillo, Greg Christensen, Geoff Doner, Dave Dubiel, Lisa Durham, Liz Flynn, Avrielle Gallagher, John Gilmore, Chip Hirzel, Sarah Holbrooke, Amy Huggins, Hieu Huynh, Ryan Jimenez, Kyle Johnson, Michael Judge, Sean Kelly, Eleanor McManus, Katherine McQuade, Virginia Moubray, Brad Parks, Jason Ravou, Sonja Reitmeier, Stephen Salvador, Sarah Schnare, Rosy Stefanatos, David Theall, Lisa Thompson, Hunter Waters, Michael Watts, and Lindsay Geier. And a special recognition to Carrie Stevenson and Allison Marsh who work on the show around the clock and never ask me why I'm calling them in the middle of the night. I love you all, and thank you so much.

Walker, my son. I love you, you are my best friend. You give me more joy than you will ever know. Thank you for being my beautiful and loving son. And I know one day you will be a famous writer!

Amaya, my daughter. I love you so much. You are a beautiful soul and a gifted singer. I cry every time I hear you sing. Thank you for being a teenager who actually loves her mama!

Larry King. There is only one of you. Our humor is our glue, your talent is my inspiration. It is an honor to be your producer and your friend. Thank you for believing in me and trusting me. And my love always to Shawn.

Randy Woods. Thank you for finally finding me and for being the nicest man I've ever known. Your support and kindness are gifts. And I can't take my eyes off of you! Thank you for making me happy every day.

Terry Brown, my sister. I love you. Thank you for always being there for me and teaching me how to be a good mother and decorator! To my mother and father, who I wish were still here but now are finally together. And my sisters, Peggy and Mary. Thank you for everything you have done for me.

Mary Heckmann. You are my beautiful soul mate and friend. Thank you for sleeping with me all of those nights! And thank you for loving me as much as you do.

Michelle Weinger, the twin sister that I never had! You are always there for everyone in your life, including me. Thank you for making me laugh and sharing your mom with me! And sharing your sweet husband, Duayne.

Jenny Craig, my mama and my wonderful friend. Thank you for making me part of your family. I love having you in my life. You are such a role model for me, from your family to your work ethic to your kindness.

To Ali, Tracy, James, Jennifer, Sammy, and Liam Fayed. You are truly my family. I love you all and have loved watching the boys grow from babies to amazing men. You have all meant so much to me in my life, and I will never forget all the priceless things you have done for me. Thank you for making me part of your life.

Sabih and Hani Masri. You both are two of the most important people in my life. You have taught me so much about the world. But most of all, you have been steadfast and fantastic friends. Thank you for being in my life.

To Suzanne Somers and Alan Hamel—being with you for a day seems like an hour. You are two of the lucky ones who have true love and you are soul mates forever. You are such good friends, and we love spending time laughing with you both. Thank you for our great friendship, your wisdom and the comfortable and good times we have together. We truly cherish our time with you both.

Katie Couric. Little did we ever know when we were starting

out that you would make history. But then, I knew it all along! Thank you for your friendship, your advice, your parents, and your love. We've had an amazing journey that isn't over yet, Kats.

Lisa Gregorisch, Sister Sledge. You are truly a gift in my life. I trust you with everything except my children, but actually, I even trust you with them! You are a huge force in this business. You are talented and honest. And such an amazing friend. Now if only I could get you to stay up long enough to go out to dinner, that would be nice.

Cindy Vance, my beautiful friend whom I adore and love. Thank you for your endless advice and love.

Trish McEvoy. Little did I know all those years ago that when you put my makeup on at Neiman Marcus that you would be such a part of my life. Not only do I love how you made your makeup brushes by cutting regular paintbrushes when you were first starting out, I am lucky to call you a friend. I am so proud of you and your accomplishments, sister, and I am loving you as my friend. Thank you so much for everything.

To Deepak Chopra and Carolyn Rangle. I pinch myself when I think of how lucky I am to have you in my life. Thank you for your wisdom, your loving friendship, and for constantly educating me about myself and how I belong in this life.

Thank you to Jan Miller, my agent. Jan, I have never seen you look anything but perfect. I want all of your bracelets! Thank you for believing in this project enough to introduce me to Hachette. And to Harry Helm, my editor at Hachette, I know you liked me because you could visit California in your shorts, but also I'm glad you took a chance on me. And a special thank you to Adlai Yeomans, the best editorial assistant in the business.

And to Andrea Cagan, my collaborator and writer, thank you

for all those nights when we sat by the fire while I told you all these stories. It was like going to a shrink, but a lot more fun! You are so talented and such a beautiful woman, inside and out. It was a privilege to work with you on this book. And to Rick Davis, my friend and colleague at CNN, who had to edit this book as well, thank you for having my back and being my friend at CNN for thirty years.

To Char Margolis, whom I met before she really knew me. You are such a good friend, and I adore you. My life is more full because you are in it.

Nathan Turner, my brother, who has the same taste as I do! I love the time we carve out for each other. Whenever I am with you and the kids and our dogs, I am home. Thank you for choosing me to be your friend.

JZ Knight. I am so lucky to have you in my life. There are only a few people I've met who are so incredibly unique and fascinating. You are clearly one of those people. Your energy has been a blessing to me. Thank you for everything you continue to do as my friend and loving guide.

To Rosa Garcia, thank you for making our home so warm and happy. And I wish everyone who reads this book could try your tortilla soup! I love every flower you have planted!

To my hometown and oldest friends whom I still see! Jennifer Kersten, Nancy Packard Rosen, Jane Riley Murray, Martha Fuerste Henry, and Mary Eby Smith. We never got caught burning the sofa in high school!

To Mary T. Browne. I know I saw you at least once at Roshek's. It's great when good friends come to you later in life, and I am blessed you came into mine. You are the best, Mare.

James Van Praagh. Not only do you see dead people, but I'm glad I have you in this life to keep me focused and laughing.

To my beautiful college friends. I always feel so close to you all, even though we don't see each other every day, and even though we were a lot cuter thirty-some years ago! To Cynthia Guill, we will always be connected to each other in a very special way. To Torrey Shuford, Dolly Horner, Sara Simpson, Susan Bance, Connie Moore, Debbie McChesney, Karin Chriss, Candy Lloyd, and Cissy Benedict.

To my Rancho Santa Fe posse! A great group of wonderful friends that I am so lucky to have. Kathy Connor, Deborah and Ron Greenspan, Martha and John Eggemeyer, Joy and Hugh Bancroft, Cathy and Brad Geier, Chrissy and Rick Nicholas, Chris Penrod, Connie and Bill McNally, Art and Catherine Nicholas, Ron and Georgia Spogli, Shelby and Bill Strong, Joani and Chuck Wafer, Marty and Pam Wygod, and Carol Thompson. And to Robin and Gerry Parsky, thank you for insisting that I stay in the Ranch to hang with this wonderful group of people. You have been terrific friends. And Gerry, thank you for my new best friend, Jerry Weintraub!

To Sheila and Bunny Pourhosseini and Tom and Jen DeLonge. Thank you for making life more interesting, by bringing music and makeup to my everyday life and the lives of my children. You guys sure make our times together unpredictable and filled with love.

To George Pratt, John Assaraf, and Ken Druck. I am so blessed with knowing you and learning from you. Thank you.

Dr. Sanjay Gupta. You are an amazing man. I don't know how you do it all. I'm so glad to call you a friend. And it's nice to have a neurosurgeon on call!

To Caryn and Jeff Zucker. Thank you for always being there for me no matter what. I love you both.

Ryan Seacrest—I wish I was thirty-five again just so I could try to do everything you do in a day. You are a joy in my life and I just love your energy. I love spending time with you.

Jeff Probst—I'm so glad your agent made me let you host the show. You are so talented and driven. It has been a joy working with you and becoming your friend.

To Roy Bank. Roysers, he's so hot right now. Besides our love for *Zoolander*, you are one creative, interesting man. Here's to all the ideas we have had and will continue to have! Roysers!

To Lisa Betyar. I know that all accountants are not like you. You are a lot prettier than most, and the things that you have done for me do not fit any job description! Thank you!

To Chelsea Handler, I want to be you...

Suzy Kelly, thank you for being such a steadfast friend for over thirty years. Love you.

Heather Mills, I will never forget how you helped me through a very rough time. Here's to happy memories with our kids and more future adventures.

Gary Foster, some things never change in life, and your friendship is one that picks right up every time. Thank you for being my friend, creep.

Lisa Ling, I have so much respect for you after seeing your courage this year. Thank you for our friendship.

Bert Fields and Howard Rubenstein—I could not have survived without you. Thank you both for your guidance and endless support.

Thank you to:

President George H.W. Bush, Nancy Crown, Beth Dozoretz, Sarah Ferguson, Tammi Fuller, Cari Klepper, Bill Maher, Dr. Babs Moosa, Gayil Nalls, Suze Orman, Dr. Dean Ornish, Dr. Pam Peeke, Ross Perot, Dr. Phil, Boone Pickens, Haim Saban, David Saltz, Ann Schooler, Bobbi Smith, Nancy, Julie and Mrs. Whitlow, Sandi Mendleson, Seth MacFarlane, Jen Snell, David and Aileen Leavitt, Jeff Loyland, Donna and Bob Holcombe, Michelle Laxalt.

Ethel Kennedy. I really owe this book to you. If I hadn't waited on you at Brooks Brothers, I would not have worked for you. And I would not have learned that I have to work harder than the other guy. And I would not have worked with the ABC producers on the RFK Pro-Celebrity and I would not have realized that I wanted to be a producer. So you are responsible for my career and my book! I am honored to have worked for you and am proud to call you a friend. You have been an inspiration in my life to reach higher and do more. Thank you so much for being part of my life.

To Jon Klein, Jim Walton and Phil Kent. No one could have better bosses. You have been supportive all the way, and a ton of fun as well. I celebrated my 30th year at CNN, largely because you have kept me there! Ted Turner once said that you should stay at CNN as long as you have something to learn. Well, I don't think any of us have stopped learning. Thank you for continuing to believe in me and sharing this journey with me. I am always eager for your new challenges, and so appreciate the honor to work at CNN with all three of you. Thank you for everything.

CNN Friends, past and present. Thank you, Ted Turner, for my incredible life. To George Watson, thank you for bringing me to CNN and showing me the way. Tom Johnson, thank you for trusting me with Larry King before I did. You always gave me the chance to do more and I am very grateful to you for everything you did for me. You are a good friend and I want to thank you from the bottom of my heart. Thank you to Charles Bierbauer, Frank Sesno, Candy Crowley, Wolf Blitzer, Carol Cratty, Kevin Bohn, Molly Boyle, Bryan Cole, Peter Morris and Jim Helling, my White House family. I carry our memories with pride and fondness and laughter. To Gail Evans, you have always had my back and I have learned so much from you. Thank you for continuing to be there for me. Thank you to Anderson Cooper, Christiane Amanpour, Sue Bunda, Jim Miklaszewski,, Bernie Shaw, Brad Ferrer, Pete Janos, Steve Korn, Rick Kaplan, David Newman, my pal Guy Pepper, Kyra Philips, Eunah Francis, Burt Reinhardt, Kandy Stroud, Mark Shields, Maggie Simpson, Pat Pinto, Erin Sermeus, Juli Gallagher, Donna Rockwell, Scott Willis, Stacey Wolf, Susan Grant, Scot Safon, Dave Bohrman, Greta Van Susteren, Ted Rowlands, Jack Womack, Greg D'Alba, and a special thank you Bart Feder, who has shown me nothing but endless patience and support.

And a note to thank those who contributed to the book by allowing us to ask them about their memories of some of these events so I could get my story straight! Katie Couric, Larry King, Suzy Kelly, Mark Geragos, Gail Evans, Sam Donaldson, Char Margolis, Gary Foster, Tom Johnson, Frank Sesno, Lisa Ling, Lisa Gregorisch, John Towriss, Charles Bierbauer, Hani Masri, and Kevin Mabbutt.

About the Authors

Wendy Walker has held a front row seat to the world's stage for the past thirty years, as an Emmy-winning broadcast news veteran and CNN senior vice president. The longtime senior executive producer of *Larry King Live,* Walker is the force behind television icon Larry King. A CNN original, she joined the network when it began in 1980, soon becoming senior White House producer and later rising to the top, helming the cable news giant's most powerful primetime program, seen around the globe. Called "relentless" by Barbara Walters, Walker has covered every major news event of the past three decades, producing interviews with every living U.S. President and countless game-changing and notable newsmakers. From statesmen and world leaders, to celebrities and everyday people doing extraordinary things—Walker has covered them all as she created some of the most remarkable, famous, and history-making moments in television.

Andrea Cagan has been writing, collaborating, and editing for two decades. She has brought a dozen books to the bestseller lists, including three *New York Times* #1 best sellers. She works and lives in Los Angeles, California, with her Balinese cat, Lulu.